809 Psy

The Psychoanalytic study of literature.

**The Lorette Wilmot Library
Nazareth College of Rochester**

THE PSYCHOANALYTIC STUDY OF LITERATURE

Edited by

JOSEPH REPPEN, Ph.D.
MAURICE CHARNEY, Ph.D.

THE ANALYTIC PRESS
1985

Distributed by
LAWRENCE ERLBAUM ASSOCIATES, PUBLISHERS
Hillsdale, New Jersey   London

Copyright © 1985 by The Analytic Press.
All rights reserved. No part of this book may be reproduced in any form, by photostat, microform, retrieval system, or any other means, without prior written permission of the publisher.

Distributed solely by

Lawrence Erlbaum Associates, Inc., Publishers
365 Broadway
Hillsdale, New Jersey 07642

Library of Congress Cataloging in Publication Data

Main entry under title:

The Psychoanalytic study of literature.

Includes bibliographies and indexes.
1. Psychoanalysis and literature—Addresses, essays, lectures. 2. Psychoanalysis and the arts—Addresses, essays, lectures. I. Reppen, Joseph. II. Charney, Maurice.
PN56.P92P74   1985   809   84-16791
ISBN 0-88163-023-3

Printed in the United States of America
10 9 8 7 6 5 4 3 2 1

Contents

Preface   v

I. FREUDIAN CONCEPTS AND THE LITERARY PROCESS

1. Freud's Reading Process: The Divided Protagonist Narrative and the Case of the Wolf-Man
   Donald M. Kartiganer, Ph.D.   3

2. Ghost Writing: A Meditation on Literary Criticism as Narrative
   Madelon Sprengnether, Ph.D.   37

II. CLINICAL APPROACHES TO CREATIVITY

3. The Psychiatrist in the Movies: The First Fifty Years
   Irving Schneider, M.D.   53

III. FREUD, PHILOSOPHY AND LINGUISTICS

4. Freud's Philosophy of Mind: Cartesianism and Unconscious Intentions
   Arthur Collins, Ph.D.   71

5. Signals of the Comic
   Roger B. Henkle, Ph.D.   89

CONTENTS

    6. The Grammar of Representation in Psychoanalysis and Literature
       Zelda Boyd, Ph.D.   107

IV. PSYCHOCULTURAL STUDIES OF INDIVIDUAL TEXTS AND AUTHORS

    7. Fantasy Work and the Crux of the Literal in Samuel Butler's *The Authoress of The Odyssey*
       Margaret Ganz, Ph.D.   127

    8. Reading the Letter: Romance and Repression in Hawthorne's *The Scarlet Letter*
       Elissa Greenwald, Ph.D.   149

V. PSYCHOANALYSIS AND SHAKESPEARE

    9. The Purloined Handkerchief in *Othello*
       Peter L. Rudnytsky, Ph.D.   169

VI. LACANIAN INTERPRETATION AND THE FRENCH FREUD

    10. The Graphic Unconscious
       Tom Conley, Ph.D.   193

    11. Burying the Treasure: Forgetting as Creative Work in Freud and Proust
       Jerry Aline Flieger, Ph.D.   215

    12. Modes of Lacanian Fragmentation in Three Texts
       Leopold Charney   238

    13. *The Ravishing of Lol. V. Stein*
       Susan Cohen, Ph.D.   255

Notes on Contributors   279

Author Index   283

Subject Index   287

Preface

"The Freudian psychology is the only systematic account of the human mind which, in point of subtlety and complexity, of interest and tragic power, deserves to stand beside the chaotic mass of psychological insights which literature has accumulated through the centuries." So observed the literary critic Lionel Trilling over three decades ago in his classic essay on "Freud and Literature." Trilling's influential verdict notwithstanding, it is within the past decade that literary critics, spurred by the work of classic and post-Freudian thinkers, have intensified their interest in the explanatory power of psychoanalysis. Psychoanalysts, for their part, have also turned more frequently to literary models in their conceptualization of the psychoanalytic process and their explication of psychoanalytic case material.

The Psychoanalytic Study of Literature is of mutual interest to psychoanalysis and literature. We extend the term "literature" to include other cultural activities and pursuits such as film, theater, philosophy, and art. Although our fundamental orientation is to literature, this volume explores the new ways that the study of literature can illuminate psychoanalysis and how the study of psychoanalysis can inform, expand, and enrich our knowledge of literature, literary theory, and critical thinking.

Joseph Reppen, Ph.D.
Maurice Charney, Ph.D.

I FREUDIAN CONCEPTS AND THE LITERARY PROCESS

Freud's Reading Process: The Divided Protagonist Narrative and the Case of the Wolf-Man

1

Donald M. Kartiganer, Ph.D.

I

"From the History of an Infantile Neurosis" (1918)–Freud's case history of the "Wolf-Man"–is the most comprehensive account we have of his interpretive procedure. While it is based on his theories of the human mind and provides important evidence for their validity, its primary value for us as literary critics lies in its detailed demonstration of Freud as reader: the analyst in the act of transforming the most baffling, disjointed forms of human behavior into a coherent and significant text. The case history constitutes, in other words, an implicit hermeneutics and a practical criticism, a theory of how to read and a detailed demonstration of how reading proceeds, what it requires, what it produces, and how its results may be measured.

One way of clarifying this aspect of the case history as example of and commentary on interpretive activity is to locate Freud's study within an important subgenre of 19th- and 20th-century narrative in which the act of reading becomes a central issue. This subgenre has been called the "divided protagonist" narrative (Scholes and Kellog, 1966, p. 261), or fiction of the "secondary first-person narrator" (Kawin, 1982, p. 34). It is characterized by the division of the traditional central figure of narrative, the protagonist, into an actor and an observer: one to carry out the events of the narrative, the other to understand and articulate their meaning. Among the many narratives that belong to this tradition are *Castle Rackrent* (1800), Hoffmann's "Don Juan" (1813), "The Fall of the House of Usher" (1839), *Fear and Trembling* (1843), *Wuthering Heights* (1847), *Moby-Dick* (1851), *The Blithedale Romance* (1852), *Heart of Darkness* (1899), *Lord Jim* (1900), *Le Grand Meulnes* (1912), *The Great Gatsby* (1925), *Absalom, Absalom!* (1936), *All the King's Men* (1946), *Doctor Faustus* (1947), *Pale Fire* (1962).

In each of these texts the actor—Heathcliff or Cathy, Ahab, Kurtz, Gatsby, Sutpen, Leverkühn, Willy Stark—bears the dramatic burden of narrative, performing its action, but bereft of the traditional capacity to comprehend it. He is enigmatic not only to the world, a puzzling, often frightening figure, he is also an enigma to himself, enacting deeds more momentous than his analytic powers can contain. In the silence of the actor's self-analysis, the observer of the action—Nelly Dean, Ishmael, Marlow, Carraway, Quentin Compson, Zeitblom, Jack Burden—who has little to do with its performance, becomes its primary interpreter. With no deeds of his own that challenge analysis, living a life far more conventional and socially bound than the actor, this observer gives himself over to an act of reading, forfeiting his own life, as it were, to his obsession with that of the actor—as if the meaning of the actor's life were somehow the key to his own.

This transformation of narrative into a dynamic exchange between actor and observer reflects a number of crucial tendencies in 19th-century thought—tendencies at work in Freud's development of psychoanalysis: the modification of the real into a continuous process of dialectically engaged forces; the modification of time, as the idea of linearity begins to bend beneath the pressure of repetition and revision; the modification of priority, as first and second, originator and successor, begin to compete convincingly for primacy.

One result of this split between actor and observer is to raise the issue of interpretation to the dramatic surface of the narrative. The very process by which meaning comes to adhere to the compelling, often violent actions of the actor becomes itself an action richly elaborated—almost to the point of overshadowing those deeds that have called forth interpretation in the first place. Once considered – according to the tradition extrapolated from Aristotle's theory of tragic drama – the soul of narrative, the action takes on the opacity of a succession of symptomatic events, arousing wonder and even shock, but lacking the coherence that alters succession into sequence, fragment into developmental stage, chaos into signifying story. This coherence must now be supplied by the observer of the action, whose very remoteness from the events seems crucial to the capacity to understand and organize them.

Clearly the observer is more than a faithful recorder of prior facts, of a history to which point and meaning gradually accrue as it approaches its foreshadowed climax and denouement. Essential to his arrival at meaning is the intrusion of his own needs and desires into that action which, at the outset, confounds him. While the status of objective and self-effacing reporter is his occasional claim, the observer's obsession with the actor is all too obvious, and with that obsession his tendency to borrow the life of the actor as an imagery for his own wishes. In the course of providing coherence and meaning to the actor's deeds, the observer is also living out vicariously those desires that would otherwise remain bodiless, unexpressed and incompletely known.

What might appear to be merely exploitation, however, a parasitism by which desire robes itself in another's courage to act, is also a form of self-sacrifice, the abandonment of one's own deeds for the sake of those larger ones that belong to the actor. As Marlow says at the climax of Joseph Conrad's *Heart of Darkness* (1899/1971): " 'And it is not my own extremity I remember best – a vision of greyness without form filled with physical pain, and a careless contempt for the evanescence of all things – even of this pain itself. No! It is his extremity that I seem to have lived through' " (p. 72). Observer and actor, in other words, meet in a relationship of appropriation and submission, a vicarious fulfillment of desire – which is also the clarification of that desire – and a relegation of self to a subservient role whose task is to praise by illuminating the Other.

Whatever the complexities of the process, its moral and epistemological implications, the act of interpretation is at least partially powered by the observer's desire, a personal bias that becomes the bridge to the Other. Moreover, interpretation is dependent on that bias. Without its effective presence as a kind of heuristic vehicle, a vague instinctual model which the actor's deeds are seen to enact, those deeds are themselves doomed to the status of fragment, the unreadable symbol that bewilders even its performer.

But the intrusion of the observer into the "text" of the actor is actually of two kinds, opposed, yet functioning together to produce the observer's reading. Both are realized in stances that originate outside and prior to the text at hand—the actor—but while one is of a decidedly personal nature, the other is a reflection of a communal identity. Both are subjective in that they introduce into the actor's history elements that preexist it; one, however, follows from a structural awareness of codes and conventions—aesthetic, moral, political, social—the other from more personal needs and desires.

In F. Scott Fitzgerald's *The Great Gatsby* (1925), Jay Gatsby's rags-to-riches career, precariously balanced on vaguely hinted criminal activity, is no more than a meaningless series of material acquisitions, extravagant parties, and vulgar posturings—all nurtured by the absurd pursuit of an old flame. Only in its translation by the more outwardly restrained and conventional Nick Carraway does this life deepen into an allegory of the noble, if doomed, American dream of recovered innocence. Carraway moves to that reading of Gatsby both through and despite the screens of a tight moral code, a need for order and a world "in uniform and at a sort of moral attention forever" (p. 2). These structures provide Nick with a context for Gatsby's behavior, but finally it is Nick's sense of "something gorgeous about him" (p. 2), a "romantic readiness" (p. 2) vivid in the loyalty to Daisy and echoing some unexpressed desire of his own, that allows Nick to bring forth a Gatsby larger and more intelligible than his visible actions. Gatsby emerges for us as the bearer of an idealism that burns as much in Carraway's desire as in Gatsby's deeds: an idealism that cannot exist at all without the collaboration of both characters.

In *Heart of Darkness*, Marlow, despite his strong attachment to the conventions of restraint, duty, and the moral imperative, follows an inner urge to defiance into a strange kinship with the outlaw Kurtz, the cultured, idealistic European turned master of barbaric rites in the African jungle. His progress to Kurtz is literally a function of Marlow's adherence to correct nautical procedure, a strict attention to "hidden banks" and "sunken stones" (p. 34) that protect him from those temptations on shore – "This wild and passionate uproar" (p. 37) – to which Kurtz apparently succumbed. Ultimately, like Carraway, disarmed of the codes that have enabled him to approach the actor, Marlow interprets Kurtz out of a powerful empathy with his willingness to descend into darkness – an empathy which, in the clarity of its expression, is the sole evidence of Kurtz's will. A life and death that might be easily understood as the evidence of moral corruption or psychic derangement is read by Marlow as the fulfillment of a search for meaning, culminating in a "supreme moment of complete knowledge" (p. 71), "a moral victory" (p. 72).

Observer and actor become the languages of each other, each the vehicle of the other's self-knowledge. The result is a kind of collaborative text: a "Marlow-Kurtz," a "Carraway-Gatsby," in which meaning is produced only by the engagement, indeed the incrimination, of observer and actor, reader and text, in each other's lives. This meaning is neither inherent in the actor-text as an implicit presence, nor merely the imposition by an observer-reader of desires preexisting his encounter with the actor. Meaning, rather, is the cooperative construct observer and actor realize in their interaction: a meaning that confers new identity on both.

The observer's stance reveals a commitment and a complicity which the voyeur, fantasizing from a distance, carefully avoids. This complicity emerges as the observer's repetition of the textual construct he has co-authored in his own activity as interpreter. The method and strategy of interpretation reflect the particular coherence the observer establishes in the actor's life, as if the price of whatever satisfaction he derives from the sense of a "right" interpretation, as well as the vicarious pleasure of witnessing his own wishes enacted, must be the need to repeat that construction in his own life. Nick Carraway, for example, finds himself imitating the high idealism of Gatsby (which he himself has inferred) by at last giving up Jordan Baker, "this clean, hard, limited person" (p. 81) with whom he is at least "half in love" (p. 179). It as if Nick's reading of Gatsby as the last embodiment of the great American dream, and his avowal that " 'You're worth the whole damn bunch put together ' " (p. 154), can only be confirmed and validated by his own abandonment of a flawed reality—of any reality that fails to be "commensurate to his capacity for wonder" (p. 182).

We see a more complex interpretive repetition in *Absalom, Absalom!* in which Quentin and Shreve explain the deepest mystery of that novel—why Henry Sutpen killed Charles Bon—by deciding that Henry and Charles were half-brothers, the sons of Sutpen, and that Bon was part black. In the course of this explanation—much of it extremely dubious insofar as the known facts, the text, are concerned—Quentin and Shreve transform themselves into "brothers," putting forth their interpretation as a cooperative venture. They proceed to enact the very love they infer in Bon and Henry and, even more striking, the ensuing conflict—that which resulted in Henry's murder of Bon. Quentin's and Shreve's fraternal activity as interpreters is the means by which they achieve the novel's great breakthrough into the "truth" of the Sutpen history, but it also constitutes their repetition of the tragedy they describe. Imprisoned in the interpretation they have so convincingly devised, the two boys cannot help but follow its logic to the end, as their own relationship—like that of the Bon and Henry they imagine—dissolves into bitterness and misunderstanding. The validity of their reading, in other words, is bound up with their reenactment of it. Their personal conditions become the cause—and the effect—of their interpretation.[1]

II

The divided protagonist narrative, despite its fictional nature, is a tradition appropriate to the complex analytic experience Freud describes in the Wolf-Man case history, as analyst and patient—versions of the fictional observer and actor—bring forth a text whose ultimate coherence is dependent on a similar dynamic. Freud's writing of such a text is, of course, not the result of any knowledge of this narrative tradition, but rather of the gradual evolution of his ideas of therapeutic technique and of the particu-

---

[1] For a complete analysis of *Absalom, Absalom!* in terms of its narrators and their contributions to the story, see Kartiganer, 1979, pp. 37–68.

lar reality—the human mind and its neurotic formations—with which he was trying to deal. In general, we can characterize Freud's development in these areas as involving, first, a gradual loosening of the analyst's control of the patient's response, allowing it an increasing freedom in determining its structure and subject matter, and, second, a growing sense of the absence of any clear-cut source for the neurotic symptoms the patient revealed.

Basic to the early *Studies on Hysteria* (Breuer and Freud, 1893–1895) was the belief that symptoms were rooted in a traumatic event the memory of which, the idea of which, had proved incompatible with the ego and was repressed—only to return in the form of a "mnemic" symptom. The symptom was a "conversion" of the offending idea into a symbolic form—inconvenient but apparently less painful than consciousness of that idea would be. The traumatic event could be recalled under hypnosis and, through the patient's verbalization of it, accompanied by the original emotional response, could be "reproduced"—but now in a complete, hypnotically induced awareness. This full and final reenactment, action and idea performed before the analyst-audience, resulted in the disappearance of the symptom.

Freud soon discovered that the traumatic event and its relationship to the neurotic symptom were far more complicated than he and Breuer had realized. Dissatisfied with the failure of the "cathartic" method to cure symptoms permanently or to prevent them from being replaced by new ones, Freud found himself invariably going beyond the recollected event, progressing backward into the patient's past in a thickening array of associations and earlier events: "If the memory which we have uncovered does not answer our expectations, it may be that we ought to pursue the same path a little further; perhaps behind the first traumatic scene there may be concealed the memory of a second, which satsfies our requirements better and whose reproduction has a greater therapeutic effect; so that the scene that was first discovered only has the significance of a connecting link in the chain of associations. And perhaps this situation may repeat itself. . ." (1896, p. 195).

However intricate the series of memories and scenes the crucial event laid down as it receded into the past, Freud remained convinced of that event's status as a real, historical moment that the analyst could infer from the patient's responses and submit to him as the ground of his symptomatic behavior. In 1896 Freud announced his conclusions as to what the content of that event was most likely to be: "For now we are really at the end of our wearisome and laborious analytic work, and here we find the fulfillment of all the claims and expectations upon which we have so far insisted. . . . I therefore put forward the thesis that at the bottom of every case of hysteria there are *one or more occurrences of premature sexual experience,* occurrences which belong to the earliest years of childhood but which can be reproduced through the work of psycho-analysis in spite of the intervening decades" (1896, pp. 202–203). The experiences were real ones, "affecting the subject's own body," initiated by an older person, sometimes even a "close relative." (Freud did not here single out the parent.) If initiated by another child, it could only be because he had himself been sexually indoctrinated by an adult. The child, in other words, was always the victim of a sexual act he was incapable of desiring on his own.

Such a ground was not only more shocking than Breuer's original notions of the traumatic event, in which the sexual factor had been deliberately underplayed; it consisted of a reality which patients literally did not remember. Referring to his use of the "pressure" technique as a modification of Breuer's hypnotic method, Freud wrote in *Studies on Hysteria* that "sometimes . . . as the climax of its achievement in the way of reproductive thinking, it causes thoughts to emerge which the patient will never recognize as his own, which he never *remembers,* although he admits that the context calls for them inexorably, and while he becomes convinced that it is precisely these ideas that are leading to the conclusion of the analysis and the removal of his symptoms" (Breuer and Freud, 1893–1895, p. 272).

But the absence of literal recollection did not deter Freud from his conviction that the guiding assumption of the cathartic method still held: behind every symptom there was a real if complex cause, susceptible to methodical, scientific investigation. These scenes of childhood sexual experience, inferable from the logic if not the letter of the patient's associations, were the only piece that would complete the puzzle of the patient's neurotic condition: "Only that one piece fills out the picture and at the same time allows its irregular edges to be fitted into the edges of the other pieces in such a manner as to leave no free space and to entail no overlapping" (1896, p. 205). In short, Freud asserted, he had come to "*a caput Nili* in neuropathology" (p. 203).

It was, of course, this solid if somewhat sordid ground for the neuroses that Freud finally saw slipping away from him in the summer of 1897. In the famous letter to Fliess of September 21, 1897, Freud disclosed "the great secret which has been slowly dawning on me in recent months" (Freud, 1954, p. 215), the fact that he could no longer accept the seduction theory. Clearly this conclusion was bound up with Freud's own self-analysis, which began in June of that year, and his discovery of the Oedipus complex, first suggested in May. The various improbabilities of the original theory—the consistency with which perverse sexual acts were laid at the door of the father, the failure of the patient to remember such moments, the impossibility finally of distinguishing in the unconscious "between truth and emotionally-charged fiction" (p. 216)—apparently combined with Freud's discovery of his own infantile sexual desires, and the Oedipus complex that described their dynamics, to produce an entirely new understanding of the origins of neurosis. As Freud described it in *On the History of the Psycho-Analytic Movement* (1914), "Analysis had led back to these infantile sexual traumas by the right path, and yet they were not true. The firm ground of reality was gone. . . . If hysterical subjects trace back their symptoms to traumas that are fictitious, then the new fact which emerges is precisely that they create such scenes in *phantasy*" (p. 17).[2]

---

[2]This crucial rejection by Freud of the seduction theory is, of course, the crux of Jeffrey M. Masson's war with the American psychoanalytic community and the subject of his forthcoming volume *The Assault on Truth: Freud's Suppression of the Seduction Theory*. His essay (1984), "Freud and the Seduction Theory," while repeating the story of Freud's and Wilhelm Fliess' ill-conceived treatment of Emma Eckstein and Freud's shameful exoneration of Fliess [revealed in letters from Freud to Fliess omitted from *The Origins of Psychoanalysis* but printed in Schur (1966)], does not make a convincing case for his thesis that Freud abandoned the seduction theory "not for theoretical or clinical reasons but for complex personal ones that had nothing to do with science" (p. 59). These personal reasons are presumably Freud's need to maintain his friendship with Fliess, whatever the cost to truth, and a desire to achieve "an internal rec-

The evolution of Freud's thinking here reveals a duality in his fundamental investigative attitude that can be seen everywhere in his work, especially in the Wolf-Man case history. From one perspective he insists on the basically scientific nature of his work: he is in search of a causative moment in time, an event in the real world that can be discovered through a method of neutral, detached observation. Behind the uncanny arrangements of the self-deluding mind, which remembers and forgets in the same symptom, lies a concealed core of objectively recoverable evidence. But from another perspective Freud's quest seems not so much the scientist's search for facts as the romantic artist's determination to subvert any scene or structure that points too surely at bedrock and the end to all investigations. Taken together they constitute the characteristic Freudian activity of constantly opening closed cases, uncovering fresh complexity beneath ap-

---

onciliation with his colleagues" (p. 56). If such were Freud's intentions, it need hardly be pointed out that he failed at both. In attributing Freud's momentous decision to his desperate need for Fliess' and his colleagues' approval, Masson minimizes drastically the possible influences of the death of Freud's father, his self-analysis, and his discovery of the Oedipus complex – all of which were taking place during this period. Masson also ignores the free association technique which Freud was evolving at the time, and which helped shape (and was shaped by) Freud's developing ideas of the nature of that reality which he was trying to explore.

In addition to these factors, there is also implicit to Freud's reversal a recognition of the possibilities of therapy, of the analytic process as a means by which patients might not only identify but release themselves from their neuroses. Freud was not insensitive to the realities of abuse, nor without compassion for the child's position of weakness in the family structure: the act of repression is performed in the name of a perfectly understandable fear. Yet Freud must have seen in the new emphasis on fantasy rather than reality an alternative to the idea of neurosis as a necessity of the past and the adult patient as the victim of an attack inflicted on him as a child. Because of his rejection of the seduction theory, Freud could stress the significance of the patient's response to the conditions of his childhood as the foundation of his potential *revision* of that response. This revision could eventually be a re-writing of the narrative of his life, culminating in his release from the incessant repetitions of the original response. For Freud, the largest, most significant freedom lay not in the privilege of identifying the true (external) villain of one's neurotic life, but in the opportunity – conceived by the process of analysis against the "fact" of an irrevocable past – of re-inventing that life so that it frees itself both from neurosis and the very necessity of a villain to account for it.

parent clarity. Every solid ground yields new layers of memory and scene. Finally, having arrived at a moment in childhood which combines the required characteristics of *"suitability"* and *"traumatic force"* (1896, p. 193), a *"caput Nili"* indeed, he soon pushes on into a further realm of compromised reality.[3]

What emerged from Freud's investigative descent into the nature of neurosis was his discovery of the astonishingly fertile inventiveness of his patients: an unconscious capacity to create fantasy lives so powerful as to determine the shape of their real ones. The kernel of that fantasy might be the most innocuous circumstance inflated by the patient, at an indeterminable moment or series of moments, into a drama of imminent love and murder, complicated by a fear of reprisals equally fantastic. And that drama, issuing from pretexts as intangible as the processes of its evolution, inscribes itself on the patient's life as its single, encompassing "event"; he will perform it at every encounter with the world, distributing its already defined roles to each new actor that moves unknowingly onto the stage.

Freud's great model for this event was a piece of theater—*Oedipus Rex*—the mystery of whose enduring power Freud found answered in the unconscious desires of its audience. The most vivid example in his work of how elaborate drama can arise from virtually nonexistent roots came in one of the possible explanations he offered for the neurosis of the Wolf-Man (not his preferred explanation, as we shall see). This was the possibility that, when the one-and-a-half-year-old infant awakened from his nap that fateful afternoon, what he saw was his mother and father in their white bedroom attire: "but—the scene was innocent" (1918, p. 58). Such "primal scenes," empty of overt sexual content, become through the intricacies of deferred influence the "source" of a life of paralyzing psychic disturbance and pain. The drama which the Wolf-Man will enact throughout his life is a drama that, in a sense, rehearses nothing, represents nothing, contains nothing but the uncanny network of its own production.

In the language of present-day criticism, Freud began in 1897 the deconstruction of the concrete cause of his *neurotica*. But the

---

[3]For a review of Freud's gradual abandonment of the seduction theory, see Schimek, 1975.

effect was not merely to commit his findings or his patients to an endless chain of fictionalized scenes, repressive in their very illumination and productive of neither health nor truth. Rather, it was to permit a more appropriate engagement with psychic reality: a condition—invariably a disease of greater or lesser degree—that did not so much originate in a historical event as perform itself anew in every present, adding fresh dimensions to its expanding past. Given the pain of these performances, and the ultimate failure of growth they usually demonstrated, they were like bitter parodies of feast days—of the "returning festival" as Gadamer (1975) has described it: "It is not an identity, in the manner of an historical event, but neither is it determined by its origin so that there was once the 'real' festival—as distinct from the way in which it came later to be celebrated. Thus it is its own original essence always to be something different (even when celebrated in exactly the same way). . . . It has its being only in becoming and in return" (p. 110).

The enormous problem that Freud had raised for himself in 1897 was how to deal with this new reality: an unquestionably real mental and/or physical pain whose cause and aetiology were made available to him only as a series of performances grounded in no verifiable event distinct from those performances. The problem did not catch Freud by surprise, for in fact, even as he was working his way through to the conclusions of mid-1897, he was also modifying the technique which was at once a response to the new conditions and the partial cause of their discovery.

On a number of occasions Freud wrote that psychoanalysis truly began when he dispensed with the use of hypnosis as a means of unlocking his patients' memories of a traumatic past. In place of hypnosis, and following a transitional period in which he employed the "pressure" technique, Freud eventually adopted the technique of free association, the great virtues of which were to permit the patient's resistance and his tendency to "transfer" to reach the surface of the analysis—to become in fact the essential content of the analysis. Freud's objections both to hypnotic suggestion and Breuer's cathartic method were based on personal predilection as well as his dissatisfaction with their results. The practice of hypnotic suggestion was not only "monotonous: in each case, in the same way, with the same ceremonial, forbidding the most variegated symptoms to exist"; it was also demeaning: "It was hackwork and not a scientific activity, and it recalled magic, incantations and hocus-pocus" (1917, p. 449). Even the more sophisticated cathartic method must have had for Freud embarrassing connotations, especially when he was unsuccessful in his attempts to hypnotize a patient: " 'But doctor, I'm *not* asleep' " (Breuer and Freud, 1893-1895, p. 108). Most important, of course, hypnosis did not attempt to deal directly with the patient's resistances to cure, an understanding of which Freud found crucial to any insight into the cause and evolution of the neurosis. Instead, hypnosis had the effect of thrusting that resistance to one side, pushing directly past the patient's strange defense of his own symptomatic pain.

Freud's adoption of the pressure technique, apparently for the first time with Elisabeth von R. in the autumn of 1892, allowed him to encounter resistances more directly, and also permitted the analysis to penetrate beyond the "initial" traumatic event to events further back in the past, ultimately to the years of childhood. What linked this technique to the hypnotic methods, and what presumably led Freud to abandon it, was its quality of focusing the analysis too rigidly. To begin with, there was the use of the symptom as starting point. More important, even as hypnosis operated by suggestion or by precise questions regarding the origins of symptoms, the pressure technique operated as an "insistence": "I proceeded as follows. I placed my hand on the patient's forehead or took her head between my hands and said: 'You will think of [the origin of the symptom] under the pressure of my hand. At the moment at which I relax my pressure you will see something in front of you or something will come into your head. Catch hold of it. It will be what we are looking for—Well, what have you seen or what has occurred to you?' " (Breuer and Freud, 1893-1895, p. 110).

As long as the analytic quest had as its ultimate goal the recovery of a real event in the patient's past, such a focusing procedure on the part of the analyst could be justified. But with the discovery that such an event had an entirely different makeup than Freud expected, that it was more fantasy than reality, and that it was constantly being revised in its reproductions in the psychic life of the patient, Freud gradually relinquished this last control on the patient's responses, permitting the analysis to open itself to the full freedom of the patient's associating mind.[4]

The key difference between free association and Freud's previous techniques was that, loosened from the analyst's focusing questions and insistences, it allowed the patient to indulge fully his unconscious passion for repetition, for the reenactment of his neurotic drama within the analytic situation. Above all, it permitted him, through the dynamics of transference, to enlist the analyst himself as a participant in that drama: to "introduce the doctor into one of the psychical 'series' which the patient has already formed" (1912a, p. 100). In other words, the analyst found himself incorporated into the very text he was seeking to elucidate. He had now to attend to *himself* in that text: what the patient had made of him, what role he had assigned him in this latest performance of the drama. As a result Freud had to modify his stance of neutral observer and move from the position of spectator of the drama to actor, abandon his seat in the audience for a position on the stage. Bound no longer to a secure origin, the text spread itself across its many incarnations in the patient's life—finally including the analyst himself among its personae.[5]

The secrets of the neurosis were thus not be unearthed by the analyst, like the solid ruins of a buried age, but to be *experienced*, to be understood existentially as an event happening now, in the imagery of the encounter between the analyst and the patient. In Kierkegaard's terms, taken from the context of religious experience, the analyst knows only by becoming "contemporary" with the object of knowing, with the "*for thee*" of the past that alone determines what is real (Kierkegaard, 1850/1944, pp. 67-68).

In this new role as participant in, as well as commentator on, the neurotic drama, the analyst could scarcely rid himself of the reality of his own experience, the particular conflicts and history

---

[4]For a discussion of the period of Freud's use of the pressure technique, see Strachey's note in Breuer and Freud, 1893-1895, pp. 10-11.

[5]For a discussion of the notion of the patient as a "text," and for the relationship between psychoanalysis and literary criticism in general, see Chabot, 1982, pp. 49-75.

which constitute his character. The actor in a play does not leave his own personality in the dressing room when he walks out on stage, but rather performs his given role through whatever links he can construct between it and himself.

This incrimination within the drama provides the analyst with his fullest access to the patient's illness, by virtue of the fact that he is now *in* it. Like the observers in the divided protagonist narratives, the analyst studies the patient-text through the privilege of his own presence in it; he submits literally to the *will* of that text, but only in and through the self he is and has chosen to be. "You are either part of the solution or part of the problem," the radicals of the 60's used to say; what Freud discovered was that he could become part of the solution only by allowing himself to be transformed into part of the problem.

The place of the personality of Freud in the analytic treatment—however greatly modified by the transferring patient—was a topic he rarely discussed, except for his warnings about the dangers of countertransference. The patient's dramas were fueled by the energy of unconscious desire, and the analyst, finding himself the object of that desire, should be careful not to gratify it even as he must not frustrate it prematurely. Recent commentators on the analyst-patient relationship, however, have emphasized the partnership of that situation, and the impossibility of the analyst's maintaining a perfect neutrality. Leavy (1980) writes:

> Freud's early approach was that of the Hippocratic physician. As soon as transference and countertransference entered into his thinking, he was working from a radically different approach. The physician is no longer outside the illness; he is part of it, to the extent that he is the bearer of unconscious images from the patient's past on the one side, and to the extent that he needs to be in tune with his own disposition to make the patient the bearer of unconscious images out of his own (the analyst's) past. Moreover, as we shall see in greater detail, the arousal of personal, historical images of one's own is not a handicap to the analytic work unless it is neglected; on the contrary it is an essential part of it. We only grasp the mental life of another through the summoning up of these private images of our own past, but they become part of the

commonality of experience only when they pass through the ordering, regulating and transforming system of language [p. 32].[6]

This view of the analyst as necessarily bound to his own history, and progressing toward a new understanding of another's drama only by means of the enlarged understanding of his own, is consistent with modern theories of hermeneutics, especially as elaborated by Gadamer (1976). Building on Heidegger's attention to the interpreter's ontological condition as a factor in his understanding, Gadamer stresses the inescapable bias implicit to the ground of interpretation, the vehicle of contact with anything outside the self:

> It is not so much our judgments as it is our prejudices that constitute our being. . . . Prejudices are not necessarily unjustified and erroneous, so that they inevitably distort the truth. In fact, the historicity of our existence entails that prejudices, in the literal sense of the word, constitute the initial directedness of our whole ability to experience. Prejudices are biases of our openness to the world. They are simply conditions whereby we experience something—whereby what we encounter says something to us [p. 9].

The entry of the analyst into the analysis was, as Freud often acknowledged, potentially the most dangerous as well as the most productive stage of the analysis: transference was "on the one hand an instrument of irreplaceable value and on the other hand a source of serious dangers" (1940, pp. 31–32); "it is precisely [the phenomena of transference] that do us the inestimable service of making the patient's hidden and forgotten erotic impulses immediate and manifest. For when all is said and done, it is impossible to destroy anyone *in absentia* or *in effigie*" (1912a, p. 108). The upshot of transference was the possibility of change: the opportunity, in the controlled situation of the analysis, not merely to repeat the old conflict and the old decision but to decide a second time, choosing a course that would "lead . . . to a better outcome than that which ended in repression" (1917, p. 438).

---

[6]On the shifting attitude toward the relationship between the analyst and the patient, see Loewald, 1960.

In conjunction with this new intrusion of the analyst into the treatment, two other factors played a part in Freud's reading process. One of them was that structural element I have referred to in my discussion of the divided protagonist narrative—in this case the elaborate theory of personality development, particularly the Oedipus complex, which remained for Freud as an expanding but enduring grid on which to plot the specific responses of the individual patient. This theory operated as an objective counterpart to his more "biased" encounter with the text. It consisted of the various complexes, phases of sexuality, alternative regressions and fixations, that preexisted the individual case and needed only to be sensitively and selectively applied in order to yield returns of coherence from apparent chaos. Always, as one commentator has pointed out, there was the assumption that all the patient's responses "possess an extraordinary degree of interrelatedness and coherence," a "radical continuity" which could be realized through the analysis (Chabot, 1982, p. 64). And although Freud himself was the chief architect of this theory, he submitted to it as to a set of tested conventions, the psychoanalytic inheritance of scores of cases, now constituting a genuine tradition.

In addition to the structural factor—which, however objective, still originated outside and prior to the particulars of the individual patient—there were the initial stages of the free association procedure, which consisted ideally of a total submission of the analyst to the patient's text. Free from expectation or personal desire, the analyst seeks to maintain an utter openness to the textual facts being laid out before him. Freud prescribed for the analyst a posture of complete receptivity, an "evenly-suspended attention," in which there is no attempt to "direct . . . one's notice to anything in particular": "He should simply listen, and not bother about whether he is keeping anything in mind" (1912b, pp. 111–112). In an image of almost sublime detachment, Freud instructed the analyst to "turn his own unconscious like a receptive organ towards the transmitting unconscious of the patient. He must adjust himself to the patient as a telephone receiver is adjusted to the transmitting microphone" (pp. 115–116).

Thus theory and theatrics, the various forms of the analyst's vantage point, must await this stage of yielding to the patient's unique, dislocated utterance: the text as a series of images unpatterned by any order-making source other than the utterance itself. "Unknown" to itself in terms of its origins or concealed continuity, it is yet acknowledged here as, in one sense at least, the complete text, the bearer of all meaning.

As for interpretation, in its objective or subjective form, "the moment for disclosing to [the patient] the hidden meaning of the ideas that occur to him, and for initiating him into the postulates and technical procedures of analysis," this could begin only when "an effective transference has been established in the patient, a proper *rapport* with him" (1913, p. 139). In other words, the analyst divulges his interpretations only *within* the text, within the newest reproduction of the illness he is interpreting. Like the observers in the divided protagonist narratives, the analyst speaks necessarily out of his own perspective, but he does so in a language already modified by his place within the drama.

III

"From the History of an Infantile Neurosis" is not an analysis but the story of an analysis: not the actual process of interpretation which the case entailed but a story of interpretation, written after the fact. The transference is not spelled out, although the results, in terms of the particular role we find the analyst adopting in the course of his reading, enable us to infer it. In general I will concentrate on how, in the given narrative of the case history, the analyst reads the patient, the way he moves through the maze of symptoms toward a meaning which both he and the patient find valid—and therapeutic.[7]

When Freud encountered the wealthy young Russian in February 1910 he had already spent years in various kinds of therapy. He was, as Freud notes at the beginning of the case history, "entirely incapacitated and completely dependent upon other people" (1918, p. 7). Of his present condition Freud tells us little, since in the case history he concentrates almost exclusively on the

---

[7]For a discussion of the relationship in the case history between *fabula* and *sjuzhet*, story and plot, see Brooks, 1979.

infantile neurosis that had subsided by the time the patient was ten years old. What he makes clear, however, is the patient's inability to function in anything like a normal manner, apparently not even being able to dress himself (Brunswick, 1928, p. 367). The two symptoms of the adult neurosis Freud reveals confirm the patient's helplessness. He had to endure a perpetual constipation, being able to move his bowels only two or three times a week, and then only with the aid of an enema administered by a servant. He also lived with the constant feeling that, as he put it, "The world . . . was hidden by a veil." This veil was torn away, he said, only when, as a result of the enema, he was able to move his bowels. Then he "felt well again, and for a very short while he saw the world clearly" (p. 99).

Freud presents the neurotic behavior of childhood in detail: a sudden transition in a boy of three from good-naturedness to irritability, turning occasionally to rage; a wild fear of the picture of a standing wolf in a picture book; terror of certain creatures such as beetles and caterpillars which he would sometimes counter by cutting them to pieces. Between the ages of four-and-a-half and ten, the boy experienced an obsessional neurosis characterized by excessive piety, occasionally undermined by blasphemy: he could not go to sleep at night before he kissed all the holy pictures in his room, and yet at times he found himself thinking such thoughts as "God-swine, God-shit" (p. 17). He also had a need to breathe rapidly out or in when in the presence of old men, cripples, and beggars. Finally, as he approached puberty – after having had a very affectionate relationship with his father – he grew to be afraid of him.

Here then we have the "actor" of the case history – a series of pathetic and grotesque behavioral and affective fragments for which Freud must find meaning, a significant explanatory relation.

The story of Freud's reading begins with an impressive demonstration of the virtues of a structuralist approach. The first third of the case history is its daytime world, in which various symptoms release their secret meanings – verifiable through the patient's recollection of certain forgotten facts – to the pressure of standard psychoanalytic patterns and inferences. The analyst's interpretive posture is one of Freud's favorites: that of the cool, detached detective who seems to do no more than allow the patient to insert his puzzling symptoms into the waiting psychoanalytic grid. Freud's tone here is one of utter confidence, not so much in his own acumen as in the theory he implements. He seems delighted with the opportunities the case has provided him: an unusually long duration, an unusual severity of illness—always necessary for learning something new!—a chance to examine a childhood neurosis through the more sophisticated linguistic capacities of the adult. In the concluding paragraph of Section I there is a quiet, even complacent pride: "On the whole the results of the case coincided in the most satisfactory manner with our previous knowledge, or have been easily embodied into it" (p. 12).

Freud enumerates calmy in Section II the incredible list of symptoms, "the riddles" it was his task to interpret, and then in Section III—enticingly entitled "The Seduction and Its Immediate Consequences"—immerses himself in the tried and true procedures of psychoanalytic interpretation, recording the first breakthrough in the case. The process begins with two screen memories of the patient responded to by Freud with a construction that proves to be incorrect but succeeds in inspiring the patient to produce some dreams. These dreams turn out to be a repetition of fantasies which the patient had at puberty of certain aggressive, sexual actions he took toward his older sister during childhood. As a consequence of this particular analytic sequence the patient suddenly recalls that in fact his sister "had seduced him into sexual practices" (p. 20) when he was a child, probably a little over three years old. Freud also adds, without telling us when the information was revealed, that soon after the seduction, the boy "began to play with his member in his Nanya's presence" (p. 24), an act which elicited from her a response easily interpreted as a castration threat.

The sequence is complex and yet typical of psychoanalytic logic: present time, puberty time, two periods of childhood; screen memory, a false but suggestive construction by the analyst, dream, fantasy, factual recollection. It is a journey through several time zones and modes of perception, concluding in a number of solved riddles. Freud speculates that the early seduction of the patient at the hands of his sister, which inspired him to approach

Nanya sexually, produced a certain sexual passivity in him. Coming at a time when he normally would be entering a period of genital organization, this passivity forced him to regress to a pregenital, anal-sadistic stage. Hence the cruel treatment of animals. Also encouraged by the acts of his sister and Nanya was a passive sexual attitude toward his father, a "feminine" desire to have sexual relations with him. Since sadism would not be an effective approach to his father, he emphasized the masochistic side of the anal phase, going into unaccountable rages in order to receive punishment from his father, and thus providing himself with a version of the sexual pleasure he desired.

At this point Freud is simply employing standard psychoanalytic principles to explain and connect events which, in themselves, in their origin, and in the process of their present revelation, Freud finds neither unusual nor especially troubling. The boy experienced no anxiety; his behavior at this time, between three-and-a-quarter and four years old, was simply marked by "naughtiness and perversity" (p. 28). Operating securely behind the interpretation as check and confirmation are the theoretical structure built from the evidence of previous cases and the patient's memory, jogged by the analytic sequence into solid recollections.

In the last paragraph of Section III, however, Freud mentions for the first time the dream which the boy had on his fourth birthday, which divides the boy's childhood in half, between "naughtiness and perversity" and anxiety "in the most tormenting shape" (p. 28). This is the dream which will give the patient his name in psychoanalytic literature; and at its first mention there is an implicit warning that something dreadful is about to happen—to the boy and to the analysis.

The boy dreamed that he was lying in bed at night. "*Suddenly the window opened of its own accord,*" and he saw outside a bare walnut tree. On its limbs were sitting "*six or seven*" white wolves with large tails; they were perfectly still. He was terrified, "*evidently of being eaten up by the wolves*" (p. 29). In the dream he screamed, and then woke up from the dream. The anxiety of his childhood dates from that moment, taking the form of a fear of wolves, and particularly of a standing wolf in a picture book he had.

Freud's reading of this dream is wholly different in its procedure and result from the sequence of suggestion, dream, fantasy, and recollection in Section III. The difference is between the credible and the incredible, between a sequence that culminates in a factual recollection contributing directly to the solution of a symptom, and a sequence that culminates in a bizarre "primal scene" which the patient is never to recall.

Freud signals the entrance of the analysis into this new realm with a startling admission, an abrupt abandonment of the detachment and easy assurance of Sections I–III. He has established with his patient some early analyses of the dream and its consequences: evidence of a homosexual urge in the patient toward his father, a fear of castration suggested by the wolf's loss of his tail (in a story his grandfather told him). Particularly important is the conviction, based on certain qualities of the dream, of the existence of some actual scene concealed behind its strange, distorting imagery. Freud is at an impasse: "I have now reached the point at which I must abandon the support I have hitherto had from the course of the analysis. I am afraid it will also be the point at which the reader's belief will abandon me" (p. 36). In the following paragraph Freud presents his construction of that hidden scene. It is the single moment in the patient's life which he will accept according to the logic of construction but which he will never actually be able to remember. The scene, presumably witnessed by the boy, was of the boy's parents engaged in repeated intercourse, at least once from the rear. The boy woke from a nap and was able to see clearly both his mother's and father's genitals. He was one-and-a-half years old.

The scene itself, Freud argues, is hardly out of the ordinary; in fact it should be seen as something "commonplace and *banal*" (p. 38). What is highly unusual is the strange process of deferral by which the scene came to exert such a powerful influence on the patient—introducing the anxiety of the wolf phobia and subsequently, as we shall learn, every symptom of his childhood illnesses and those of his adulthood which Freud mentions.

Originally, at the age of one-and-a-half, the child did not find the scene disturbing; in fact, a motivating factor for the dream at four is an unconscious memory of a forgotten image of pleasure. At the age of four, however, in his dream recollection of it, he experiences complete terror. What has occurred, according to Freud, is that the boy has wished for some kind of sexual contact with his father—a desire which in Section III Freud has traced to the seduction by the sister and the threat from Nanya, both of which have inspired sexual passivity in him. The dream *should* serve its usual function of satisfying an unconscious wish—in this case allowing to surface, in the available, "innocent" imagery of a nursery tale and the imminence of Christmas, a previously witnessed scene which will provide him with a knowledge of what sexual intercourse with his father would be like.

But the dream is converted from wish-fulfillment to anxiety because in the interval between the primal scene and the dream certain incidents have occurred—the seduction, the threat from Nanya—which have introduced to the boy the possibility of castration. The scene, which has been recalled in order to provide gratification, is now recognized as the evidence of castration, of the mother who indeed has intercourse with the father, but only at the cost of being herself castrated—or so the absence of a penis suggests to the four-year-old dreaming boy. The content of the scene, the same as it was two-and-a-half years earlier, has been revised—not in action but in meaning—has altered in accordance with the altered knowledge of the boy whose dream refers back to it. The boy responds by repressing the homosexual wish which initiated the dream, and the repressed material immediately returns in the form of a wolf phobia: fear of castration. "*In great terror, evidently of being eaten up by wolves, I screamed* and woke up" (p. 29). In a sense the boy has reinvented a past which will, as a direct result, drive him into a severe neurosis.

The difference between this analytic sequence and the one in Section III is crucial. In III the patient winds his way, through combinations of dream, direct suggestion, and two types of delusion (screen memory, fantasy) to a real occurrence at the age of three-and-a-quarter, which contributed directly to certain kinds of abnormal behavior shortly thereafter. Here, in Section IV, dream, association, and analytic construction take the patient into an unverifiable, virtually prehistoric past, whose revised content has an impact infinitely greater and more immediate than the real scene he remembered in Section III. This primal scene, so central to the entire history, is rooted in insubstantiality, plays havoc with time and perception.

According to Freud, this scene spills across the patient's childhood, inscribes itself, in one distorted form or another, in each of his symptoms—finally including even those adult symptoms which Freud mentions. Each phase of neurosis takes sustenance from this problematic center and, in return, rebuilds it—without changing a single fact in its makeup. Every symptom, once perceived as unintelligible and unrelated, now discovers itself as one layer of the primal scene, planting itself within it in order to know itself in its own present: the wolf phobia, the religious obsession, the anal eroticism, the adult dependency on and strange response to the regular enemas—everything returns as a new edition of the crucial conflict (between a desire for homosexual gratification and a fear of castration) which organizes the primal scene in the boy's dream at four years of age.

Within the primal scene, as we gradually learn from the case history, lies the boy's fear of castration, his sexual passiveness as well as his sexual activeness, his homosexual as well as his heterosexual tendencies, his identification with and imitation of both his father and mother in their respective roles in the intercourse. The heavy breathing in the presence of old men, beggars, and cripples is in part an identification with the vigorous breathing of the father; the intestinal difficulties refer to what the infant assumes to be sexual penetration in the anus (although the four-year-old's fear of castration knows differently) as well as to the infant's form of response—a defecation—to the original scene. The posture of his mother in intercourse will lead him to the maid Grusha bending over her work, and forever after to peasant women as heterosexual object choices; his fear of castration attaches itself both to his mother—deprived of a penis—and to the father, who apparently loses his in the act of intercourse.

In the suffering of his present symptom—the constant enemas—the Wolf-Man repeats and reinterprets every element of the primal scene. With the enema, usually administered by a man, the Wolf-Man creates fantasies both of a return to the womb and of rebirth. He is himself penetrated, like his mother, and gives birth to a "child," who is also himself. He is at once within his mother's womb, having intercourse with his father and, according to the rebirth fantasy, having intercourse with his mother, the product of which is again himself. During these enemas the Wolf-Man claimed that the "veil" which hid the world from him was broken: "he saw the world and was re-born. The stool was the child, as which he was born a second time, to a happier life" (p. 100). According to Freud, "the tearing of the veil was analogous to the opening of his eyes and to the opening of the window. The primal scene had become transformed into the necessary condition for his recovery" (p. 101).

The construction of this primal scene and the recovery in it of each of the Wolf-Man's symptoms signal the shift in the case history from one mode of reading activity to another. Although he is still masterfully employing everything he has learned about the structure of dreams, their relationship to subsequent symptoms and the phases of personality, the brunt of Freud's interpretation is now gathering its force primarily from the power of his own personal stance and desire. Although the Wolf-Man collaborates in and confirms Freud's reading, his inability to remember the primal scene represents a denial of what was always a primary aim of the analysis, namely, the patient's ultimate recollection of the event of repression. Nevertheless, despite the absence of recall – or perhaps because of it – Freud absolutely insists on the central influence of this scene and, for the most part, on its literal occurrence. Now he is no longer the detached detective, methodically plugging symptoms and memories into a master plan, but a committed, desiring individual, caught up in a contemporary dispute within the psychoanalytic community and exercising a very personal and characteristic mode of behavior.

The first of these has to do with the conflict during the early years of the Wolf-Man analysis between Freud and Adler and Jung; the second has to do with Freud's stance of intellectual daring, a willingness to defy what is perhaps a more pleasing and even plausible interpretation in order to reach what he always insisted must be a disturbing, even intolerable truth. Both stances shape Freud's reading in accordance with what he requires of the case, the meanings he needs to see realized in the neurotic drama, *and* with his sense of what the case requires of *him*: what the actor-text, the patient, requires as an interpretive force that will generate an order to his life and a possible revision of it. In other words, Freud's intrusion into the interpretation is not merely an exploitation of the Wolf-Man's convenient neurosis, but a response to the needs of the text, to that actor within whose transferential drama Freud is performing his interpretive role.

The crux of the disagreement between Freud and his former followers was the issue of sexuality, particularly childhood sexuality and its impact on adult neurosis: whether in fact it was a primary cause of neurosis, as Freud argued, or whether it was itself the product of neurosis, projected by the adult back into the past as part of his refusal to confront the difficulties of the present. In the childhood neurosis of the Wolf-Man, with its clear sexual origins—whether the primal scene be thought of as literal or a projection from the age of four—Freud believed he had found irrefutable evidence for his position.

This debate with Adler and Jung—obviously peripheral to the immediate problem of the patient and at times seemingly petty and unworthy of Freud—becomes much more central when Freud links it to the need of the analyst, *and the patient*, to proceed with more boldness and risk than the conditions of the analysis will allow. Freud's attack on Adler and Jung, in the form it takes in this case history, is really an attack on any purportedly psychoanalytic approach—whether it be Jung's recourse to "actuality and regression" or Adler's to "egoistic motives"—which backs away from what Freud calls "the revolutionary and inconvenient advances of psychoanalysis" (p. 53). The view which locates "the causes of neurosis almost exclusively in the grave conflicts of later life" would, among other things, "involve the disappearance . . . of much that raises resistance to [psychoanalysis] and alienates the confidence of the outsider" (p. 49).

Of course, any procedure that avoids resistance and conciliates the outsider is immediately suspect for Freud. The issue here is not one of intellectual acuity or psychological perception; it is one of courage. The error of Adler and Jung lies in their unwillingness to descend to those depths at which psychological findings are both "inconvenient" and incapable of being absolutely grounded. The all-embracing significance of the primal scene, in its content and its ontology, remains, by Freud's own admission—I would say "boast" – in the twin hells of the unbearable and the unknown: places which only the boldest interpreters dare to invade.

It is in this emphasis on investigative courage that Freud joins his quarrel with Adler and Jung to his relationship with the Wolf-Man. For the daring Freud insists on as crucial to psychoanalytic investigation is the daring he insists on with his patient. It is the core of their relationship: the stance he offers the patient as stimulus and model, as the clarifying rationale for what the patient's chaotic life *might be taken to be*. In return – for the analysis is finally the cooperative construct of a story – the patient becomes for Freud the perfect embodiment of precisely that courage Freud is trying to bring into palpable being.

As in the divided protagonist narratives a complex exchange is taking place. Freud is the imaginative, articulate observer who discovers in the tortured life of the actor the living image of his own interpretive daring; the Wolf-Man is the actor who reconstructs that life on the armature of Freud's desire, transforming it from a series of fragments into a coherent design.

From both observer and actor a leap is demanded, a departure from what can be known and verified, into a world where meaning is a test not only of perception but of what one is willing to know – about oneself and the world one inhabits and investigates. Interpreter and actor, Freud and the Wolf-Man, make their descent together: the actor in order to understand who he is and why, the observer in order to discover in that identity the nature of what and how he knows. Together they retrace consciously the same path that the Wolf-Man's neurosis has blindly repeated forward, this time grounding the encompassing and signifying design of that path on the never-to-be-recollected scene of its possible beginning.

Toward the end of the case history Freud explicitly links his own interpretive courage with the courage of his patient, as if fully aware of the reciprocal action that is taking place. Returning to the dispute with Adler and Jung, Freud hypothesizes what their interpretation of the Wolf-Man's history would be. He suggests that they would see his patient's present fantasies of a return to the womb and rebirth (his response to that tearing of the "veil" which his enemas brought about) as a symptom of his "flight from the world" and a model on which he "concocted" the primal scene (p. 102). They would regard the construction of that scene as the supposed origin of his symptoms not as the mark of the patient's insight into the cause of his neurosis but as a way of protecting himself from some risk of adult failure: "He was driven to embark on this long backward course either because he had come up against some task in life which he was too lazy to perform, or because he had every reason to be aware of his own inferiority and thought he could best protect himself from being slighted by elaborating such contrivances as these" (p. 102). Two paragraphs later Freud, aware that his own attempt to describe "such early phases and ... such deep strata of mental life" is being challenged, writes that "it is better to perform that task badly than to take flight before it"; he insists that he will "put a bold face on it and show that I have not allowed myself to be held back by a sense of my own inferiority" (p. 104).[8]

What Adler and Jung would call the Wolf-Man's cowardliness in the face of some life task is, for Freud, precisely the opposite. His fantasies are the once unintelligible return to the origins of his life; and his courage in tracing these fantasies to their source is identical to, and supportive of, the courage of Freud himself—who will accompany him, as interpreter, every step of the way. The patient becomes the hero of his life as he becomes the image and action of the analyst's heroic desire.

The crucial, determining relationship in the Wolf-Man's life was that with his father, and presumably it is this relationship that is being repeated in the analysis, with Freud playing some version of the father's role in the patient's childhood. For the most part we can only infer the dynamics of transference from the case history account, yet I would suggest that the particular stance we have seen Freud taking as interpreter is one that is not only con-

---

[8]In the German text: "*Der Patient beklagt seine Weltflucht in einer typischen Muttërleibphantasie. ... Zu diesem ganzen Rückweg musste er sich entschliessen, weil er auf eine Lebensaufgabe stiess, für deren Lösung er zu faul war, oder weil er allen Grund hatte, seinen Minderwertigkeiten zu misstrauen und sich durch solche Veranstaltungen am besten vor Zurücksetzung zu schützen meinte.*"

"*Und es ist besser, man löst sie schlecht, als man ergreift vor ihr die Flucht... Man zeigt also lieber kühnlich, dass man sich durch das Bewusstsein seiner Minderwertigkeiten nicht hat abhalten lassen.*"

sistent with that father's role but reflects as well the necessary revision of the original relationship which must occur if the analysis is to be not only enlightening but therapeutic.

The patient's relationship with his father varied critically from the expected Oedipal conflict; instead of hating his father and desiring to get rid of him so that he could enjoy his mother exclusively, the patient felt a strong sexual attachment to him. It was this homosexual desire that the patient repressed when, in his childhood dream, he confronted the apparent evidence of castration. Therefore, in his relationship with the Wolf-Man Freud's reflection of the father is not as a seducer figure as in the "Dora" case history, nor an adversary figure as in the "Rat Man," but the figure of partner and comrade, befitting the Wolf-Man's repressed desire for his father. Freud's interpretive stance, which I infer as a reflection of the transferential stance, is also a model for the patient of the kind of activity necessary for the analysis and an active inducement to that activity.

The great problem in the analysis, Freud tells us, was the unwillingness of the patient "to take an independent share in the work": "His shrinking from a self-sufficient existence was so great as to outweigh all the vexations of his illness" (p. 11). Freud's response to this unwillingness is an authoritarian one, of naming a precise date for termination of the analysis. But that response, which had excellent results, is also a lesson in daring, for it demonstrates Freud's willingness to violate a cardinal rule of psychoanalysis (one he has just described in detail), namely, the need of the analyst to "behave as 'timelessly' as the unconscious itself" (p. 10). It is this daring, this willingness to risk, which gradually becomes the crucial dimension in Freud's interpretive role; it is a daring which he successfully inspires the patient to emulate and which becomes the basis of their relationship. The role obviously emerges from Freud's own personality, but it also speaks directly to the need of the patient, who must somehow break out of the paralysis of his nearly total dependency. He must discover for the analysis what he has been unable to discover for his life.

The function of the transference is not merely to repeat the old relationship but to revise it. Freud and the Wolf-Man reenact and rewrite the old, repressed homosexual bond, altering its fundamental spirit and paralyzing results. Freud's emphasis on interpretive courage is a reading of the reconstruction of the life of the Wolf-Man as itself an act of courage, a long, painful retracing of the past by analyst and patient that constitutes a remaking of it. Once the prisoner of a buried sexual desire for his father, the Wolf-Man revises that pathological past into the new and more productive relationship of comrades. As the Wolf-Man commented, long after the analysis, "I can only say that in my analysis with Freud I felt myself less as a patient than as a co-worker, the younger comrade of an experienced explorer setting out to study a new, recently discovered land" (Gardiner, 1971, p. 140).

Perhaps the best example of the Wolf-Man's growth within this "repetition" comes toward the end of the case history when Freud tests the problematical reality of the primal scene by raising the possibility that it "was a phantasy of [the patient's] later years," the result of "an observation or an experience by the patient of the administration of an innocent enema." The patient, who earlier has to be prodded into taking an "independent share," "looked at me uncomprehendingly and a little contemptuously when I put this view before him, and he never reacted to it again" (p. 95). The primal scene has come into being as the cooperative construct of the Wolf-Man and his analyst, and no one, not even Freud, can take it away.

There are two places in the Wolf-Man case history where Freud seems to threaten to unravel the rich, all-embracing construction that he and his patient have built—by seriously challenging the reality of the core of that construction, the primal scene. When Freud published the case history in 1918 he added to the draft of 1914 two notes in which he hedges somewhat on the literal occurrence of the scene, even while insisting that proof of childhood sexuality as a cause of neurosis is in no sense affected by that issue: There is a clear indication of some kind of sexual determination to the neurosis beginning at age four. The notes have attracted a good deal of attention from recent commentators, especially those of a deconstructivist bent, who have seized them as evidence that Freud ultimately centers the case history in a fiction, converting into fantasy the constructed univocal pattern of the Wolf-Man's life. The case history dissolves, as the current critical shibboleth has it, into "Undecidability."[9]

I do not think the notes support such a reading. To begin with, although Freud introduces various arguments against the position he takes throughout the case history, he by no means reverses himself. The first note suggests that the boy of four may have transferred onto an innocent scene a memory of sheepdogs copulating; yet the note concludes with the rather too coy *"non liquet"* and indicates that new disclosures will be forthcoming (p. 60). Moreover, Freud observes that, with the primal scene shifted from reality to fantasy, "how greatly the demands on our credulity are reduced," not to mention the elimination of what "was a disagreeable idea for many of us" (p. 58). Any expression of concern by Freud for our sense of what is plausible and decorous must always be taken with caution.

The second note focuses on the crucial episode with the nursery maid Grusha, the sexual nature of which, despite again the possibility that copulating dogs were the cause of the boy's apparent desire, leads Freud to reaffirm the primal scene: "I cannot deny that the scene with Grusha, the part it played in the analysis, and the effect that followed from it in the patient's life can be most naturally and completely explained if we consider that the primal scene, which may in other cases be a phantasy, was a reality in the present one" (p. 96). In the concluding paragraphs of the note Freud raises the possibility of a "phylogenetic heritage" in which racial memory supplies what personal experience has omitted. But Freud's last word on the subject hardly makes a case for a decentered case history: "Finally, I cannot feel surprised that what was originally produced by certain circumstances in prehistoric times . . . should, since the same circumstances persist, emerge once more as a concrete event in the experience of the individual" (p. 97).

The question to be raised here is not why Freud "erases" the primal scene into fantasy, but the very opposite one: why Freud insists on maintaining its literalness—even as he marches out all

---

[9]See, for example, Carroll, 1975; Brooks, 1979; and Culler, 1981, pp. 179–183.

the arguments against it. Freud makes abundantly clear that neither understanding of the Wolf-Man's life nor the cause of childhood sexuality requires a literal scene; and since 1897 he has recognized the possible fantasy nature of the sexual experiences of childhood. In the *Introductory Lectures on Psycho-Analysis* he asserts that, fantasy or reality, there is no "difference in the consequences" (1917, p. 370). Clearly we would all be more comfortable without the scene. But that, in this case history, is precisely the point. It is the very daring of Freud's insistence—indeed a somewhat gratuitous daring—that is crucial here. For it is perfectly consistent with the tenor of this case history: the role the analyst has chosen, the relationship between analyst and patient, the desire on which the patient has traced the explanation of his life. For Freud, recourse to the empirically verifiable fact is in some ways the last resistance analysis must overcome.

But there is another, and more serious, expression of doubt—one that did not need to be added in 1918. It comes in the final paragraphs of the case history as once again, as if fully implicated in the history's narrative compulsion, Freud returns to the primal scene. He takes up the matter of "phylogenetically inherited schemata" and their capacity to override individual experience, sexualizing innocent scenes. But then he shifts to a new problem "not far removed . . . but . . . incomparably more important." He considers again the four-year-old boy confronting the scene in a dream, the one-and-a-half-year-old infant confronting it in the flesh: "It is hard to dismiss the view that some sort of hardly definable knowledge, something as it were, preparatory to an understanding, was at work in the child at the time" (p. 120).

In this speculation about a "knowledge" which the boy or infant already *brings* to the scene—a knowledge which must imply a determination, a cause—Freud pushes past the scene that is the key to his construction. He is not questioning the *reality* of the scene but its *primacy*. He is not converting the scene into fantasy but into one more of those events in our lives that does not explain so much as it is something to be itself explained.

This is Freud the reader caught in the rhythm of his reading, forcing his way, as if compelled by his own interpretive logic, to reopen the stucture he has contrived and defended with such skill. He is now within the control of his own imagination, driven by the impulse of intellectual daring into a new subversion of the very history it has generated. It is as if Freud is no longer determining but *following* the action of the Wolf-Man, who has freed himself from the paralysis of the single repeating structure. Like the fictional observers of divided protagonist narratives – who confirm their imagined structures by succumbing to their power – Freud finally follows and validates the reading which is this case history by breaking through it into the new, unexplored territory that lies on the other side.

REFERENCES

Breuer, J., & Freud, S. (1893–1895). *Studies on Hysteria*. S.E., 2.
Brooks, P. (1979). Fictions of the Wolfman: Freud and narrative understanding. *Diacritics*, 9:1.
Brunswick, R. (1971). A supplement to Freud's "History of an Infantile Neurosis." In M. Gardiner (Ed.), *The wolf-man by the wolf-man* (pp. 263–307). New York: Basic Books. (Original work published 1928).
Carroll, D. (1975). Freud and the myth of the origin. *New Lit. Hist.*, 6:513–528.
Chabot, B. (1982). *Freud on Schreber: Psychoanalytic Theory and the Critical Act*. Amherst: University of Massachusetts Press.
Conrad, J. (1971). *Heart of darkness*. (R. Kimbrough, Ed.; rev. ed.). New York: Norton. (Original work published 1899).
Culler, J. (1981). *The Pursuit of Signs: Semiotics, Literature, Deconstruction*. Ithaca: Cornell University Press.
Fitzgerald, F. S. (1925). *The Great Gatsby*. New York: Charles Scribner's Sons.
Freud, S. (1896). The aetiology of hysteria. *S.E.*, 3.
_____ (1912a). The dynamics of transference. *S.E.*, 12.
_____ (1912b). Recommendations to physicians practising psychoanalysis. *S.E.*, 12.
_____ (1913). On beginning the treatment (further recommendations on the technique of psycho-analysis). *S.E.*, 12.
_____ (1914). On the history of the psycho-analytic movement. *S.E.*, 12.
_____ (1917). *Introductory Lectures on Psycho-Analysis*. S.E., 15 & 16.
_____ (1918). From the history of an infantile neurosis. *S.E.*, 17.
_____ (1940). *An Outline of Psycho-Analysis*. S.E., 23.
_____ (1954). *The Origins of Psychoanalysis*. New York: Basic Books.
Gadamer, H-G. (1975). *Truth and Method*, Eds. G. Barden & J. Cumming. New York: Crossroad.
_____ (1976). *Philosophical Hermeneutics*, trans. & ed. D. Linge. Berkeley: University of California Press.
Gardiner, M. (1971). *The Wolf-Man by the Wolf-Man*. New York: Basic Books.

Kartiganer, D. (1979). *The Fragile Thread: The Meaning of Form in Faulkner's Novels*. Amherst, MA: University of Massachusetts Press.

Kawin, B. (1982). *The Mind of the Novel: Reflexive Fiction and the Novel*. Princeton: Princeton University Press.

Kierkegaard, S. (1944). *Training in Christianity and the Edifying Discourses which "Accompanied" It*, trans. W. Lowrie. Princeton: Princeton University Press. (Original work published 1850).

Leavy, S. (1980). *The Psychoanalytic Dialogue*. New Haven: Yale University Press.

Loewald, H. (1960). On the therapeutic action of psycho-analysis. *Internat. J. Psycho-Anal.*, 41:16–33.

Masson, J. M. (1984). "Freud and the Seduction Theory." *The Atlantic:* 253 (February 1984):33–60.

Schimek, J. G. (1975). The interpretations of the past: Childhood trauma, psychical reality, and historical truth. *J. Amer. Psychoanal. Assn.*, 23:845–865.

Scholes, R., & Kellog, R. (1966). *The Nature of Narrative*. New York: Oxford University Press.

Schur, M. (1966). "Some Additional 'Day Residues' of the 'Specimen Dream of Psychoanalysis.'" In: *Psychoanalysis—A General Psychology*, Eds. R. M. Loewenstein, L. M. Newman, M. Schur, & A. J. Solnit. New York: International Universities Press, pp. 45–85.

2 Ghost Writing: A Meditation on Literary Criticism as Narrative

Madelon Sprengnether, Ph.D.

> *And what should dream or writing be if, as we know now, one may dream while writing.*
> Jacques Derrida, *Of Grammatology*

> *But poems are like dreams: in them you put what you don't know you know.*
> Adrienne Rich, *"When We Dead Awaken"*

This is an essay about narrative, specifically the kind of narrative that we call literary criticism. It is at the same time an example of autobiographical writing and a form of storytelling, my point being that the practice of literary criticism participates in both these forms: fiction and autobiography. In order to demonstrate the interweaving of these forms, I have chosen first to examine some of my own critical writing in the light of my understanding of my concerns at the time of writing, then to consider the process of narrative formation through the efforts of my young daughter towards interpretation, and finally to discuss the "ghost" in narra-

---

An earlier version of this essay was presented at the Modern Language Association in 1979 in a session on "The Self in Criticism," sponsored by the Division on Psychological Approaches to Literature. A grant from the University of Minnesota in the form of a single-quarter leave has enabled me to complete it.

tive, the way in which writing is haunted by the unconscious. In telling this story I shall be recreating in some measure the process of my own discovery: my shock at recognizing the shapes of my desire revealed in my critical writing, my fascination with my daughter's narrative constructions, which I came to see as a model for self-creation, or the creation of an ego, and my conviction finally that this ego (as Lacan has claimed) is haunted or shadowed from the moment of its creation by a kind of ghost. I see writing in this way as the product of both conscious and unconscious activity, a design inhabited by dream and desire. By opening literary criticism (a form of narrative usually excluded from such discussion) to this kind of understanding I would hope to open it as well to a sense of movement and play.

I recognize, of course, that my own essay, as a story or a series of parables, has its own ghost, a shape of desire, apart from my stated intention, that urged it into articulation, that haunts it still at the moment of this writing. Once named, however, this ghost shifts its location, as each self-creation ceases to be true from the moment it is apprehended. This interplay—between the ego and its shadow, writing and its ghost, criticism and desire—interests me. I would like the reader to regard the essay that follows in the spirit of Montaigne, as an experiment, a trying out, a movement towards some understanding of this interplay.

Many years ago, when I was in graduate school, I began to be troubled by the sense that my critical writing bore no relation to my daily life. While I wrote cheerfully and prolifically about unities and harmonies in texts, I felt my life to be full of dissonance. The wisdom I professed in my seminar papers about human relations and which I claimed to discover in the stories, poems, and novels I read, was nowhere evident in my relations with my family or my friends. Not knowing how to resolve the apparent split between what I said and what I did, I tried to accommodate myself to this schizoid condition. For a while this was not only possible, it was encouraged by the critical mode in which I had been trained to read: the New Criticism.

I was living, in 1964, in a fairly sheltered environment, one which permitted the exclusion of both personal and political concerns from the realm of literary interpretation. By 1968, the time at which I left graduate school, this illusion had been shattered, primarily by the pressure of the Vietnam war, a pressure which I, and the people I knew, experienced in every area of our lives. The kind of genteel separation between life and work with which I was familiar, at a time when people were marching on Washington, burning draft cards, and refusing induction orders, seemed not only impossible but absurd. I will not lay claim, however, to any sudden revelation, only to an increased awareness of the problem from which I was suffering.

Other events in my first year of teaching contributed to this awareness. In the spring of 1969, I gave birth to a daughter, whose presence in my life has altered my relation to myself and to my profession. The lines of demarcation I had drawn between my thoughts and feelings, my intellectual and emotional life, my lectures on the human condition and the nitty gritty of changing diapers, cooking, and housekeeping, began to blur, even in the absence, in those years preceding the rebirth of the women's movement, of a rhetoric in which to discuss these matters. It was in the area of teaching that I first found a language more congenial to my needs.

The books I was reading at that time were mainly about children and dealt with the relationship between learning and trust. I read Holt (1968), Kozol (1967), Dennison (1969), Herndon (1968), Kohl (1967), Erikson (1950), and Piaget (1968), and paid attention to my daughter and her apprehensions of the world, making connections where I could between these intimate contexts of learning and the ways in which my students seemed to learn. The books I was reading all dealt in some measure with the emotional climate in which learning (a seemingly abstract process) takes place. I was drawn to these texts because they offered models of interaction that included more aspects of experience than the ones with which I was familiar. While I began teaching at an opportune moment, given the amount of educational innovation which characterized that period, I was not myself a great innovator. But I did try to personalize my teaching a little, holding some classes at my house and getting to know some students as friends.

In the meantime, I was struggling to complete my dissertation, a process I found extremely painful and which was accomplished only through an enormous effort of will. Its subject matter, I now think, reflects this sense of struggle, dealing with works that pose significant barriers to form: Nashe's picaresque tale *The Unfortunate Traveller*, Sidney's mammoth and unfinished *New Arcadia*, and Spenser's metamorphic *Faerie Queene*. In each work I argued for a concept of emergent form, an order that becomes apparent to the reader in the process of reading, out of an initial sense of disorder or fragmentation. Later I abandoned this argument, feeling uneasy about my insistence on a harmonious resolution in texts which seemed more clearly problematic. I felt I was forcing the issue, as though I were trying to fit the Renaissance back into a medieval framework.

It was in the period following the completion of my dissertation, moreover, that I experienced my most severe writing problems. The first essay I wrote for publication underwent at least five rewritings before it made any sense. Through the first three rewritings, it became progressively more incoherent: stilted, garbled, and abstract. Finally, after teaching a course on the picaresque, I was able to write my way out of the dilemma. Given my sense of internal division, it seems no accident to me now that this essay concerned problems of narration in a mode which exhibits an unstable relation between style and subject.

Nashe's picaresque narrator, I argued, remains willfully ignorant or unconscious of the increasingly violent and deterministic nature of his encounters. This stance seems designed to rescue him from despair, from the realization that, as I phrased it then, "We are all unfortunate travellers, embarked on a course of suffering, loss of liberty, and death." I did not perceive when I wrote this how much I felt drawn to such a vision and unaccountably moved by the grisly scenes of torture and execution so characteristic of this book and of Nashe's style generally. What saved me from this realization is what saves Jack from a similar awareness, a half-willed decision not to see, a fundamental evasiveness in the interests of hope. I, like Jack, relied on "wit," on all the verbal strategies at my command to distance myself from the vision of punishment which so deeply informs his world, and perhaps my own.

It was not until two essays later that I began to observe the ways in which the works I chose to write about and the problems that drew my attention reflected some of the issues with which I was wrestling personally. Not long after I started psychotherapy, I wrote again about Sidney's *New Arcadia*, focusing this time, not on the triumph of order, but on the convolutions of the narrative as an index of Sidney's interest in a kind of psychological fiction for which he had no adequate models. I became interested in mannerism as a style which formalizes disjunctions such as this between form and content and which raises questions of interpretation in deliberately non-transparent modes of fiction. This interest also manifested itself in a continuing fascination with Spenser's allegory, another narrative mode in which things are not what they appear to be.

The experience of psychotherapy as a reinterpretation or radical rewriting of my life contributed to my absorption with strategies of narrative duplicity or opacity. In terms of personal narrative I was dealing with a text that no longer made sense to me, one that seemed to obscure rather than to illuminate my history. In writing about *Euphues*, I found myself describing the euphuistic style as a kind of verbal camouflage, designed to protect both speaker and listener from direct understanding. It was in the course of writing this essay, moreover, that I first perceived the extent to which I was writing myself through the process of interpreting a literary work.

I had stopped in the middle of a paragraph to read over a passage which I had composed with unusual ease, when I recognized with a shock the parallel between what I had just written and a particularly painful aspect of my recent history. I was first embarrassed by this realization, then anxious that I was too revealed, that my readers would know more than I wanted them to know about me from reading this essay. Then I began to notice how few people shared my understanding about the autobiographical aspects of literary interpretation, and I felt protected by their ignorance. Also, during this period, I felt vaguely ashamed of the habit I was forming of shifting perceptions I had about my relations with people with whom I was intimate into the realm of literary understanding. Since they were my clearest insights I was not about to give them up, at the same time that the whole process somehow seemed illegitimate, or at the very least not something I should talk about.

I was still haunted by the paradigm of objectivity I had inherited from my graduate training. I needed a critical language that permitted a greater degree of latitude in discussing matters of emotional complexity. It makes sense that I should have turned at this point to psychoanalytic theory. While I had, in a nonsystematic way, read a good deal of Freud in the previous ten years, I began my serious reading of psychoanalytic theory with Winnicott. I started with *Therapeutic Consultations in Child Psychiatry* (1971b), the book that describes the squiggle game, in which child and therapist participate in the creation of an image by adding to one another's doodle marks. This game, according to Winnicott, engages the child's unconscious fantasies when he or she becomes absorbed in it to a sufficient degree. Winnicott describes this stage of absorption as something like the moment of passage from consciousness to unconsciousness we experience in going to sleep. I was struck by this description, in part because my daughter was at an age at which she voiced her fantasies as easily as her more ordinary perceptions about her world. I began to listen in.

One day, after she had gone to a three- and four-year-olds' birthday party at a fish hatchery, where each child had had the opportunity to catch a small fish, she started talking, as she was falling asleep, about what she had seen. At first she described how, after a fish was caught, the man who was helping them would clean it, slitting the fish open, and letting it bleed in the water. Then gradually, with no apparent transition, she began talking about vampires and how it is safer to kill them with a knife than with a gun because with a gun you might miss. This perception in turn led her to her final observation that if someone were to cut her open like the fish, she would die. It seemed to me at the time that I was hearing the process Winnicott described—the moment of elision between the world of reality and that of dream. My daughter was at that moment weaving the events of the day into her fantasy life in a way that amounted to an interpretation.

I became more attentive to these childish attempts at interpretation. One morning, as I was making breakfast, absently listening to her chatter, I caught the phrase "God's wife." I stopped and asked, "Does God have a wife?" "Well, yes," she said. She paused for a moment and then explained, "Because what about the queen and the baby?" I realized that the image of the queen and the baby had come from a book of mine with reproductions of illuminated manuscripts, in which Mary is depicted as the queen of heaven, holding Jesus on her lap. My daughter's assumption, from the little she had heard about God was that he was the king of heaven and that Mary, being a queen, must be his wife, and Jesus their child. She had constructed a family image replete with sexuality, where orthodox Christianity has taken some pains to disjoin these elements. Her interpretation, on the whole, seemed the more sensible one.

I had not noticed until this point the extent to which she had become engaged in the formation of religious myth—neither my husband nor I had offered her any religious training. Some of her most profound thoughts on the subject came, I later discovered, from the movie "Jesus Christ Superstar," which she saw with a teenage friend. What impressed her most about this film was the portrayal of the crucifixion. For weeks, she would announce solemnly, at random moments, "God died," except that her word at the time for die was "dive." At the same time, a good friend of ours that fall had died, and she would, in the same reverent tones, refer to the fact that "Paul dive" and "God dive." While she was in some sense coming to terms with the idea of death, she had not yet encountered the idea of resurrection. This concept entered her consciousness from a different direction.

One day at the beach a little boy she knew nearly drowned. By the time he was pulled out of the water, he had stopped breathing and had to be revived with mouth-to-mouth resuscitation. Later he was taken to the hospital, where he made a full recovery. My daughter was extremely impressed by this scene and for a long time afterward would talk about how when you die you are taken to the hospital where the doctors bring you back to life. She was similarly impressed for a while by the children's room of the local natural history museum, where there were many animal pelts and bones for the children to handle. This led to another serious meditation in which she concluded (until I explained otherwise) that when people die their skins are taken off, but their faces are left on—like the animal skins she had seen at the museum. This meditation was also coupled with a reflection, drawn from a different source, that "we are all covered with blood when we are born."

Slowly I realized that the theories she had constructed were not, as I supposed, based on my attempts at realistic explanation, but rather that they were drawn from a multitude of sources, some of which were unknown to me, and that they underwent various transformations internally until they emerged in a form which bore the marks of her particular character and intelligence, as well as reflecting in some fashion the problems with which she was struggling at the time. Sometimes she would be engaged in a process of interpretation for months without my being aware of it. The most poignant example of this silent labor concerned our move from Vermont to Minnesota when she was two-and-a-half. We had, I thought, explained to her why we were moving, that we had better jobs in Minnesota and that we thought of Minneapolis as a good place to live. One day as we were driving home, she asked again why we had moved and I repeated this explanation, at which point she asked if the old home was broken.

I would be tempted to use the word "bricolage" to describe my daughter's interpretive strategies, if it did not sound as though I were attempting to raise an infant structuralist. But the word does describe something of the way in which she fashioned explanations of her world out of the random bits of information available to her, from her parents, her friends, her cultural environment. Her vocabulary is simultaneously idiosyncratic and plagiarized. Her picture of the world is a collage composed of the accidents of her gender, race, nationality, the historical moment in which she lives, and the personal histories of her parents, as well as her own. She alludes to all of these elements, embedding them in her essays towards understanding, in the way, perhaps, that a more sophisticated author such as Montaigne might allude to classical texts in his essays explaining himself and his relations to the world. For she is, of course, an author, like the small Gabrielle, in Winnicott's posthumous case study called *The Piggle* (1977), struggling to articulate her perceptions in a fashion comprehensible to herself and others.

What I have said about my daughter is no doubt obvious to psychoanalysts and to most parents. It does not seem to be as obvious to literary critics, many of whom will affirm the radical instability of texts, while implicitly affirming the stability of their method of interpretation, seeking a metaphysical basis in the process of interpretation which is immune from the accidents of personality. To the extent that the deconstructionist mode is practiced in this fashion it resembles the New Criticism in its insistence on the objectivity or impersonality of the interpreter.

What I came to understand about my own writing (and here I mean journal writing, notes I make to myself about teaching, poems, and personal essays, as well as literary criticism) is that it is perhaps the primary way I have of apprehending myself in relation to the world. By creating a narrative, composed of elements both internal and external, I am also creating a self, or perhaps a series of selves, since this process, like that of psychoanalysis, is properly speaking interminable. When I accepted this, the act of writing itself became easier for me. It also became more revealing. I have begun to think recently, for instance, about my obsession with interpretation itself and why it is that I first wrote about texts which pose such obvious barriers to understanding. I remembered that when I was in high school I loved the fiction of Henry James because his protagonists were so often immersed in an ambiguous and confusing linguistic environment, requiring heroic efforts at interpretation. This world seemed to me at the time to be completely familiar and thus realistic. It felt like my family, in which indirect discourse was the norm. I was used to translating what was said into what was meant, assuming throughout that I was dealing with two texts, one of which was unstated. If my taste for James has waned, it is because of other changes in my life. The texts I am most drawn to at any given period of my life seem to be the ones that give form and expression to problems or issues I only dimly perceive in myself. In this sense, they act as extended metaphors or objective correlatives, and my engagement with them an attempt through narrative to draw into consciousness some of the buried metaphors by which I live.

Thus literary interpretation strikes me as a refracted form of autobiography. The text of psychoanalysis itself—the product of a complex interplay of internal and external observation, informed with metaphor—may be read in this fashion. Derrida (1978) makes this point (among others) about Freud's *Beyond the Pleasure Principle*. By reconstituting the web of relations among Freud, his favorite daughter Sophie, who died shortly after the birth of her second child (Freud's favorite grandson, who shortly thereafter also died) and the first child Ernst, who played in earnest his game of absence and return, Derrida reveals the melancholy undersong of this most melancholy book. Metapsychology for Freud reads as poetry, a shaking loose of metaphor that acts as personal narrative, no less powerful or persuasive for being so. That Derrida's essay in turn may be subjected to this kind of scrutiny has been efficiently demonstrated by Johnson (1977) in her reading of Lacan's reading of Poe.

We are by now becoming accustomed to reading Freud as a literary text. How long will it take for us to read Derrida in this fashion? To what extent does repetition compulsion, for example, characterize the career of a literary critic? Does the figure of Sophie, for instance, disappear from Derrida's text on Freud to return in the guise of Nietzsche's veiled figure of woman as truth (Derrida, 1979)? Does this Sophie, related by Derrida himself to Freud's mother and by implication to the triple goddess of the essay on the three caskets, in any way resemble the forever absent mother of Rousseau (Derrida, 1976)? If so, what significance could one attribute to such a pattern? What significance could one attribute to my interest in tracing such a pattern?

There is, as Johnson (1977) indicates in her discussion of frames of reference, no privileged position from which to read this series. While de Man (1971) refers to this awareness in terms of the critic's blindness, I prefer to think of it as the necessary inscription of the unintended. Literary criticism, like every other form of writing, bears its freight of unconscious meaning. The dream of total objectivity is a dream of total outsidedness, whereas the message of modern psychoanalysis is one of participation, of complicity, of the simultaneous elusiveness of boundaries and of the self. While Lacan (1977) seems engaged in guerilla warfare against the domestication of consciousness, Derrida systematically dismantles the structures of Western thought which have permitted such a cheapening of our mental life. Derrida, in particular, by "othering" writing, reveals its resonance.

It is, I believe, the necessary inscription of the unintended in any text which creates the quality of resonance, that rich wake of meaning which rocks our conscious life and disturbs us in our dreams. Passionate readers are aware of the brooding presence of certain texts in their lives, of the extent to which their lives may be organized around lines of poetry, situations in novels, characters in plays, which alter and accrue meaning through time just as the events of their childhood, altering in memory, reverberate throughout their lives. We do not distinguish, in such instances, between real and fictional events, any more than we do in our dreams.

Sodium pentothol, I am told by a forensic psychiatrist, was abandoned as a truth serum for legal purposes when it was discovered that under its influence people revealed their fantasies as readily as their actions, according them the same weight, the same validity. Harold Bloom, a reader of Blake and Hart Crane at six, once said to me that for him at that age these books constituted what was real. My daughter at age two could not distinguish between the wolf on stage in a production of *Peter and the Wolf* and a real wolf who might eat her. She finally resolved her anxiety, while watching the performance that day, still believing in the reality of the wolf, by claiming that she was too big for him to eat. Such innocence in the face of fantasy is of course dangerous, but so is the denial of dream altogether, which produces even stranger fantasies, like that of the solitary rationalist Descartes, annihilating the disappointingly fallible world from his armchair in order to reconstruct it on a basis of mental certitude. And still he couldn't be sure he wasn't dreaming.

Winnicott (1977), in his seventies, sat on the floor to play with a three-year-old child who was terrorized by her own dream creations. He attempted to enter her world in order to help her understand her own symbol-making mind, not to destroy it, but to relate it to what she already knew. The conversations between this elderly man and this little girl reveal a process of communication which, like sodium pentothol, does not respect the boundaries between fantasy and reality, in which communication on fantasy levels in particular is necessary for health, if by health we mean the capacity to live relatively comfortably with other people in the world.

Winnicott's fascination with sliding states of consciousness emerges elsewhere in his formulation of transitional space as the locus of cultural activity and play (1971a). A relaxed acceptance of this condition of blurred boundaries, he would argue, is a prerequisite for artistic production. Milner (1957), in an essay dealing not with writer's block, but with painter's block, talks about the inhibiting effect of fear of the unintended, of not allowing room for the expression of the unanticipated in one's work. She relates this to fear of one's own unconscious mind.

Looking back now on my own writing in graduate school and my subsequent difficulties, it seems to me that the feeling of hypocrisy from which I suffered had to do with the weight of everything I could not say, in part because of the inadequacy of my critical vocabulary, but also because of my fears about myself and my dreams. I was afraid, even in an impersonally styled essay, of revealing anything but my belief in unity, harmony, and grace. To have done otherwise, at that time, would have undermined my fragile sense of self. It was a long time before I could give up my fiction of control, the illusion that there was nothing hidden either in my writing or in my life. I had to acknowledge the presence of some of the ghosts in my life before I could allow them to inhabit my writing.

I have also had to admit that I will never know them completely. While the language I invent for them allows them to speak, it is not their native tongue. They are liars and plagiarizers, borrowing my words for their existence, compulsively telling their story. To this extent, all writing is simultaneously fiction and autobiography. To accept this condition perhaps is to be able to play, in the unself-conscious world-making way that children do. The understanding of the small Gabrielle, as reported by her mother, about the voluminous notetaking activity of Winnicott during their sessions together was that he was writing his autobiography, as of course he was, reading himself through her as she through him. Gabrielle's summary of this mutually dependent and illuminating interpretive process was this: "He used to write and I used to play" (Winnicott, 1977, p. 201).

REFERENCES

de Man, P. (1971). *Blindness and insight*. New York: Oxford University Press.
Dennison, G. (1969). *The lives of children*. New York: Random House.
Derrida, J. (1976). *Of grammatology*, trans. G. C. Spivak. Baltimore: Johns Hopkins University Press.
_____(1978). Coming into one's own. *Psychoanalysis and the question of the text*, ed. G. Hartman. Baltimore: Johns Hopkins University Press.
_____ (1979). *Spurs: Nietzsche's Styles*, trans. B. Harlow. Chicago: University of Chicago Press.
Erikson, E. (1950). *Childhood and society*. New York: Norton.

Herndon, J. (1968). *The way it spozed to be*. New York: Simon & Shuster.
Holt, J. (1968). *How children fail*. New York: Pitman.
Johnson, B. (1977). The frame of reference: Poe, Lacan, Derrida. *Yale French Studies*, 55-56:457-505.
Kohl, H. (1967). *36 Children*. New York: New American Library.
Kozol, J. (1967). *Death at an early age*. Boston: Houghton Mifflin.
Lacan, J. (1977). *Ecrits*, trans. A. Sheridan. New York: Norton.
Milner, M. (1957). *On not being able to paint*. New York: International Universities Press.
Piaget, J. (1968). *Six psychological studies*. New York: Vintage.
Winnicott, D. W., (1971a). *Playing and reality*. New York: Basic Books.
_____ (1971b). *Therapeutic consultations in child psychiatry*. New York: Basic Books.
_____ (1977). *The piggle: an account of the psychoanalytic treatment of a little girl*, ed. I. Ramzy. New York: International Universities Press.

II CLINICAL APPROACHES TO CREATIVITY

3 The Psychiatrist in the Movies: The First Fifty Years

Irving Schneider, M.D.

The last decade of the 19th century saw the birth of two inventions that were to have a profound effect on the social and cultural life of the 20th century: motion pictures, and modern psychiatry and psychoanalysis. Not only do their histories cover virtually the same time period, but they show many striking developmental parallels (Schneider, 1977).

The new motion picture system was first demonstrated publicly by Lumière and others in 1895, the year in which Freud wrote his *Project for a Scientific Psychology*, the prototype of his later theoretical system. And in 1900, when Freud published his monumental *The Interpretation of Dreams*, George Méliès made, among other films, *The Miser's Dream of Gold*, *The Rajah's Dream*, *The Christmas Dream*, and *The Man with Wheels in His Head*.

So strong has been the affinity between psychiatry and the motion picture that from the very beginning of their joint history they have turned to each other for subjects and concepts. Dream screens, frame analysis, and flashbacks have infiltrated psychological analysis; amnesia, hallucinations, dreams, madness, and odd motivations have not only contributed to many good movies, but have also provided scriptwriters with oft-needed relief from the pressure of constructing plausible scripts.

As early as 1900, five years before the proliferation of nickelodeons, Clifford Beers testified to the psychological power of the new medium in his groundbreaking *A Mind That Found Itself* when he described his psychotic break in these terms: "I imagined that these visionlike effects, with few exceptions, were produced by a magic lantern controlled by some of my myriad persecutors. The lantern was rather a cinematographic contrivance. Moving pictures, often brilliantly colored, were thrown on the ceiling of my room and sometimes on the sheets of my bed. Human bodies dismembered and gory, were one of the most common of these" (1907, p. 30).

The first motion picture treatment of psychiatric subjects consisted mostly of one-reel comic chases in which asylum patients, dressed as Napoleon in some films, outwit their attendants in escaping from their custody, lead them a merry chase through the countryside, sometimes tormenting them along the way, and then return to the institution. Since successful films of the day were shamelessly copied by competitors, some in this genre, such as the Biograph *The Escaped Lunatic* and Edison's *Maniac Chase*, were identical scene for scene.

More serious and dramatic treatments of psychosis appeared in D. W. Griffith's 1909 *The Maniac Cook* and *The Reformation;* these, however, were the exceptions. Méliès had made *Under a Hypnotist's Influence* in 1897, but hypnosis was only a device to get a young woman out of her clothes; and Edwin S. Porter had made *The Kleptomaniac* in 1905, and Griffith *What Drink Did* and *A Drunkard's Reformation* in 1909, but their interest was in the social rather than the psychopathological.

It was not until the 1906 chase film *Dr. Dippy's Sanitarium* that a psychiatrist, or at least the asylum doctor, was actually portrayed. It, and the January 1909 Griffith one-reeler *The Criminal Hypnotist* represent the earliest depiction of psychiatrists that I have been able to find.[1]

Dr. Dippy's Sanitarium opens with Dr. Dippy hiring a new attendant. The poor man is immediately introduced by the doctor to four patients, one female, who leave their cells to meet him and to perform comic lunatic turns. As soon as the hapless attendant is

---

[1]Rabkin (1967, 1979) has written interestingly of the November 1909 film, Griffith's *The Restoration*, which portrayed an acute psychotic episode brought on in a neurasthenic man by a jealous act of rage. It is cured by a nonpsychiatric physician through the reenactment of the traumatic scene.

left alone with his charges, they overpower him and the three male patients chase him through the countryside. They, in turn, are chased by the now comical doctor and two veteran attendants. At the end the patients return the new attendant to the hospital, tie him up, and begin throwing knives at him. It is only the arrival of Dr. Dippy and the attendants with pies to distract the madmen that saves the new man, upon which he quits his job. In this film, Dr. Dippy's role is peripheral to the action, but it has implications that I shall presently discuss.

The Criminal Hypnotist is a more complex film. In its opening scene a young, black-bearded gentleman is entertaining appreciative guests at a party by hypnotizing several of them into performing silly tasks. The following day, the young hostess of the party encounters the hypnotist on a New York street. He immediately hypnotizes her and lures her into his apartment. Briefly considering a sexual pass, he turns quickly to more serious business, inducing her to steal her father's money from the desk drawer in which he keeps it locked. In an obvious trance, she goes home and starts to take the money, but cannot bring herself to complete the task. She returns to the hypnotist without the money, upon which he deepens her hypnotic trance, accompanies her to her father's room, takes the money himself, and leaves her behind. When the father enters the room he finds his daughter in a strange state and sends for a doctor. The puzzled doctor throws up his hands and instructs the maid to fetch a specialist. The next scene shows the maid entering a house on whose wall is a shingle identifying the occupant as a "Mind Specialist," a designation apparently more meaningful to audiences of the day than the term psychiatrist or alienist. The large, stocky, bearded specialist quickly follows the messenger to the troubled household. He immediately recognizes the problem and lightens the trance, preserving enough of it to enable the troubled young woman to lead him, the father, the doctor, and a policeman to the hypnotist's lair. As the policeman takes the villain off, the "Mind Specialist" fully clears the young woman's mind and she falls happily into her father's embrace.

What is especially interesting to me about these two crude films is that they present, at the very outset of the film depiction of psychiatrists, the three dominant models of the profession that were to recur throughout film history. For purposes of typology I will refer to these three prototypes as Dr. Dippy, Dr. Evil, and Dr. Wonderful.

Dr. Dippy, as his name implies, shares more than his professional subject matter with his patients. He lives on in the common observations that psychiatrists are as crazy as their patients, or that you have to be crazy to see a psychiatrist. He is foolish, trivial, lacks common sense, and is either overly serious or harmlessly crazy. The patients he works with are not really sick, or they may even possess some greater wisdom. He commonly appears in courtrooms or in California. A prime example is the psychiatrist in *Mr. Deeds Goes to Town* who testifies in court that Mr. Deeds, that paragon of common sense, is insane, but ends up appearing sicker and more foolish than his patient.

Although the criminal hypnotist is not in fact a psychiatrist, he does serve as the prototype for that eminent screen psychiatrist, Dr. Evil. In the public perception, both are identical in their ability to control minds, and to bend them to their will.[2] Dr. Evil, as he has appeared in so many movies, has an urge to master or control, often for criminal purposes, but just as often for the sheer pleasure in power. Like Drs. Caligari and Mabuse who will be discussed later, he is willing to experiment without regard to human consequences, and the poor souls who come under his influence are often driven to murder, suicide, or crime. Sometimes, as in the 1957 *I Was a Teen-Age Werewolf,* they are even transformed into monsters, for Dr. Evil's goals are seldom ordinary. He is prepared to explore those secrets of life that are best left untouched. When insane, his illness takes a malevolent form: Where Dr. Dippy is silly and pompous, Dr. Evil is ruthless and grandiose. When he treats patients he is likely to use methods seen as coercive – ECT, lobotomy, drugs.

The appearance of Dr. Wonderful in movies has been marred by the fact that very few filmmakers have known how psychiatrists work. So, while they easily depicted comedy and melodrama, filmmakers were retarded in their presentation of good psychiatric treatment. Added to that was the obvious difficulty in

---

[2]Throughout the history of movie depictions of psychiatry, the titles and functions of psychologists, psychiatrists, and other psychotherapists have been assigned indiscriminately. In *The Dark Mirror* (1946), for example, Lew Ayres is presented as Dr. Scott Elliott, M.D., Psychologist.

presenting the "talking cure" in the age of silent movies. With a few exceptions, then, the dramatically successful presentation of the work of psychiatry had to wait for the forties. As he evolves, however, Dr. Wonderful emerges as humane, concerned, earnest, selfless, modest, intense but human, and almost always in touch with the patient's problem. He is wonderful at improvisation, in coming up with a clever maneuver or interpretation at just the right moment. He is especially adept at uncovering traumatic events, and thereby achieves instant cures. His patients are in real psychic pain, but he treats them with non-coercive methods, almost always the talking cure. Occasionally he will use hypnosis, "truth serum," or environmental change, but only in a deeply caring way. He is always ready to ride to the rescue, and like his two colleagues he does not seem to have a life ouside the office. But if he had one, we know it would be ideal.

What we see emerging then at the very beginning of motion picture history are three major prototypes. What they represent is in large part an attempt to cope with the anxiety aroused by an authority figure who has the power and skill to deal with the human mind and its irrational manifestations. Scientists, mad and otherwise, have been subject to similar treatment, but it is power over the mind that makes the psychiatrist especially threatening and that calls forth primitive defenses.

Defensive ridicule is Dr. Dippy's province, but the unbelievably bad Dr. Evil, and the impossibly good Dr. Wonderful are manifestations of splitting, the psychological defense that has been increasingly emphasized in recent years in the literature on the borderline personality. In this defense, both objects and impulses are split, so that good objects and bad objects are maintained separately in the mind. In an all-or-none approach, people are perceived as either all-good or all-bad, sometimes alternatingly, rather than as simultaneously combining in an integrated way good and bad traits.

In the Kleinian scheme, splitting constitutes a normal defensive operation characteristic of the early ego. While it would be heartening to think that splitting occurred in movies principally in their infancy, it has, in fact, continued to the present day. One recent view (Gabbard and Gabbard, 1980) finds that stereotyping of the psychiatrist has increased in recent years with the full emergence of cultural narcissism, but I see the defensive portrayal of the psychiatrist as a constant phenomenon throughout motion picture history.

One variation on splitting that appeared early is the film in which the audience cannot be sure if the psychiatrist is crazy or sane. The most famous of these was the 1919 *The Cabinet of Dr. Caligari* which launched the post-World War I German film industry into international prominence. It tells the story of a somnambulist who commits murders under the influence of a mad psychiatrist, Dr. Caligari. At the end, in an unexpected turn of plot, Dr. Caligari emerges as the kindly director of a mental hospital in which the teller of the tale, previously seen as the hero of the story within the story, is a patient. The film is noteworthy not only because it presents the theme of psychiatrists who may be crazy/evil, but also because it presents psychological states through expressionist distortions of sets, makeup, and acting styles.

Interestingly, the last film made before Hitler came to power was also a film about a power-mad psychiatrist. Realizing that Fritz Lang's *The Testament of Dr. Mabuse* (1933) was not just a thriller, but also an indictment of anti-democratic forces, Goebbels destroyed all available copies. The film survives only from a print shipped to France prior to the ban.

In the same year as *Caligari*, Douglas Fairbanks appeared in *When the Clouds Roll By* which tells of a mysterious doctor of the mind who designs a scientific experiment to demonstrate that even a young man as healthy and ebullient as Fairbanks can be driven to suicide. Just when the experiment is about to succeed, the mind expert is unveiled as an escapee from the New York Insane Asylum.

Even *Spellbound*, that 1945 landmark psychiatric film directed by Alfred Hitchcock, was drawn from a novel about a madman taking over an insane asylum. The resultant film dropped that emphasis and emerged, in Hitchcock's own words, as "just another manhunt story wrapped up in pseudo-psychoanalysis" (Truffaut, 1967, p. 118). He incorrectly believed he was making the first picture on psychoanalysis, but what a crew he assembled: Ingrid Bergman as a psychoanalyst, Gregory Peck as her amnesiac patient/lover, Ben Hecht as scriptwriter, and Salvador Dali as designer of the dream sequences that are the key to the mystery. And in place of the sane/insane split, *Spellbound* offered two psychiatrists, Leo G. Carroll and Michael Chekhov, as Bergman's father figures, one emerging as a murderer, the other remaining an unblemished mentor. Together they present only slightly upgraded versions of our split pair, Dr. Evil and Dr. Wonderful.

The first film about psychoanalysis had actually been made in Germany in 1926. The previous year an executive of UFA, the principal German film company, had suggested to Karl Abraham that he participate in making a film that would illustrate some of the mechanisms of psychoanalysis. Freud did not discourage the idea, so the project proceeded with Abraham, Nicholas Kaufmann, and Hans Sachs (who was increasingly involved because of Abraham's illness) acting as consultants. The resultant film was the famous *Secrets of a Soul* (*Die Geheimnisse Einer Seele*), directed by G. W. Pabst, who had introduced the young Greta Garbo in her first non-Swedish role the previous year. (Ironically, after a brief stint in Hollywood in the thirties, Pabst ended his career directing films in Nazi Germany.)

The story, taken from life according to the credits, is of a chemist who develops a knife phobia, impotence, and homicidal impulses, and is cured by psychoanalysis. Dream analysis plays a significant role in the treatment, and interestingly, the dream sequences in this earlier film are richer in symbolism and technically superior to those in *Spellbound*, and they are interpreted with restraint.

The first movie appearance of a bona fide psychoanalyst is an auspicious one. The tormented chemist, Martin Fellman, is sitting in a bar drinking alone, while at a nearby table, a stocky, Slavic-looking man sits drinking and silently observing him. When Fellman gets up to pay his check, in his agitated state, he spills the contents of his pocket and leaves his house key behind. In the next scene, we see him in front of his home searching his pockets for his key. Just then, the stocky man from the bar comes up, hands Fellman the key, and observes, "You have reason for not wanting to return home." "How do you know that?" the startled chemist asks. "I am a Psychoanalyst," the man says.

Needless to say, that man, Dr. Orth (*sic*), becomes Fellman's analyst and cures him of his torments.

The film encountered some outside criticism for what was felt to be the unseemly participation of psychoanalytic leaders in a commercial project, but more telling was the internal criticism. In what has been all too typical of the psychoanalytic movement, Storfer, director of the *Internationaler Vorlag,* and Bernfeld, who had written a script, immediately launched a drive to make a new film to correct the errors of the first. Had they succeeded we might have seen a series of increasingly refined analytic films, but fortunately nothing came of their effort.

Germany continued to make somber psychological films – the Dr. Mabuse films, *Warning Shadows, M* – a style which contributed to the American *film noir* genre of the forties and fifties. Meanwhile, the American films of the twenties seemed largely to ignore psychiatrists, and what few they depicted were mostly Dr. Dippys. In 1925, for example, *The Boomerang* used for the first time the term psychoanalyst, but the story it tells is of a doctor who, lacking patients, decides to set himself up as a psychoanalyst. He opens a sanitarium and becomes quite successful, but a clairvoyant woman who wants to get into what she regards to be a racket, signs on as his nurse. Predictably, they fall in love, and after complications, marry.

In another film of the period, the 1930 *Free Love,* a woman consults a psychoanalyst and for a fee of $800 learns that she is an "intuitive introvert," and that her husband is an "infantile extrovert." She thereupon decides to leave her husband and take her children with her.

The first American film to deal seriously with mental illness and its treatment was probably Walter Wanger's *Private Worlds,* made in 1935. Starring Claudette Colbert, Joel McCrea, and Charles Boyer as psychiatrists whose own personal problems are interwoven with those of the patients in the private mental hospital where they work, it presented them as humane, compassionate, and competent professionals.

Other films of the pre-World War II period continued the Dr. Dippy tradition. Psychiatrists made fools of themselves testifying in the courtrooms of *Mr. Deeds Goes to Town* (1932) and *The Amazing Dr. Clitterhouse* (1938); Fred Astaire played a singing-dancing psychiatrist in *Carefree* (1938); and Katharine Hepburn confounded the profession in *Bringing Up Baby* (1938). And after presenting the story of a tormented woman psychiatrist who gets too involved with a neurotic young couple in *The Flame Within* (1935), MGM withdrew its recognition of the specialty and assigned its psychiatric cases to Drs. Kildare and Gillespie. In *Dr. Kildare's Strange Case* (1940), they even allowed Dr. Kildare to treat a mental patient with insulin coma therapy and brain surgery.

Two exceptions to the trend did appear. *Blind Alley*, a movie about a dangerous gangster who is psychoanalyzed into passivity was made in 1939, and was sufficiently appreciated to be remade in 1949 as *Dark Past* with William Holden as the gangster and Lee J. Cobb as the psychiatrist. More noteworthy, 1942 saw the release of *Now Voyager* a classic tearjerker starring Bette Davis, Paul Henreid, and Claude Rains. Best remembered for Henreid's two-cigarette technique with Bette Davis, it did much to make psychiatry respectable. Though we never see Claude Rains work his cure, he is an attractive, warmhearted psychiatric role model, a true Dr. Wonderful, so much so that a colleague confided to me recently that he decided to become a psychiatrist after seeing this film.

Once World War II began, the popular interest in psychiatry began to accelerate. The stage had been set for it by the arrival in America in the thirties of refugee European intellectuals, psychiatrists, and psychoanalysts, but the more immediate cause was probably the impact of the rejection rate of draftees because of mental illness and the growing awareness of psychiatric casualties of the war.

The result was a rising tide of psychological films during the mid- and late forties. It is seldom possible to delineate neat beginnings to new trends, but probably the first of the landmark films showing psychiatrists at work was the 1944 musical *Lady in the Dark*, closely followed by the already discussed *Spellbound*. Reportedly written in tribute to author Moss Hart's own analyst, *Lady in the Dark* boasted music and lyrics by Kurt Weill and Ira Gershwin, and starred Ginger Rogers in the role of a career girl who turns to psychoanalysis for help because she is torn between her work and three different men. Barry Sullivan in the role of the analyst presented him as a compassionate, intelligent, sophisticated man.

With a plot superficially similar to *Lady in the Dark* but a style totally dissimilar, the British produced in 1945 the moving and influential *The Seventh Veil*. In it, a beautiful classical pianist runs away from a harsh guardian, James Mason, and finds herself unable to choose between boyfriends. The ensuing emotional breakdown is skillfully and sympathetically treated by an analyst and the situation is brought to a happy and surprising ending. A great hit when released in the United States, the film did much to glamorize psychotherapy.

Significant in the late forties and early fifties was the sharp reduction in the number of Dr. Dippys. The only one of any distinction was the psychiatrist in *Harvey* (1950) who was silly enough to think something wrong with a man who has as a companion a six-foot invisible rabbit.

Instead, most psychiatrists of the period were wonder-workers, but with a significant intermixture of evil, criminal types. The preponderance of the psychological films of the period were shallow, trashy romances or suspense dramas that emphasized lurid symptoms and dramatic cures. Psychologists and psychiatrists protested the depiction of their professions (Kubie, 1947), but the situation was best summed up in an article in the screenwriters' trade journal. In reviewing twenty-two films of the genre, Sward (1948) wrote: "What we should look for in the neurotic personality—or what Hollywood is telling us to look for—is murder, suicide, alcoholism, lying, kleptomania, amnesia and functional paralysis or thoroughgoing break down."

To treat these conditions, Sward goes on to point out, the studios came up with the image of "the mental wonder-worker who is half physician and half super-sleuth [who raises] the dead by resurrecting the single traumatic incident.... The central character is only a hair's breadth this side of psychosis. Yet each is cured in a flash the moment a certain repressed memory is dragged forward or upward into his conscious mind."

In this generally disheartening situation, however, a few outstanding, if not landmark, films were made. Perhaps the most important of these was *The Snake Pit* (1948). Based on a novel by Mary Jane Ward, it featured sensitive performances by Olivia de Havilland as the patient committed to a state hospital, and Leo Genn as her psychiatrist. By exposing the dehumanizing effects of inadequate mental hospitals, it did much to arouse public opinion and to set up a climate for change, but it also presented an educational overview of then-current psychiatric care and theory. In the course of the hospital stay, de Havilland receives psychotherapy, narcosynthesis, and ECT, and except for the last, each helps her uncover important memories and understand better the psychological roots of her difficulties. In the end she is cured not by her doctor, but by the environmental shock of being placed in a back ward inhabited by patients not too unlike those first encountered in this survey in *Dr. Dippy's Sanitarium*. In the earlier film these incurables were played for laughs, but here, experienced from the inside, they are symbols of despair and neglect.

The doctor's explanations of how de Havilland's illness came about seem facile to modern audiences, but this is less due to the shallowness of the film than to a change in our views of mental illness. The much-admired National Film Board of Canada's *Mental Mechanisms* series made between 1947 and 1950 offered essentially similar explanations of psychiatric disturbances.

Another memorable Dr. Wonderful appeared in 1949. Responding to both declining profits and an awareness that movies with adult themes were doing well at the box office, Hollywood decided to tackle the race issue. The result was a contest among the major studios and independents to be the first to complete a movie on the subject. The unlikely winner was a small independent company led by the thirty-five-year-old Stanley Kramer, and the screenwriter Carl Foreman. Filming in great secrecy on a very low budget, they completed in less than a month the powerful and successful *Home of the Brave* (see Leab, 1975).

The story for the film was adapted from an unsuccesssful play about a Jewish soldier who cracks up in combat. By changing the Jew to a black, it now told the story of a black soldier suffering from amnesia and hysterical paralysis following a dangerous mission on an enemy-held island. He attributes his symptoms to a racial slur, but the psychiatrist informs him that his difficulties are due to the more universal survivor guilt. (This explanation was to turn up again in the 1980 film *Ordinary People*.)

Under pressure of time, the doctor decides to treat the soldier with narcotherapy, but this succeeds only in lifting the amnesia, not in restoring locomotion. Then, in one of those clever maneuvers so typical of a Dr. Wonderful, he steps back and calls the soldier "a dirty nigger," which provokes him to begin walking angrily toward him.

At a time when the psychiatric literature was hailing narcosynthesis, and when John Huston's famous documentary about army psychiatric casualties *Let There Be Light* was demonstrating its effectiveness — even in a case of hysterical paralysis like the one in *Home of the Brave* — it is noteworthy that these landmark films, *The Snake Pit* and *Home of the Brave*, attribute only partial success to the method. In both it is ultimately a form of environmental shock, a bad therapeutic milieu as it were, that restores the troubled protagonists to effective functioning.

One other trend of the period deserves mention, the development of the genre that has come to be known as *film noir*. While the dark, pessimistic, cynical films of the genre were concerned mainly with crime, a significant number of them branched out into the world of madness, and corrupt, disturbed patients and evil therapists. For a time it seemed that every film whose title included the adjective "dark" dealt with neurosis, crime, and psychiatrists: *Dark Waters* (1944), *The Dark Mirror* (1946), *Dark Delusion* (1947), *Dark Past* (1949).

The outstanding film of the genre also bears a somber title, the 1947 *Nightmare Alley*. With a directness uncommon for its time, it dealt with religious charlatanism and professional misconduct in a story of a con man, played against type by Tyrone Power, who teams up with an unscrupulous psychotherapist to use her confidential records to bilk her patients. In the end he is defeated, and deteriorates to the point of becoming an alcoholic and a carnival geek, the man who bites off the head of live chickens.

What is particularly impressive about the film is the power ascribed to the therapist, much of it derived from her possession of disc recordings of her patients' sessions, and her utter unscrupulousness. Her name Lilith, later used for the destructive patient in the 1964 film of that title, serves as a powerful symbolic equivalent to Dr. Evil, for in Semitic mythology Lilith is a female demon dwelling in deserted places and attacking children. What more telling image can we imagine for an evil therapist! And with what was probably conscious irony, the author of *Nightmare Alley* gives the doctor the surname Ritter, a chivalrous knight in German. Finally, in line with the role of splitting in the genesis of the Dr. Evil and Dr. Wonderful models, we learn that in Jewish folklore Lilith is Adam's first wife before Eve was created. In the Beginning was the split.

3. THE PSYCHIATRIST IN THE MOVIES

With this group of movies we come to the end of the first half of the century. As we sum up the history of the first fifty years of the romance between psychiatry and cinema, we find surprisingly little progress in Hollywood's depiction of the profession. The stereotypes present at the beginning continue as the dominant images of the psychiatrist. The doctors of *Harvey, Nightmare Alley,* and *Home of the Brave* are more sophisticated and more fully drawn, but they are not essentially different from the mindworkers we first encountered in *Dr. Dippy's Sanitarium* and *The Criminal Hypnotist,* nor is their treatment method much more complex than the reenactment of the traumatic scene in *The Reformation.* What is still lacking is a sense of what the everyday world of the psychiatrist is like, what happens when the average patient meets the average psychiatrist on an average day, or even when the unusual patient meets the average working psychiatrist on a special day. Poor box office we might say, but many fine movies on other subjects were drawn from just such material.

What is especially ironic about the predominantly unrealistic portrayal of the work of psychotherapy is that it occurred at the same time that so many members of the Hollywood community were themselves in psychoanalysis. It is unlikely that what they were experiencing in their own treatment much resembled what they were portraying on the screen.

There were exceptions, of course. *Secrets of a Soul,* despite its lurid symptomatology and formulaic exposition, did present a reliable picture of psychoanalytic thinking and methods. And though not a very good movie, and overinclined to melodrama, *Spellbound* did give the mass audience for the first time some notion of then-current psychiatric work. What stands up today as the period's most convincing portrait of the psychiatrist at work appears to my mind to be *The Snake Pit.* Though marred by an overdidactic function, Leo Genn comes across as concerned and attentive, without great power in his own institution nor the ability to cure his seriously ill patient, but able to help her along on her own path to recovery.

At the half-century mark Hollywood had already peaked: From 1949 on, the average weekly attendance at the movies showed a steady drop. Within a few years the psychoanalytic model in psychiatry, most powerful in the forties and fifties, began to show a similar decline. For the motion picture industry, television was the threat, and an effort was mounted to recapture the lost audience by turning to new technologies and more daring themes. The psychoanalytic model in psychiatry, in turn, found itself confronting the proliferation of alternative treatments, the pressures of community expectations, and the resurgence of biological models.

The movie depiction of psychiatry was to reflect these changes. Instead of the seriously disturbed patient of the past, people suffering from the psychopathology of everyday life were to seek varieties of therapeutic experience in the films of Paul Mazursky (*Bob & Carol & Ted & Alice, An Unmarried Woman*); complex human beings attempted to resolve their often serious problems in a series of well-wrought case study films (*Face to Face, A Woman under the Influence*); and problems of authority versus freedom got serious if sometimes sensationalized attention (*One Flew over the Cuckoo's Nest, A Fine Madness*). Some of the best portrayals of the psychiatrist were played by psychiatrists themselves (Don Muhich, Dean Brooks). And, of course, for every well-intentioned film there were a number of exploitation films, but that is in the nature of the mass media.

It would be encouraging to complete this look backward with the conclusion that we have come a long way from the stereotypes of the first half-century. Unfortunately, a glance at the most popular psychiatric films of 1980 turns up the Dr. Dippy of *Love at First Bite*, the Dr. Evil of *Dressed to Kill*, and the Dr. Wonderful of *Ordinary People!* Plus ça change.

REFERENCES

Beers, C. (1975). *A Mind That Found Itself*. Garden City, NY: Doubleday. (Reprinted from 5th rev. ed., New York: Longman, 1907).

Gabbard, G., & Gabbard, K. (1980). From *Psycho* to *Dressed to Kill*: The decline and fall of the psychiatrist in the movies. *Film/Psychology Review*, Summer-Fall, 157–166.

Kubie, L. (1947). Psychiatry and the films. *Hollywood Quarterly*, January, 113–117.

Leab, D. (1975). *From Sambo to Superspade*. Boston: Houghton Mifflin.

Rabkin, L. Y. (1967). The movies' first psychiatrist. *Amer. J. Psychiat.*, 124:545–547.
_____ (1979). The celluloid couch: Psychiatrists in American films. *Psychocultural Review*, Spring, 73–90.
Schneider, I. (1977). Images of the mind: Psychiatry in the commercial film. *Amer. J. Psychiat.*, 134:613–620.
Sward, K. (1948). Boy and girl meet neurosis. *The Screen Writer*, September.
Truffaut, F. (1967). *Hitchcock*. New York: Simon & Schuster.

III FREUD, PHILOSOPHY AND LINGUISTICS

4 Freud's Philosophy of Mind: Cartesianism and Unconscious Intentions

Arthur Collins, Ph.D.

It seems bold to say so, but Freud's thinking about the mind is quite inadequate from a philosophical point of view. The great source of the defects in Freud's philosophy of mind is the burden of traditional views he accepts without reflection and without even realizing that he has accepted anything philosophical at all. Freud's ideas should be a source of support to philosophers who are trying to liberate our understanding of mentality from longstanding traditions as stultifying as they are tenacious. This has not been the case because Freud adopts these stultifying views himself and seems to believe that he depends on them. Nor are these traditional philosophical ideas just so much superfluous baggage in Freud's thinking: They create general strains and obscurities and generate particular inconsistencies. Although Freud's thinking is plainly intelligible in spite of the defective philosophical setting in which he presents it, the future development of psychoanalytic theory is hampered by the retention of an unsatisfactory philosophy of mind.

Freud's ideas are related to the philosophy of mind chiefly in connection with the concept of the unconscious. When Freud mentions philosophy he often expresses impatience and disappointment with it. He thinks that philosophers mostly identify mind and consciousness and thus rule out the very possibility of unconscious mentality without investigation. He once said that psychoanalysis is midway between medicine and philosophy, but even this remark is made in the context of criticism of the unreasonable philosophical exclusion of the unconscious mind. Freud thinks that the possibility of communication between philosophy and psychoanalysis is largely destroyed by philosophers' intractability on this point. His opinion, however, that philosophers mostly rule out the unconscious mind is certainly false. It is so very wide of the mark that we will have to ask what Freud really means by speaking as though it is generally characteristic of philosophical thought to oppose the unconscious.

Thinking about the mind has been at the heart of philosophy since the Renaissance. Much philosophical, psychological, and scientific thought is still decisively influenced by the Cartesian ordering of things according to which men are, in the first instance, acquainted only with the contents of their own consciousness. The familiar schedule of solipsistic and egocentric problems that characterize modern philosophy are generated by this Cartesian starting point. These are the problems of the external world, of other minds, and of mind-body interaction. They depend on the supposition that each man only knows at first hand the contents of his own mind and that the existence of anything extramental is something that has to be argued. Waves of revolutionary resistance to this Cartesian scheme of things have taken the form of idealistic reductions of matter to mind and materialist reductions of mind to matter. None of these movements has succeeded in permanently unseating the fundamental Cartesian presumptions and most of the revolutions have come to appear to be only variations on a Cartesian theme. It is Descartes' egocentric subjective perspective that moved the mind to the center of modern philosophy. From this perspective other branches of philosophy and all of the sciences, including psychology, are intelligible only in terms of a preliminary philosophy of mind.

In considering Freud, two things about the Cartesian tradition deserve mention at the outset. First, Freud's thinking is essentially Cartesian, and, second, the Cartesian program and the tenor of modern philosophy has been more encouraging than not to the idea of an unconscious mental life. It is well known that Freud tried to construct a wholly physiological theory of mind in his unfinished *Project for a Scientific Psychology* (1895), and that he always thought that his own psychological concepts might be replaced by physical concepts when physiology was sufficiently advanced. Thus, Freud was plainly not a committed dualist whereas dualism is more prominent than anything else in Descartes' thinking. As I have already suggested, however, materialist reduction of the mental to the physical can be only a Cartesian variation in spite of its rejection of dualism. Descartes interprets mentality in terms of an *inner* reality of which the subject is conscious, at least sometimes. Materialist philosophers characteristically accept this conception of the inner life and differ only on the metaphysical status of the inner items which they assert to be physical events and activities and which they say take place inside the head. Thus materialism avoids any commitment to an ethereal mind-stuff and, as a consequence, appeals to the scientifically minded, Freud among them. But in many ways the crucial thing about the Cartesian picture is the idea of an inner realm of subject matter on which each man reports only in his own case. The identification of this Cartesian inner realm as being made of this or that substance (matter or mind-stuff) is of secondary importance. Materialist philosophers of mind tend to accept the more fundamental conception even while they differ with Descartes and all dualists on the constitution of the inner world. Freud plainly thinks of unconscious mental things in the setting of this Cartesian picture of the inner life. Some Cartesians, and perhaps Descartes himself, thought that all the inner items which comprise the mental are items of which the subject is conscious. Freud asserts that this is not so. We do not know about all our inner states and activities. Perhaps most of them are unconscious. This is a difference within the Cartesian framework. But it is not a challenge to the correctness of that framework.

What is the typical Cartesian stand on the unconscious? For Descartes, extension or the filling of space is a necessary characteristic of any material object. That is, such an object might lose or gain other characteristics without ceasing to exist but if a material thing ceased to take up any space it would be nothing at all. Extension is *essential* to the existence of anything material. Descartes is a dualist, so extension is certainly not a property, much less the essence, of the mind or any mental thing. For much of the Cartesian tradition, the essence of mind is supposed to be, in some sense, *thought*. Therefore, to say that a particular mind ceases to think is to say that that mind ceases to exist. At the same time, we are supposed to have such knowledge of minds as we do through our own conscious experience, which is plainly not continuous. For instance, it is interrupted by dreamless sleep. Unconscious mental activity, it appears, will have to be posited to fill the gaps between disconnected episodes of consciousness. Philosophers who do not accept this posit but rather identify the mind and consciousness, as Freud says most philosophers do, will not be able to explain why we think the mind endures when consciousness ceases.

Express commitment to unconscious mental things and activities is especially characteristic of German philosophy. Leibniz presents a theory of unconscious *"petites perceptions."* He finds that the understanding of a priori and innate knowledge requires unconscious thoughts and ideas, and he articulates a defense of the unconscious mind against Locke's views. Kant inherited this pattern from Leibniz. His critical philosophy has it that the world of scientific investigation is a system of phenomena that are in some sense constructed from primitive input by the creative powers of the mind. The various Kantian syntheses which accomplish this vast stage-setting task for human knowledge are all unconscious mental activities. The great flowering of German systematic philosophy in the 19th century is virtually unanimous in its support and, indeed, enthusiasm for the unconscious. Hegel, Schelling, Fichte, Schopenhauer, and Nietzsche, and ever so many lesser figures, are all advocates of some form or other of unconscious idea, reason, will, or the like. Eduard von Hartmann achieved popular success in 1869 with the publication of his *Die Philosophie des Unbewussten,* which surveys and employs dozens of philosophical appeals to various types of unconscious mentality. Of whom does Freud speak when he asserts that philosophers generally assert a definitional equivalence of mind and consciousness?

For himself, Freud adopts a view which is as opposed to the definitional equivalence of mind and consciousness as is possible. In various works, Freud explains his conception of consciousnesss by analogy with perception. Consciousness affords us apprehension of inner mental things just as perception affords us apprehension of outer physical realities. Consciousness does not constitute mental reality, nor is consciousness essential to the existence of a mental reality, any more than vision constitutes or is essential to the things we can see. Just as there are many outer things which we do not happen to perceive or are unable to perceive, so too are there mental realities of which we do not happen to be conscious, or of which we cannot be conscious. Repression, for instance, puts things out of the reach of consciousness just as visible objects might be put out of the range of our sight.

This analogy brings out Freud's Cartesianism. Mental things and activities are inner realities although consciousness does not reveal them all, as perception does not reveal all outer things. To understate the case, the analogy is imperfect. We can use its shortcomings to bring out the problems concealed in Freud's version of the Cartesian philosophy of mind.

The force of the analogy comes from the clarity with which we grasp that vision, for instance, is access to, and not creation of, visible things. Understanding this much about perception, we transfer the pattern that fits outer things to the alleged inner things of which we are apprised in consciousness. But the idea that consciousness is *like* perception neglects the fact that perception is itself counted among mental activities and that perception is itself conscious, at least sometimes. So the analogy has to mean that other instances of consciousness are like perceptual consciousness. Perceptual consciousness does not constitute its objects, for they are plainly independent outer things. So consciousness of the inner need not be thought to constitute its objects. Inner objects can be as independent of consciousness as outer objects are.

But why is it that perception is counted as a mental activity at all? As we see, perception is certainly not a mental activity by virtue of its objects. It is not because rocks and trees are involved as things we see that we think of vision as a mental function. Visual perception is counted as mental *because it is conscious*. But this tends against the very point Freud wants to make in his analogy. The essential thing about perception that makes us count it as mental is that it involves consciousness and not that it involves certain kinds of objects. If that is so, and if we follow the analogy, we should conclude that apprehension of the inner is mental because it is consciousness of things and not because the things apprehended are inner things. Why is it that all sorts of inner activities like secretions and peristalsis are not mental activities? Is it not plainly because they are not conscious activities? This conclusion is plainly the reverse of the one Freud wants.

Freud might respond to this difficulty in a way which is extremely familiar in the history of Cartesian philosphy of mind. He might provide an inner object for perceptual consciousness so as to make it clear that the mental status of perception does come from the inner object. Strictly speaking, he would say in this vein that it is visual experiences or visual impressions of which we are conscious. Visual experiences or impressions are not out in the exterior world. They are inner things. The immediate object of perceptual consciousness is the thing that would exist even if, due to some aberration, there is no physical object present at all. Supposing that we accept this understanding of perceptual consciousness as ranging over experiences and perceptual impressions rather than rocks and trees, we will not be able to rehabilitate the analogy of perception and consciousness that Freud wants. For on this interpretation, perception no longer offers an example of objects of apprehension which are not dependent on our consciousness for their very existence. On the contrary, my visual experience of a rock does not continue to exist without consciousness, and visual impressions of trees exist only while conscious subjects are aware of them. So, were we to introduce an inner object to play the role of the immediate object of awareness in visual perception, the analogy of consciousness with perception will again seem to imply that consciousness is essential to the mental, which is just what Freud seeks to deny.

The only place that I know of in Freud's writings that clearly suggests the idea of the innerness of the objects of perceptual consciousness is in the *Project for a Scientific Psychology*. Freud speculates that a class of neurones manage to introduce into our experience what he calls "quality." The external world and most of physiological reality consists of objects and forces which can be exhaustively described in quantitative terms. These neurones are assigned the task of transforming some quantitative input into the qualitative (sensuous) aspect of our representations. This aspect of our representations is not possessed by outer realities. Such an account has a long philosophical pedigree. It is a version of the theory of primary and secondary qualities and a cornerstone of the Cartesian philosophy of mind. The traditional intention was to filter away the sensuous, as scientifically unmanageable but merely mental, so as to make intelligible the success of mathematical science, which deals with quantitative, mathematically describable features of reality only. As a consequence the theory always provides a mental object of perceptual consciousness as the bearer of qualities not found in the outer world. Of course, Freud abandoned the *Project*, but there is no evidence that he ever abandoned the underlying Cartesian outlook on the inner and the outer, and much of what he says shows that he did not abandon it.

To sum up this point, Freud's analogy of consciousness and perception is unsuited to his own objectives. If objects of perception are supposed to be outer mind-independent things, then the mental status of perception will come down to the fact that perception is conscious, and if the object of perception is supposed to be inner, then perception does not illustrate the apprehension of mind-independent objects and the analogy accomplishes nothing.

Let us now return to the question, Why does Freud incorrectly assert that philosophers generally exclude the unconscious by definition? When Freud was a medical student in Vienna he attended the lectures of Franz Brentano, a philosopher now known best for his revival of the scholastic concept of "intentionality" and his use of this intentionality as the essential mark of the mental. In the general chorus of approval of the unconscious in German philosophy, Brentano stands out as a dissident voice. He denies the existence of mental things of which we are not conscious. It appears from his writings, however, that even Brentano thought of this as a difficult issue—he argued it at great length, and he did not simply start from a definitional equivalence of mind-consciousness. Nonetheless, Brentano's view and his influence on the educated Viennese with whom Freud would have conversed may provide an understanding of Freud's assertion. In order to see this, let us look at Freud's use of the concept of unconscious mentality in his explanations of slips and accidents.

Freud (1901) likes the psychopathology of everyday life as an expository vehicle for his conception of the unconscious because his explanations in this area make no appeal to expert knowledge of psychiatric matters. The explanations remain within the context of things that everyone knows about. My guess is that when Freud told people about these explanations of everyday things he often encountered a certain form of objection. I think these objections would turn on definitions or claims about concepts which are loosely "philosophical" and which would rule out the unconscious mental things to which Freud adverts in his explanations.

Many of Freud's explanations proceed by ascribing an intention to the subject. (This is the everyday sense of "intention" and has nothing to do with Brentano's revived scholastic concept.) For example, an appointment is forgotten because the subject did not want to keep it. In some sense, he forgot it in order not to have to keep the appointment. A slip of the tongue which would be insulting if taken literally was made because the subject was hostile or angry. In some sense, he intended to insult. A switch is accidentally thrown the wrong way, causing damage to equipment that makes the rest of the day's work impossible. The switch-thrower did not want to continue the work. When Freud complains that philosophers identify mind and consciousness he is probably alluding to logical or conceptual objections which people make to these explanations. For example, many people must have said to Freud that what is accidental cannot be done for some reason because to call behavior accidental logically entails that it was not done for any reason. Freud's explanation starts by assuming that the characterization "an accident" is justified and fits the switch-throwing in question. He does not claim that there was no accident. On the contrary, behavior would not even be a candidate for his radical explanation unless it were really an accident. If the subject just threw the switch as he did in order to ruin the equipment, then the case would not be fodder for Freud's new explanations at all. But then the explanation itself goes on to contradict this status by viewing the behavior as the successful fulfillment of an intention to ruin the equipment.

In the same way, a slip of the tongue is "by definition" an utterance which is not what the speaker meant to say, not what he intended to say. This must be established before the business of explaining a slip can get under way. If we think that the utterance may have been what the speaker intended to say, then we are not certain that we are confronted by a slip of the tongue at all. Therefore, in his explanations of slips of the tongue Freud contradicts the characterization of them which he also accepts. The case of intentional forgetting is even more vexed from a conceptual point of view. In order to conceal a fact from someone intentionally a man surely has to know what fact he is concealing. One might intentionally mislabel the drawers of a file cabinet in order to foil spies, but to do so requires knowing that there is a disparity between the labels and the contents of the file drawers. In the absence of this explicit knowledge, a mislabelling might still foil spies, but it could not be done with that intention. So in order to intentionally forget something one must know what it is that one is to forget. If he does not know just what he is forgetting, then, however well his forgetfulness serves his desires, it cannot be intentional forgetting. It is as though intentional forgetting calls for remembering what to forget. This is not coherent.

No doubt Freud would like us to understand that these philosophical objections are vitiated precisely by our failure to recognize that he is invoking unconscious intentions in all these explanations. The relevant accidents, slips, and forgettings would not be describable as accidents, as slips, and as forgettings if the subject had a conscious intention. To say that a man consciously intended to throw a switch accidentally would be incoherent. Similarly, for the other cases. Generally speaking, I think that Freud is entitled to this rejoinder. The philosophically important point, however, is that he would not be entitled to it if the Cartesian conception of mental things that he adopts were correct. It is because he accepts a Cartesian idea of the inner mental life that critics can rightly say that his explanations seem to involve contradictions.

In the Cartesian theory an intention is an inner mental item of which a man may be, but is not necessarily, conscious. If a man is not conscious of his intention, then he will not be able to state his intention even if he makes an honest effort. So, if I have said something which you find offensive, and I have said it intentionally in order to offend you, I will not be able to give this correct explanation of my behavior if I do not know about my intention in this case. I will say that I did not mean to utter what I did and did not intend to be offensive. Under the heading "slips" Freud wants to include cases like this where the subject cannot state the intention that he did have. An accidental switch-throwing provides a similar case such that, if it was done intentionally, the subject who threw the switch does not know that he had the intention and cannot honestly say that he did. In this account Freud comes close to the view that there really are no slips or accidents. He reprimands those who try to insist that some behavior was *only* an accident. Such a view insists on chance occurrences and thereby discards the perspective of scientific determinism, which requires a cause for anything that happens. When he says this sort of thing, Freud clearly implies that his explanation shows how the apparently random behavior is a causal consequence of an antecedent intention. When he adopts this understanding of the explanation of behavior, Freud is saying that the ordinary distinction between accidental and intentional actions reduces to an underlying distinction between consciously and unconsciously intended behavior. For he says that those who reject intentions for slips and accidents are removing them from the domain of causality altogether.

If we think of intentions as inner items of which we may or may not be conscious, then Freud's provision of unconscious intentions for slips and accidents is just as incoherent as the provision of conscious intentions for slips and accidents. On that Cartesian understanding we would merely be able to say that the subject is sometimes in error when he says that his behavior was not intended and was a slip. Imagine a case in which a man quickly forgets the intention with which he acted. As a consequence he claims that what he did was an accident. Surely there is no sense in which this claim is true. The fact that I fail to report the inner item that was my intention in acting as I did goes no way at all toward showing that there was anything unintended or accidental about it. The existence of the intention is decisive and my recollection of it is irrelevant to the status of the behavior.

We should emphasize that Freud himself uses the forgotten as a common illustration of the unconscious. It seems that, as long as the intention is forgotten, behavior will qualify as accidental. But if a man purposely wrecks some equipment by throwing a switch the wrong way and then conveniently forgets his intention, his behavior does not become an example of an accident. Maybe we should bear in mind that forgotten intentions are only a special case of unconscious intentions since the subject knows about a forgotten intention until he forgets it. This detail may be duly noted, but it does not bear on the question of the accidental status of behavior. Suppose the switch-thrower's intention has been unconscious from the start but that, quite suddenly, in the middle of Freud's explanation of the accident, the subject is aware of the intention. The subject, in this circumstance, will no longer join in explanations of his accident for he will now know that it was no accident at all. Therefore, when we and the subject, and Freud too, speak of a slip or an accident, that description is irrevocably conditioned by the thought that the speaker did not intend what he said or did. The characterization a "slip" or an "accident" will be withdrawn if that condition is not satisfied. If I have acted with a certain intention, if my action exists because it fits and tries to fulfill my intention, if it is what my intention calls for, then my action is not a slip or an accident and the unconsciousness of the intention cannot make it into a slip or accident.

Freud thinks that the absence of an intention for the behavior he explains would amount to the absence of a cause, and that such a case would violate the general causal determinism which science endorses or presupposes in his view. He is confident that there must be unconscious intentions for actions that go awry unless we mean to set aside the whole scientific world view. Is this a reasonable stand? In normal cases where intentions are conscious we have no natural inclination to think of the intended behavior as *determined* and as an example of scientific causality. I do not mean that consciously intended actions are widely regarded as instances of some metaphysical freedom or as evidence of gaps in the causal order. The stating and understanding of intentions is simply irrelevant to all that. On the whole, we only expect explanations in terms of conscious intentions in those cases where we think that the agent might not have acted as he did and was not under some absolute compulsion. If we found that some utterly compelling causal factor induced a man's behavior, we would not think of it as his act and would not look for any intentions. At the same time, if a man does act intentionally, if, for example, he raises his arm in order to get the attention of the chairman of a meeting, he need not deny that there is any causal explanation for the motions involved that draw on the actions of muscle and nerves. The ultimate reconciliation of intentions and physiology is an outstanding philosophical problem. At the very least, we can say that conscious intentions are not universally thought of as determining causes. Where intentions are so regarded it is by theorists like Freud himself who are responsive to the demands of their theoretical schemes and not to any natural plausibility of the idea that what is intended is thereby determined and caused.

When Freud provides unconscious intentions lest behavior go uncaused, he is again faithful to the Cartesian picture of the mind. Once we think of an inner world of events and activities, we are likely to think of these things as causally related to the outer world. Indeed, we will think this inevitable, for how else could mental things be connected to the outer world? The inner perceptual experience must be an *effect* of outer things and events, including events in the organs of perception. And an inner intention must be the *cause* of muscle contractions in some way. This is the straight Cartesian story. Once we are committed to the inner world we will have to have what Ryle called "paramechanisms" in order to understand its relevance to the world outside. Once they are inner things, mental items are certain to be thought causes and effects of outer things.

If the mind is not an inner theater, then how are we to understand it and how will another understanding fit Freud's views? This is a big question, but we can find some suggestions by looking at Freud's own thinking again. One important source of evidence for unconscious mentality in Freud's early thinking was Bernheim's demonstrations of hypnosis. Freud says that he was particularly impressed by the fact that Bernheim pressed his subjects to recall things that took place during the hypnotic sleep. He refused their claims that they did not remember. Bernheim's persistence was rewarded and his subjects eventually did remember what he inquired about. Freud says this shows that the subject remembered all along. Bernheim's interrogation enabled the subject to gain access to the memory which was there in his unconscious. Of course, we can see in this not only a source of Freud's idea of the unconscious, but also a source of the technique of psychotherapy as well. But is Freud's description of Bernheim's demonstrations satisfactory? The first thing to note is that it is certainly another manifestation of Freud's Cartesianism.

What is remembering and what is forgetting? If I knew something and, when asked about it later, I can state what I knew without any promptings or external aids, then I remember. And if I cannot state what I knew, though I would if I could, then I have forgotten. When I have forgotten, the sought-for-information may come to me later so that, though I had once forgotten, now I remember and without any intervening assistance. But I remember only when and insofar as I can produce the facts. Why should we allow Freud to describe the situation as one in which I remember continuously through periods in which the memory is unconscious? Why not say I did not remember and then, later, remembered again? Freud's description is determined by the fact that he thinks of consciousness as mere apprehension of inner realities. On this scheme, a memory is an inner item which we might "perceive" or not. Failure to be able to state the facts does not prove that one does not remember, for the memory may be there "in the mind" undetected. A later ability to state the facts without assistance means that the memory, which was there all along, has become an object of consciousness.

Many ideas are mixed together in Freud's understanding of the memories of Bernheim's subjects. Plainly it is true that the later capacity to report an earlier event shows that there has been some kind of storage that has endured through the interval in which efforts to remember were at first unavailing. Just as plainly, we all surmise that this storage takes place in the brain. Let us say that what endures is a brain trace. Furthermore, it seems very plausible and perhaps logically obligatory to suppose that the difference between the case in which a subject cannot state the facts in question, though the brain trace is present, and the situation in which he can state the facts has something to do with the ways in which the stored brain trace is connected with other neural goings on. But such general considerations, and detailed scientific versions of the same sort of material, are considerations of the physiological underpinnings of the capacity to remember. They are not discussions of the concept of a "memory" and do not give us any reason to identify a memory with some item or stage of the physiological activities contemplated. In particular, although we suppose that the brain trace has an indispensable role in explaining the capacity to remember, we do not have any reason to think of the brain trace as an inner thing of which the subject is conscious when he remembers.

Outsiders will say that the subject remembers when he is able to say what he remembers, that is, when he gets it right. Outsiders, it seems, must confine themselves to this standard because they cannot have consciousness of the memories and other items in the subject's mind. But on closer inspection, it does not seem to be true that the subject uses a different standard. From his point of view, as with the outsider, he remembers if he gets it right. He cannot insist that he remembers because he detects something inner. The test of whether he remembers or not is objective and not a matter of inner impressions. If I have forgotten a poem I knew, I will know when I remember it again because I will be able to say the lines of the poem. They will count as remembering, not because they are based on an inner item, but because they *are* the lines of the poem. If I recite them to myself and not aloud, then my memory is private and, in a sense, inner, but the reason for which it is a memory remains the same. The standard of memory has nothing to do with innerness. The role of inner brain traces has the same hypothetical scientific character for the subject as for anyone else. The fact that I may realize that I can recite the poem and that I do recite it to myself is incidental. What I do for my own benefit is, vis-á-vis memory, exactly what I do publicly. It is a case of remembering because it reproduces the poem and not because it is inner.

It is important to stress that we do not want to deny that there is any inner private life and subjectivity. There are many things that I may not tell others and my secret intentions, my disreputable cravings, my private opinions, and other "mental" things are prominent among the things that I keep to myself. There is no doubt that the very existence of privacy has been an enormous encouragement to the Cartesian conception of mind. The long dominance of Cartesian thinking leaves us susceptible to the idea that the facts of privacy definitively establish the inner-realm picture of mind. What privacy and innerness really amount to and how we should fit these things into our conception of ourselves are enormous questions which remain unaddressed if we make the leap to the Cartesian inner-theater idea. I make no pretense to contribute to the answer to these questions here. The point for us is just that the innerness (that is, potential privacy) of things such as memories and intentions is not their essential character. With respect to intentions and memories, we could have much the same mental lives even if we had no inner life but always stated our intentions publicly and recited what we remembered aloud.

We are tempted by the idea that my intention is an inner detectable item because that would *explain* why I can know about it more easily than you can. We think of the case where I say to myself, I want X but I don't want them to know, so I'll pretend it's Y I want. Of course, this can happen and you may be deceived. But my having the intention is not the same as my thinking it over and laying plans in silence. When I say that I intend to reach such and such an objective, either aloud or to myself, I am saying that my behavior will have that outcome insofar as I have anything to do with it. I am telling you or myself what my actions are aimed at and not what they are caused by. I am not saying that I expect certain behavior to develop because I detect an inner item which leads to that sort of behavior. Intention statements get their explanatory force from the fact that human behavior can be flexible and can compensate for obstacles so that an outcome is attained in spite of those obstacles. A statement of intention is a complex conditional statement that captures this compensatory outcome-oriented structure of behavior. It is certainly an extraordinary feature of human life that men are able to make statements with this degree of complexity about their future behavior and generally be right. But it is the structure of behavior and not any inner item that gives footing to discourse about intentions.

If we discard the supposed inner item, we attain a conception of intentional behavior that is far better suited to Freud's explanations than the Cartesian theory of mind. If it is the structure of behavior and not connection with an inner item that is at stake in assertions about intentions, we can understand how it is that others can sometimes assess a man's intentions better than that man himself. The psychoanalytic explanations are not merely an outsider's attempt to determine the presence of an inner item that lies undetected in the inner world of another. This Cartesian conception implies that there is always an unbridgeable gap between the most sensitive psychoanalytic assessment of a man's intentions and the facts assessed. For on Cartesian principles, the psychoanalyst can never be conscious of any of the mental contents of another. All of his statements about the unconscious mind of another are hypotheses which are uncheckable in the most fundamental way. They all assert the existence of inner items which can only really be verified by the supposed inner-turning perception that the Cartesian philosophy of mind posits. With the burden of Cartesianism the very idea of unconscious mental things must retain an ineliminable conjectural status. For if mental items are inner things, then no one has ever been acquainted with an unconscious mental item and no one ever will be. All discourse about unconscious intentions and the like will be equivalent to saying that it is *as though* the agent has such and such intention. For the fact of the matter has been identified with the inner item, which, since it is unconscious, is not accessible to the subject, and since it is inner, is not accessible to anyone else.

At least in explanations of everyday psychopathology there is no reason to think that Freud must confine himself to this disappointingly external and conjectural viewpoint. How does Freud or anyone else come by these explanations? The unconscious intention is suggested by the structure of the behavior in question. The psychoanalyst must base his assessment on what is publicly accessible. Publicly accessible things might plausibly lead to revised estimates of an unconscious intention or to the withdrawal of an ascription of unconscious intention. This is the proper and sufficient locus for claims about unconscious intentions. The existence of something in an inaccessible inner realm has no role to play. An unconscious intention is an *intention* because it shows the structure of behavior and its organization with respect to an outcome, and it is *unconscious* because the agent whose behavior is in question cannot give this account of his intention spontaneously. In the ordinary case a man is simply able to say what his intention is. A satisfactory psychological and physiological explanation of this human capacity remains to be given. It is just mythology, however, to suppose that we look into an inner realm and find or fail to find our intentions there.

In *The Interpretation of Dreams* (1900) Freud mentions another side of Bernheim's demonstrations that we can use in trying to understand unconscious mentality. Subjects carry out orders of the hypnotist after they have emerged from the hypnotic sleep. This is post-hypnotic suggestion. Freud is particularly struck by the fact that, if asked why they do what they do in such cases, subjects do not say that they have no idea but, instead, invent an explanation for their behavior. Suppose that in such an explanation a subject offers an intention. No one would imagine that this subject finds a bogus intention in his inner world and Freud does not say any such thing. The situation should help us to see how gratuitous the inner world is when it comes to intentions. Suppose that the subject did look within and did find the intention that he gives for his action. This would not lead to the acceptance of his explanation. We would still know that the subject was carrying out an order given during the trance and that his explanation is only a rationalization. The presence of an inner item would not change matters. If we believed in inner items we would say that, in this case, the inner intention has been cooked up. But that just shows that the public viewpoint will overrule even what the subject finds in direct consciousness of the mental thing itself. The essence of the intention is to be found in publicly accessible matters and not in an inner realm.

It seems that what actually happens in the case of post-hypnotic suggestion is something like this. Quite a bit of our outward behavior has the unmistakable cast of action and control. This includes speech, locomotion, and all relatively delicate manipulation of things. This component of total behavior comprises roughly what a man *does* as opposed to what merely *happens*. We are all deeply committed to the idea of a web of purposes and intentions that confers intelligibility on behavior of this sort, whether our own behavior or that of others. In the case of the incorrect explanation of the action performed under post-hypnotic suggestion, the subject has naturally tried to extend this web of intelligibility to a difficult case which calls for explanation because it falls into the right class of actions. The subject is not pretending to find something within him which he does not really find. Nor does he normally consult any inner source of information in order to explain what he is doing. When a man states his intention he tells us how to regard his behavior. When we so regard it we will see his intention in his behavior. We will not see through his behavior to some hidden locus of mental things themselves. Since intentions are in behavior in the normal case, Freud is not contradicting the very idea of intentions when he ascribes them in the face of honest repudiations by the agent. If a man's behavior is sufficiently organized to bring about a certain result, then that is what he is doing, whether he realizes it or not. This conception of the mental, conscious and unconscious, is well-adapted to Freud's thought. The ill-considered Cartesianism that permeates his work is not.

REFERENCES

Freud, S. (1895). *Project for a Scientific Psychology*. In: *The Origins of Psycho-Analysis: Letters to Wilhelm Fliess, Drafts and Notes, 1887–1902*. New York: Basic Books, 1954.

_____ (1900). *The Interpretation of Dreams, S.E.*, 4&5, 485.

_____ (1901). *The Psychopathology of Everyday Life, S.E.*, 6.

5 Signals of the Comic

Roger B. Henkle, Ph.D.

The problem is as old as comedy itself: How does a text indicate that it is treating its material comically? How is a comic frame established? What are the signals? In some instances it is quite clear: tonal qualities, such as exuberance, archness, mock grandiosity, nonsensical play; settings, such as interludes of carnival, or at the other end of the social scale, of preciousness and foppery. But there are subtler signals of the comic that are more difficult to pick up and yet *are* picked up by sophisticated readers. To ascribe such sensitivity merely to the sophistication of the audience, as Meredith and Bergson and Freud do, is to beg the question. For we need to know what the sophisticate perceives: To what attitudes or situations is he attuned? Such inquiries become especially crucial when, as is so often the case in 20th-century writing, the work provokes contrary responses—it is perceived as primarily comic by culturally sophisticated readers, but disquieting and unnerving—not in the least comic—by other readers. Indeed, such works often seek to induce this ambiguity of response, coupling amusement with uneasiness, humor with dread: the rictus of the comic mask inscrutable.

These are the texts that are particularly compelling if we are to discover any clues to comic response, and if we are to go beyond the subjectivity of the beholder. That is why I propose to focus first on one such modern text, Iris Murdoch's novel *A Severed*

Head (1961), the expression of a writer whose work has been consistently comic, but which many readers find disturbing, even (in extreme reactions) depressing. *A Severed Head* chronicles the disintegration of Martin Lynch-Gibbon's ordered, elegant, upper-middle-class life, in which he discovers that his wife has been having affairs with his close friend Palmer Anderson and with his brother Alexander; in which he loses his mistress Georgie Hands; and ultimately gives himself up, almost sacrificially, to an unattractive and domineering woman anthropologist, Honor Klein. It is a tale of repeated humiliations for Martin, and of the incestuous game-playing of an overly civilized London social stratum, and it certainly has its disquieting implications. Yet it is also a kind of arabesque of social complications, almost farcical at times. The novel resides in the mind as a comedy, even for those who feel uncomfortable reading it. Perhaps, by examining the opening pages of *A Severed Head*, we can find the sources of this ambiguity and in the process isolate some of the signals of the comic, factors that may in turn be applicable to other problematic texts—specifically Franz Kafka's *The Trial* (1925).

A Severed Head opens with Martin, the narrator, describing a langorous afternoon with his mistress Georgie. Self-revelatory, self-explaining first-person narration may in itself tilt a modern text toward the comic, especially when, as in this case, the narrator puts great emphasis on his subjective apprehension of the life around him. After a brief exchange of remarks with Georgie, Martin comments that "I liked the dry way in which she accepted our relationship. Only with a person so eminently sensible could I have deceived my wife" (p. 3). Such self-congratulation suggests that Martin is riding for a ludicrous fall; at the same time, his pleasure in the refinement of his own responses seems to swathe the narrative in a complacency that will cushion all shocks to his psyche. We may be inclined, moreover, to treat such accounts as less "serious" because of the special relationship modern readers have toward subjective accounts: Once the crucial issues are seen as those affecting the psychological state of an articulate and perceptive narrator, we can assume that we will not be forced into any traumatic encounter with subjects or situations that have threatening social implications for us. The narrator, after all, has emerged relatively intact, since he is able to speak of such things so calmly, and since he will presumably be mediating them throughout the text. And since psychological patterns and distresses are all too familiar to the sophisticated late 20th-century reader—we have a language for them, we have schemes to explain them, we have been through accounts of them before—a narrative so located, in a subjective framework and essentially describing the consequences to one ego, and thus *personal* to the protagonist/narrator, is at an important remove from a narrative that would engage us directly with larger social situations whose implications could not be presumably worked out within that mediating consciousness.

Martin's consciousness does, in fact, provide us almost immediately with reassurance that the psychological and social atmosphere in which most of us live will not confront us with disturbing challenges. Martin and Georgie are lounging around, presumably after sex, gazing fondly at each other and discoursing idly on a variety of topics. They are in Georgie's digs, symbolically curtained away from the "cold raw misty London afternoon" (p. 4)—the outer social world. Martin's attention wanders from objects in the room to Georgie's hair to recollections of the "purple underwear and black openwork tights which drove me mad" (p. 7). The conversation drifts from Martin's wife to her psychiatrist Palmer, then to Palmer's sister Honor Klein. Martin must keep in mind the time, for his wife's session ends at five, and " 'I should be back at Hereford Square soon after that. She always wants to discuss it. And we have a dinner engagement' " (p.4). All this is the ambience of modern existence: distracted, dispersed. The mind cannot attend to any one thing for long, but is diverted onto appointments, gossip, recollections, objects, whatever attracts it. In such a condition can anything of major social importance be impinging upon the actors? Murdoch puts us into a state that is all too familiar: the fabric of our ordinary lives, usually full of mundane preoccupations, none of them terribly important. We think of it as the very quality of modern existence; Benjamin (1955) has suggested that it is the nature of modern apperception, making us critically distant, almost absent-mindedly disengaged. In this slightly bemused mode, the level of intensity slackens. Indeed, there is an underlying sense of well-being. The self will usually get through ordinary life's minor confusions with minimal psychic expenditure; in all that we do there is a matrix of repeated and familiar concerns. What more identifiably comic ground can there be than that of our everyday life—locus of the situation comedy, theater for human foibles, the home base of humor? Dozens of theorists from Aristotle on have postulated that comedy deals with man in ordinary situations, at his normal level of mental and spiritual effort. In this, a sense of some level of personal inferiority may be crucial. Freud has led the way to analysis of comedy in terms of preservation or gratification of the individual ego, asserting its own invulnerability. In his important later paper "Humor" (1927), he suggests that "humor has in it a liberating element. . . . It is the triumph of narcissism, the ego's victorious assertion of its own invulnerability. It refuses to be hurt by the arrows of reality or to be compelled to suffer" (p. 159-166). The superego assists in this process by enabling one to recognize and smile at the triviality of the concerns which might confront the ego—to create an attitude of humorous indulgence toward the actions of others.

The reality that Murdoch initially evokes is one in which the challenges to the ego would not seem to be substantial. In a life so absorbed with myriad trifling distractions, the capacity in all of us for concentrated energy is diminished. Scarcely any activity is significant enough in itself to pose a challenge to one's identity or fulfillment. The condition, presumably, is general: we live in a context in which few men act with intensity and single-minded direction. Thus, if the inclination of each human organism is toward self-realization, then it should be gratified in a setting in which it is not vulnerable to the domination or opposition of other wills. How often has it been the business of comedy to break down characters with overwhelming egos, whose fixed absorption with their own interests or desires must be exposed or dispelled? Comedy's favorite target is the obsessive, self-absorbed being, who would make ordinary existence unbearable. The nonreflexive, unambiguous nature of the determined, compulsive ego is inimical to comedy's reflexive play. Happily, the modern London society of Martin and Georgie is not a place in which such behavior is symptomatic; indeed, the mind can rarely be concentrated so.

To be sure, the ego does need its little victories, its stretches of concentrated assertion, and that is what a sexual affair provides for Martin. The passion and illicitness actually compose the mind for short periods—Martin observes that he and Georgie could gaze at each other in total absorption: "Antonia and I never looked at each other like that. Antonia would not have sustained such a steady gaze for so long..." (p. 8). But here the will is merely exercising itself. Martin has no intention of jeopardizing his marriage; he shall be home at five, aperitifs at the usual time. In fact, the excitement of the affair comes from its relationship to his marriage; his dalliance is in constant tension with his life in Hereford Square. When, finally, Martin's marriage dissolves, the affair dissolves as well. Socially controlled exercises of willpower or of the ego are symptomatic of modern middle-class existence, for that class has long adjusted itself to limitations on its capacity to act independently and aggressively. Its literature, particularly the novel, has accustomed the middle-class reader to vicarious experience, to contained adventure and mediated (often displaced) self-assertion. The novel, with its capacity for extended projection of the individual ego, has provided the field in which such self-elaboration can occur, outside of society, explicitly within a fiction that reminds us of the nature of fictions. Martin's romance is just such a life-fiction: the exercise of power, a bit of a risk, by a comfortable but restless man, within prescribed parameters.

And so we find ourselves in a well-established comic setting. The world we enter in the first pages of *A Severed Head* is one in which the hazard of destructive ego domination seems to be rather remote. Psychic energies are dispersed by the thousand diversions the modern mind is heir to; sexual power is a matter for an afternoon's play, a tingling little fiction in which the id and the superego are both well accommodated. Martin's dramas will be "psychological," and that does not seem to be very serious—certainly not to him, for he observes gaily to Georgie that Antonia's sessions with Palmer are going along " 'fizzingly. She enjoys it disgracefully. Of course it's all for fun anyhow' " (p. 4.)

But *A Severed Head* is one of those texts that mixes its signals, and, as Ernst Kris (1952) says that comic writings so often do, it veers uncannily toward that "double-edge" between the comic and the disturbing. Since comedy originates, according to Kris, in a "position midway between pleasure and unpleasure," probing "the conflict between instinctual trends and the superego's repudiation of them" (p. 182), it is often in danger of venturing into areas that have not been sufficiently reduced in intensity—that produce an "uncanny" effect. On this edge, the anticomic seems to define itself. Of its two elements the first is, of course, the power of the concentrated will, a will with the capacity, and the intention, to damage the protagonist's sense of self-identity, to strip him of his self-defined "integrity," to debase or humble him to such an extent that he loses his sense of form. Lying on the floor in front of Georgie's gas fire, Martin and Georgie drift almost ineluctably into speculations about power. First they muse about Palmer's strength, Martin saying, without real conviction, that Palmer " 'has real power in him,' " (p.5). Georgie wondering aloud about the potential insidiousness of analysts who think they can set people free: " 'I don't trust these professional liberators. Anyone who is good at setting people free is also good at enslaving them, if we are to believe Plato' " (p. 5). But Palmer isn't the real threat; he is only a psychoanalyst. Their conversation moves on to focus on the truly dangerous figure in the novel, Honor Klein. And there it settles, for neither of them can quite come to terms with Honor, whom Georgie knew only casually at Cambridge and found uncomfortable: " 'she was supposed to organize my work and help me with my moral problems. God!' " (p. 6). Georgie, whose instincts are shrewder than Martin's is sure of one thing: " 'Anyway *she* certainly has power in her' " (p. 6). And at that point they are plunged into reverie.

Honor Klein, an awful, asexual figure, apparently immune to the human frailties that characterize the rest of Murdoch's cast, emerges as an indomitable force in the novel. In an episode that is ludicrous, but only partially amusing, Martin wrestles with her in a dark cellar, as if something quite vital were at stake. She is the wielder of the Samurai sword, used in decapitation, and the symbolic instrument of the castration that is the other meaning of a "severed head." This leads us to the second element that seems to define the anticomic. As an anthropologist specializing in savage cultures, she represents the mysteries that lie beyond the ken of our civilized modes of apprehension.

Cassirer (1944), like many others writing about the comic, fixes its realm in the familiar: "Comic art . . . can accept human life with all its defects and foibles, its follies and vices. . . . We see this world in all its narrowness, its pettiness, and silliness. We live in this restricted world..." (p. 192). In this realm the processes of normal comparison and analysis can be used for amusement and free play: Here, for instance, the clever mind can establish disjuncture and incongruity. Here it can exercise the power to juxtapose those disparate frames of reference that Koestler and others suggest is the trigger for laughter (Koestler, 1964; Milner, 1972). But there is another realm into which at least modern comedy may not as easily venture: that of the uncanny, the spiritual, the mysterious. Divine laughter does not seem to be available to our secular consciousnesses, and in the face of death or of the spiritual, of that darkness outside the civilized light of our familiar patterns, we find it difficult to project our comic pleasure. An outlook so wedded to the concrete as is the comic will shrink to nothing in the void of spiritual mystery. Honor Klein posits that opposition, for she is in tune with the savage mind, not the civilized mind. " 'You cannot have both truth and what you call civilization' " (p. 75). she says. And when that darkness is coupled with the power of the will, it portends terrible dissolution for Martin. " 'Being a Christian,' " Honor tells Martin, " 'you connect spirit with love. [Eastern mystery cults] connect it with control, with power' " (p. 116). And then she provides a third meaning for the book's title: " 'I am a severed head,' " she asserts, " 'such as primitive tribes and old alchemists used to use, anointing it with oil and putting a morsel of gold upon its tongue to make it utter prophecies. And who knows but that long acquaintance with a severed head might not lead to strange knowledge. For such knowledge one would have paid enough. But that is remote from love and remote from ordinary life' " (p. 221).

Ultimately Honor Klein enthralls Martin Lynch-Gibbon, and in a splendidly ironic closing scene, he is at her feet, speaking of her in terms of love that have become insidiously ambiguous: she "compels" him with her smile; he "worships" her; he is intoxicated with her (pp. 247–48). When she says that their existence together will have " 'nothing to do with happiness, nothing whatever,' " he answers " 'I wonder if I shall survive it' " (p. 248). All Martin's former life is in wreckage now: Palmer has seized control of Georgie, who is nearly catatonic after a suicide attempt; Antonia is off with Martin's brother; the house in Hereford

Square is deserted; Martin's occupation as an importer of elegant artifacts has been left behind. The carefully constructed former self exists no more. And yet, as I have said, the novel retains its predominantly comic outlook. How the anticomic forces of willpower and mystery are incorporated within that outlook furnishes us with several more "signals of the comic" in a text.

These signals can also be found at the very beginning of the novel. The opening scene in Georgie's apartment contains two long paragraphs in which Martin muses on the objects in her flat. He notes first a trio of candles glowing on the mantelpiece "as on an altar," and a pair of "Chinese incense holders in the form of little bronze warriors, who held aloft as spears the glowing sticks of incense" (p. 3). These are objects that evoke an age of spirituality and mystery, yet they have been transformed into objects of art. We are made dimly conscious of modern Western civilization's ability to reduce the formerly potent into decor, into pieces in a collection, and this acquires added irony when reread in the light of Honor Klein's invocation of Oriental power. Murdoch's writing is rich in allusion in this way, and it attunes us to the disposition of modern art to engage in these translocations, to pull in spheres of cultural reference.

The second long paragraph in the early pages appears to engage in the same process, but with a slight difference of emphasis. Again Martin is surveying Georgie's decor, but lamenting in his mind her "relentless lack of taste" (p. 7). He has provided her with "numerous Italian prints, French paperweights, pieces of Derby, Worcester, Coleport, Spode, Copeland, and other bric-a-brac," but whereas anything he and Antonia bought "found its place at once in the rich and highly integrated mosaic of our surroundings, Georgie seemed to have no such carapace" (p. 7). He resolves anew to continue this futile educative effort, but reflects that in a way such lack of worldly pretension in Georgie was rather engaging, "the very image and symbol of my relation to Georgie, my mode of possessing her, or more precisely the way in which I, as it were, failed to possess her" (pp. 7–8). The motif of possession of another human being, specifically in terms of remolding her, is established right away. Later that notion will become ominous when Honor Klein sets to work, but here it is not so, precisely because it *is* a motif. It is a motif that arises in the contexts of objects of art and of refashioning Georgie to Martin's artistic tastes. Having arisen in this way, it acquires a distinctively artistic or, rather, literary tone. Presently the motif recurs when Martin visits his brother Alexander's sculpture studio, and finds there "a clay head in the first stages of composition, the early stages when the wire framework has been roughly filled out and the clay laid over it in various directions in long strips until the semblance of a head appears. This particular moment has always seemed to me uncanny, when the faceless image acquires a quasi-human personality...." (pp.48-9). Here the relationship of "making" (or remaking) a personality to art is explicit. If, as sophisticated readers, we consider the old truism that very often artists write about the processes of art, then another, neatly involuted plane of interpretation is possible: that Iris Murdoch is dealing in part with the problems of characterization. (This is an even richer vein to pursue if we are aware of Murdoch's (1959, 1961) own complaints about modern authors who do not give their characters "free life," and instead reduce them to vehicles for ideas – an issue also taken up by her husband John Bayley [1960] in his *The Characters of Love*. But this is another level of reading sophistication that we need not expect of most readers.)

The motif acquires greater resonance as one moves through the novel, for we persistently encounter descriptions of the characters as gods or goddesses. Indeed, Martin, in the first chapter, calls Georgie a "river goddess" (p. 8). A fuller set of literary (or at least cultural) allusions begins to aggregate, for Palmer and Antonia are often associated with the capricious Greek deities who sported with mortals, and Martin (a name derived from Mars) seems to be traveling between the world of mortals and that of Olympus, often in a dense London fog, or in the cloud of his own intoxication. The references call up Greek mythology explicitly – for it is the seat of that Hellenistic civilization in which the Martin Lynch-Gibbons thrive – but there is substantial play among spiritual figures of primitive as well as civilized cultures. Martin comes upon the unfaithful Antonia and Palmer in his bedroom, and "they seemed in that momentary vision of them alike deities upon an Indian Frieze, enthroned, inhumanly beautiful, a pair of sovereigns, distant and serene" (p. 67). In this the types of reference in the two long paragraphs at the opening of the novel are conflated. The capacity of the culture to transform formerly potent materials into mere *objets d'art*, and the specific power of the literary imagination of transmute human activities onto literary and symbolic planes generate a process—that of artistic metamorphosis—which provides an ultimate control over all the matter in the novel's world.

The comic process and the creative process share much in common, as Koestler, Kris, and others have pointed out. They often begin with a reductive transformation of a solid or sacred subject—for their materials are the concrete—and they engage in a process of elaboration by which the subject is transformed, sometimes again and again, often in a spirit of play. The power to transfigure one's material inspires the joy of mastery and control, while divesting the material itself of its immobility, its potency of being and form. The ego can assert itself in a pleasurable way by demonstrating the capacity of the individual psyche to transform what lies outside it, and it does so in a way that the culture determines to be non-threatening to others: Play is defined as an activity displaced from significant social concerns.

Thus perhaps the most vital comic indicator is the capacity of the shaping intelligence in the text to engage in cultural conversion and literary metamorphosis, which we immediately see to be operating in *A Severed Head*'s allusions to the way sacred objects are made profane in Western consumer societies, and its evocation of literary parallels. Both processes involve forms of repetition. We recall similar cultural and literary conversions of the past. We are reminded of similar situations, which have now become part of our literary heritage: They are psychic tools for our use. Even the breaking down of Martin Lynch-Gibbon can be controlled by this means. Honor Klein calls him the "Knight of Infinite Humiliation," (p. 133) and in doing so suggests a comparison with Don Quixote, our culture's archetypal comic figure. In this frame of reference, comedy is the only apt term.

The question nevertheless remains: How useful are these signals of the comic when applied to other problematic texts? To carry the inquiry further, then, let us look at another text that appears to rest on that borderline between the comic and non-comic, Franz Kafka's *The Trial* (1925/1973). In this case, readers and critics generally find the novel to be disquieting and unnerving.

5. SIGNALS OF THE COMIC

There is an account by Kafka's friend Max Brod describing Kafka reading portions of *The Trial* to close acquaintances and evoking continuous hilarity, but the novel has usually fallen on the other side of the comic. Again, let us look at the opening sentences of the book to see how the tone is established:

> Someone must have traduced Joseph K., for without having done anything wrong he was arrested one fine morning. His landlady's cook, who always brought him his breakfast at eight o'clock, failed to appear on this occasion. That had never happened before. K. waited for a little while longer, watching from his pillow the old lady opposite, who seemed to be peering at him with a curiosity unusual even for her, but then, feeling both put out and hungry, he rang the bell. At once there was a knock at the door and a man entered whom he had never seen before in the house. He was slim and yet well knit, he wore a closely fitting black suit, which was furnished with all sorts of pleats, pockets, buckles, and buttons, as well as a belt, like a tourist's outfit, and in consequence looked eminently practical, though one could not quite tell what actual purpose it served. "Who are you?" asked K., half raising himself in bed. But the man ignored the question, as though his appearance needed no explanation, and merely said: "Did you ring?" "Anna is to bring me my breakfast," said K., and then studied the fellow, silently and carefully, trying to make out who he could be. The man did not submit to this scrutiny for very long, but turned to the door and opened it slightly so as to report to someone who was evidently standing just behind it: "He says Anna is to bring him his breakfast." A short guffaw from the next room came in answer; and it rather sounded as if several people had joined in. Although the strange man could no have learned anything from it that he did not know already, he now said to K., as if passing on a statement: "It can't be done." (Pp. 1, 2).

To begin with, of course, we do not have a first-person narration and thus not as clear an indication that the novel's concerns will be limited to the psyche of a controlling consciousness. Hence we are not reassured of the capacity of that mediating consciousness to survive the events of the story—indeed, K. does not survive. Still, first person-narrative is not determinative, and we do have a narration that adheres rather closely to the point of view of the protagonist, Joseph K. The novel also has a strong psychological component, but its effects appear to be mainly upon the reader, in itself a possibly significant shift of impact. In part this shift occurs because of the instability of many of those elements that we discovered to be operating in Murdoch's novel. The functioning of the superego, for instance, so crucial an element in Freud's explanation of humor, is particularly problematic in the main character. He describes himself as a conventional man, well situated in the Bank, in a position of responsibility, and he demonstrates at times an almost fatalistic determination to go by the rules of society. When summoned to an interrogation after his "arrest," he readily appears; indeed, he searches it out, for its time was never divulged to him. The next week he will appear unsummoned and discover that no hearing is being held. Yet the context of his society, the patterns of normal activity, are curiously obscured in the novel, and K. has little sense of family and community. He has a lover, who is a woman of dubious reputation, and whom he essentially deserts during the "trial"; his family connections consist principally of a busybody uncle who appears abruptly and proves to be of little use. K. is not integrated into a social order in the way that Martin Lynch-Gibbon is. Moreover, K.'s motives are unclear; he behaves erratically and impulsively. This is most evident in his ludicrous erotic encounters—on the night of his arrest he finds himself drawn to Fraülein Burstner, a fellow boarding-house tenant, and kisses her "first on the lips, then all over the face, like some thirsty animal lapping greedily" (p. 29). In the empty courtroom, he is similarly drawn to the wife of the courthouse usher, and proposes to go off with her until she is carried away on one hand by a dwarfish law student. And while waiting to discuss his case with his lawyer, he is lured into a side room by Leni, the attorney's companion, who drags him down to the floor in lust. K. is told that accused men are unusually attractive to women, but that does not quite account for the compulsive and usually inopportune onrush of sexual desire that distracts K. throughout his ordeal, and tha suggests that the normal psychological checks upon his impulses are not operative.

The inability of K.'s superego, or his socially regulating instincts, to incorporate a body of social values, or to be able to provide coherent, mediating control, deprives him of the kind of perspective that will allow the ego to deal with threats from outside and with its own obsessions. Consequently, K. is in a situation in which outer forces have an uncanny effect upon him, and in which his own assertions of will and self-interest consistently undo him. One of the ironies of *The Trial* is that the "authorities" establish a situation, through the initial arrest of K., in which the protagonist seems to be at the mercy of stronger forces, of other wills; yet the disintegration of K. occurs largely through his own willing of it. He involves himself more and more deeply in his trial; he becomes complicit with the forces of his own undoing. Kafka allows us to see the way in which his character constructs an oppressive force almost immediately. Rather than challenge his arrest effectively (although he often makes fitful attempts to do so), K. raises the question of "what authority could [these men] represent?"(p. 4) and consistently aggravates his condition. In the earlier chapters of the novel, K. oscillates between resistance and submission, but as the novel progresses he adjusts more and more to their authority over him. So confident are the authorities that they can induce K. to use his own will to destroy himself, that the assassins pass the knife to each other in front of him, anticipating that he will seize it and plunge it into his own breast.

Can we imply a comic intention from this ironic play with the issue of the working of will in the novel? It was not only the apparent absence of a strong, manipulative will in Murdoch's world that gave us a signal of the comic, but it was also the assumption—which we gathered from a variety of sources—that Murdoch's civilized world was amenable to a special kind of subjective ordering. As *A Severed Head* unfolds, we discover that a variety of egos interact in normal social situations. These interactions counteract and modify the activity of self-assertion, creating a matrix of balancing and mediating forces. In such a milieu, no single human will can dominate, and even the workings of authority have been modified by the self-interests and the highly developed and supple superegos of the upper-middle-class characters. And in such a setting, the presence of psychiatry is almost emblematic of the capacity of a complex society to mediate the adaptation of various individuals. Further, psychiatry symbolizes in Murdoch the regulation of society through *subjective* ordering; it preserves and keeps alive the strength of ego of various individuals—allows them to find gratification through expression and ordering—while continuing the mediation. Indeed, what is, in part, most disquieting about Kafka's world is the inability of K.'s subjective order to provide a pattern of meaning to the novel's society. Bersani, in *A Future for Astyanax* (1976), his perceptive reading of the psychological patterning of modern fiction, observes that our normal assumption in reading novels is that meaning will inhere in characterology—particularly in the protagonists. Such an assumption proves to be a correct one in Murdoch's novel, for what Martin experiences—what he undergoes—supplies the reader with a pattern of meaning that allows us to interpret the novel and essentially all elements in it. This is not the case in *The Trial*, which we are haunted by the sense of something not encountered. There is a disjuncture between K.'s characterization and the events which presumably arise out of it or affect it, and this in turn raises doubts about the meaning of his activities *and* of the events of the novel. In a novel so obsessively absorbed with the actions of one man, it is doubly disconcerting to suspect that meaning in the novel is not related to subjective ordering.

Such difficulties occur on the level of narrative as well. The narrative tone is puzzling, for as detached as it is, there is, at least in this translation, an almost jocular quality to it. The persisting ambiguity of the narrative tone contributes to the difficulties in gauging what our response should be. Similarly, the treatment of everyday life produces mixed signals. The sentence describing the clothing of the man at the door—"a closely fitting black suit, which was furnished with all sorts of pleats, pockets, buckles, and buttons, as well as a belt, like a tourist's outfit, and in consequence looked eminently practical"—is a nice instance of comic preoccupation with nonsensical details, and does, in fact, present the visitor as a bit of a buffoon. But there is also something slightly ominous in Joseph K.'s worry over the fact that his breakfast had not been brought to him by the landlady's cook at eight o'clock. Indeed, we are told in the first sentence that the pleasure of repetition has been broken by the arrest, and thus Joseph K.'s often obtuse insistence on routine and on the familiar ways of dealing with problems provides not the comfort of recognizable everyday operations but rather frustration. That frame of the comic has been broken away.

K.'s mode of coping, as we can see, is lamentably insufficient. If only he had some breakfast under his belt. On another occasion, he fancies that wearing an impressive black suit will carry the day. As reassuring as such mundane touches might seem, they are scarcely equal to the imaginative recourses that are necessary to lift him out of the denigrating pattern in which the authorities have thrust him. K. is unable to develop alternative fictions to serve in interpreting and possibly transmuting his experience, and this deficiency is crucial. There is scarcely anything more ludicrous than his interview with the printer Titorelli, a seedy bohemian who provides K. with his most "concrete" suggestions about his predicament and how to proceed. As Titorelli rambles on discursively on the three possibilities for K., "definite acquittal, ostensible acquittal, and indefinite postponement," (p. 152) they all seem to be insufficient: The first course requires insisting on one's innocence, and the Court rarely listens to that and such determinations are never recorded; ostensible acquittal means that the case can still be reopened by a judge at any later time, making K. liable to another sudden arrest for the remainder of his life; postponement eliminates that uncertainty, but it means as well that K. will never be free of the charge. Yet it is the best that K. is able to come up with, given the paucity of his own imagination.

Titorelli's projections cannot provide K. any imaginative recourse from his present predicament because they are all legalistic fictions—hypotheses ungrounded in the emotive and experiential realities of ordinary life. K. is always floating loose in those abstractions, unable to tether them to recognizable existence. Murdoch's characters, on the other hand, prove to be able to orient their life fictions to a setting and a range of experience that we, as middle-class readers, find familiar, and this in itself may provide the orientation necessary for a comic response to their situation. As we noted, Kafka's world, while full of material details, does not turn out to be recognizable; we cannot easily visualize it, we do not feel as if we have been there—except perhaps in a dream. Characteristic is the "living room" of the Court usher and his wife, which serves during Hearing days as a barren anteroom to the courtroom. The furniture is thus moved in and out on short notice, as it is in Fraülein Burstner's room, where K. is first interrogated. Thus comedy not only concerns itself frequently with the trivial and the everyday, it requires that we be able to situate ourselves psychically there. Correspondingly, purely abstract fictions cannot assert the control necessary for the comic. Fictions must be able to build off of, and perhaps transform, recognizable materials. Ironically, this suggests that the modern writers from Flaubert on who have sought to rid their scenes of the materiality of middle-class culture, may need that materiality for comic orientation. Even Beckett's Molloy must play with his bicycle and his sucking stones.

Nowhere is this more evident than in the nightmarish "first interrogation," in which K. tries to seize the day by challenging the right of the authorities to arrest him. The audience at the interrogation seems to be transfixed by K.'s rhetoric, and the examining magistrate is apparently thrown into confusion: "K. . . . was elated by the breathless attention of the meeting; in that stillness a subdued hum was audible which was more exciting than the wildest applause"(p. 45). This is the moment when K. thinks himself to be on the verge of transforming his persecution into tactical advantage. But the subdued hum that K. notices is not a murmur of admiration, but of incredulity. The audience is composed of those very officials K. is excoriating, and while he makes his passionate plea for justice, someone in the back of the hearing room is forcibly seducing a washerwoman, a tableau that quickly distracts the audience and reduces K.'s defense to a shambles. As ludicrous as such a dissolution is, the effect is to produce that quality of the uncanny of which Kris spoke: Transformation cannot produce control unless it is responsive to the will of the protagonist, and unless it achieves a state that accords in some way with our sense of ordinary life. The concrete particularities of this scene are only absurd and incongruous: the image of the washerwoman writhing in the back of a filled courtroom, or of K. himself noticing—for the first time—that everyone to whom he has been pleading his case wears the official badge of the examining magistrate. If the power of transformation is to be able to reduce the potency of a situation that is threatening or mysterious, it must be able—in a comic text—to incorporate those mysteries and threats into familiar, explicable human context—or, as in Murdoch's world, into manipulable objects: Chinese incense holders and such. In almost no instance in *The Trial* is control of power achieved in the latter way, through commodification, through the transformation of ideas and influences into personal possessions. K.'s world is curiously devoid of such objects.

Nor, ultimately, does the power of *literary* transformation achieve the prominence in this novel that it does in Murdoch's. *The Trial* is relatively spare in allusions to other texts, and although it eventually accumulates some resonance in this respect, it yields very little for the reader seeking literary referentiality. The ritual of trial is itself a means of cultural organization, but a highly ambiguous one, especially when it seems, as here, to be scarcely more than a mock ceremony leading to the humiliation and destruction of a scapegoat. As the reader struggles to orient the story within the context of other stories, he is obliged fiinally to exercise his *own* fiction-making capacity – and thus we have developed out of this and other works the literary fiction of the "Kafkaesque."

The comparison of these two problematical texts demonstrates how closely related the comic response is to our essential middle-class conceptualizations. Such elements of our ordinary existence as the mediation of individual will, commodification of the alien, the building of projective fictions, and the transformation of anything disturbing into banal, recognizable modes of behavior, are significant factors in the establishment of a comic reading of such texts. Psychological interpretation functions as an analogue of this process when it is foregrounded, as it were, in *A Severed Head*. One can argue that it ultimately functions in the same way in the case of Kafka's writings, when we transform otherwise disquieting works such as *The Trial* into formulations of the "Kafkaesque" – cultural incorporations of particularly uncanny psychological states. But this latter process is a secondary one; on the immediate textual level, the signals, however ambiguous they may sometimes be, provide rather clear indications of the way in which we can be presumed to interpret a novel such as Kafka's. The relationship of the various signals of the comic to middle-class conceptualizations, including that of the practice of psychology, brings us around, finally, to a new understanding of that old criterion of Freud, Bergson, and others that had seemed to beg the question: Comedy requires a "special" audience. Such an audience is not necessarily more sophisticated than the average reader, but it does share certain suppositions about the character of modern everyday existence, and a certain awareness of the processes of cultural and literary transformation, that allow it to pick up those signals in even the most ambiguous circumstances.

REFERENCES

Bayley, J. (1960). *The characters of love.* London: Constable.
Benjamin, W. (1955). The work of art in the age of mechanical reproduction. In H. Zohn (Trans.), *Illuminations.* New York: Schocken.
Bersani, L. (1976). *A future for astyanax.* Boston: Little, Brown.
Cassirer, E. (1944). Art. In, *An essay on man.* New Haven: Yale University Press.
Freud, S. (1927). Humor. *S.E.*, XXI, 159–66.
Kafka, F. (1973). *The trial,* trans. W. & E. Muir. New York: Knopf. (Original work published 1925)
Koestler, A. (1964). *The art of creation.* New York: Macmillan.
Kris, E. (1964). *Psychoanalytic explorations in art.* New York: Schocken Books. (Original work published 1952)
Milner, G. B. (1972). Homo ridens: Towards a semiotic theory of laughter. *Semiotica,* 5:1–30.
Murdoch, I. (1959). The sublime and the beautiful revisited. *Yale Review, 49,* 247+.
―――― (1961). Against dryness. *Encounter, 16,* 16–20.
―――― (1961). *A severed head.* New York: Viking, 1963.

6 The Grammar of Representation in Psychoanalysis and Literature

Zelda Boyd, Ph.D.

> *It seems to me there is an area today where all philosophical investigations cut across one another—the area of language. Language is the common meeting ground of Wittgenstein's investigations, the English linguistic philosophy, the phenomenology that stems from Husserl, Heidegger's investigations, the works of the Bultmannian school and of the other schools of New Testament exegesis, the works of comparative history of religion and of anthropology concerning myth, ritual, and belief—and finally, psychoanalysis.*
> —Ricoeur, Freud and Philosophy
>
> *Thus, from patient to analyst, and from analyst to patient, the entire process operates through language.*
> —Emile Benveniste, *Problems in General Linguistics* (1971)

It seems to be agreed that language, as used in literature and psychoanalysis, offers a crucial link between the two disciplines. But beyond that assertion, there is little agreement either about how language informs these disciplines or what elements of language the two share. The linguistic connections that are made between literature and psychoanalysis fall into three categories: the analysis of symbols, the analysis of word play, and the analysis of the grammar of discourse. Of the three, the first two have been considered at far greater length than the last, not surprisingly, since symbols and word play are easier to identify and easier to discuss than the larger semantic and syntactic units of discourse.

Recently, however, attention has turned to the third category, namely, the language of representation—that is, the grammatical structures by which both patient and text define and reveal themselves. In this essay, I willl first review briefly the ways in which language has served as a focus for psychoanalytic thinking, beginning with the more familiar cases of word play, word association, metaphor, and symbol. I will then take up the question of discourse, particularly the question of how the analysis of sentence structures might yield useful literary and psychoanalytic insights. The "action-language" of Roy Schafer (1976) is a natural starting point for such an inquiry, for Schafer was among the first to recognize the extent to which the grammatical structures we use represent our reality, and among the first to apply grammatical insights to psychoanalysis. My own discussion is an extension of Schafer's work, although it is derived not from Schafer but rather from the linguistic/philosophical sources he uses. I draw my examples from literature because there we find texts in their richest forms; the points, however, are by no means restricted to literary language. On the contrary, I believe that the sort of grammatical attention I propose can prove fruitful in any field centrally concerned with questions of language and meaning.

If we return to the first category mentioned above, we find that Freud's *Interpretation of Dreams* sets the model for the connection between literature and psychoanalysis as shared symbol systems, reading the patient as text, the text as patient. In both instances, Freud concentrates on the unspoken, the taboo, the text behind the text. Such a procedure is perfectly legitimate as long as we remember that the analogy between the patient and text is based on the extended metaphorical sense of "read" (understand or interpret), as when we speak of reading someone's face or mind, reading a situation, reading between the lines. In this sense of the word, we read both patient and text the same way— namely, semiotically, as an organization of signs to be decoded.

Freud himself demonstrated how fascinating such a "reading" could be in "The Theme of the Three Caskets" (1913), where he interprets that motif in *The Merchant of Venice* and elsewhere. The

6. THE GRAMMAR OF REPRESENTATION

caskets, Freud argues, most immediately represent women, and the correct choice is always the plainest casket/woman: for example, the lead casket in *The Merchant of Venice* of which Bassanio says, "Thy paleness moves me more than eloquence," or in *Lear*, Cordelia who "loves and is silent." Freud goes on to draw an analogy between the text and the patient, using psychoanalytic insights to interpret the literary text: "If we decide to regard the peculiarities of our 'third one' as concentrated in the 'dumbness,' then psychoanalysis has to say that dumbness is in dreams a familiar representation of death" (pp. 294–95). Freud moves from the specific text to mythology (he cites, as an instance, the three Fates, the third of whom is the Goddess of Death), then to his analytic experience with patients' dreams, looking first for the motif – patterns of three, either women or objects which stand for women – and then examining the language with which these objects are described. He does what most literary critics and psychoanalysts do. He pays close attention to what is said in order to discover what is not being said, and he leans heavily for his evidence on the language of metaphor or symbol.

More than half a century later, Ricoeur (1970) singles out this procedure of Freud's, the search for the symbolic, as "the common meeting ground" for the human sciences, and, like Freud, locates the point of juncture in language. As Ricoeur notes, although the dream is the "model ... of all disguised, substitutive and fictive expressions of human wishes or desire," the dream itself is in fact unavailable, private, beyond interpretation, so that "it is not desires as such that are placed at the center of analysis, but rather their language" (p. 6). So far, Ricoeur's argument seems obvious and straightforward, but actually his purpose lies elsewhere than in language. For him, language, like desire itself, is by nature always veiled, always double, and "this region of double meanings" is epitomized by the symbol. Here, Ricoeur's claim for the primacy of language dissolves, for symbols are not language-dependent. While his symbols – earth, heaven, water, life, trees, and stones – may be expressed *in* language, they are not linguistic in any necessary way.

In addition, Ricoeur's emphasis on the symbolic, on language as a system of double meanings, restricts the range and kind of language he considers. In effect, it rules out the largest area of language, which is unambiguous, non-symbolic, unitary in meaning, and yet of great significance to the literary critic, the psychoanalyst, or anyone else interested in how people do things with words.

Granted that every utterance can be interpreted as something other than what it says, to do so is to move from the linguistic to some other level. The *reductio ad absurdum* is the old joke in which three psychiatrists meet. The first says "Good day," at which the second turns to the third and asks, "Now what does he mean by that?" The second psychiatrist is not entirely mad. That "Good day" may have been used to serve all kinds of purposes, aggressive, friendly, hierarchical—the list is virtually endless—but whatever the utterance "means" in this sense is non-linguistic. That is, the situation would not be radically altered if the first psychiatrist had simply smiled or nodded in passing instead of speaking. The relation between the words themselves and the meaning alluded to is purely contingent, and to call this linguistic is not merely a misnomer. It literally misdirects our attention from what is in fact involved, namely, the analysis of motive or intention. It also blurs the distinction between the meaning of the words, which is not negotiable, and the meaning (intention) of the speaker in using them, which is open to all sorts of interpretation.

We find Freud closer to the linguistic substratum when he turns to the second category: words *as words*: puns, homonyms, word-substitutions, phonetic transpositions—the kind of word play so familiar in both psychoanalysis and literature. To take a relatively linguistic example, in "The Antithetical Sense of Primal Words" (1910) Freud points to a very odd phenomenon: that there are a " 'fair number of words with two meanings, one of which says the exact opposite of the other' " (p. 156). He cites from the work of the philologist Karl Abel the examples of the Latin *sacer*, which means both sacred and accursed, the English prefix *with*, which originally meant not only together but against (as we can see in frozen forms like "withstand" or "withhold"), *cleave*, which means both to separate and to cling to, or, to add to Freud's examples a more recent instance, *to dust*, which refers either to taking away or putting on (the difference between dusting the room and dusting the crops). As Freud rightly intuits, whatever is operating to create such paradoxes is not only a linguistic curi-

6. THE GRAMMAR OF REPRESENTATION   111

osity, but also offers a tantalizing insight into the workings of the human mind. While the peculiarity Abel discusses is built *into* language in a way that symbols are not, it lies, at least for the moment, beyond our power to theorize about it in any useful way. Equally linguistic and perhaps more easily interpretable are the instances of individual word play. This is certainly one point at which the interests of literature and psychoanalysis converge – in the word.

Following Freud's lead, Lacan (1977) has brought the analysis of the word into prominence for both fields. His reading, for example, of the multifold meanings of the word "foil" in his essay on *Hamlet* is an example of what linguistics, literary criticism, and psychoanalysis can do at their best to cross-fertilize one another. Lacan remarks that "the funny thing is, it's there in the text," in Act V where Hamlet uses "foil" in its literal sense of a fencing rapier and then puns on it, "I'll be your foil, Laertes" (p.32). Lacan goes on to exfoliate all the possibilities of the word and to demonstrate the centrality of this and other punning, riddling, and mocking to the play. Lacan could not have chosen better, for *Hamlet* is par excellence self-reflexive, a play on words as well as of them. Unfortunately, both in the *Hamlet* essay and in his other important essay on language, Lacan, after insisting on the significance of the letter, wanders away from it to psychological issues which are far richer. For all Lacan's amazement that "it's there in the text," the text doesn't hold him. Perhaps the problem is that the letter, or even the word, is not a sufficiently rewarding field of inquiry. Whatever the case, the Lacanian impulses, like Ricoeur's, to emphasize the omitted has the effect of moving attention away from the text while claiming to fix attention on it. If Lacan's "desire" is that which is always absent, that which makes its presence felt by omission, theoretically one could at least locate the lacunae in the text. But Lacan's readings are not sophisticated enough syntactically to pinpoint the gaps.

The insistence on the letter in all its literal, figural, and magical senses has its roots in the work of 19th-century philologists like Karl Abel and Max Müller, and the effect, both in 19th-century philology and in 20th-century criticism, has been to deflect consideration from larger units of language, in particular, from syntax. The question which needs to be asked is how language functions more broadly, as discourse, both in psychoanalysis and in literature. This question does not move us away entirely from double meanings, or from the act of interpreting the overt in terms of the covert, but it does require us to look more specifically at the syntax of sentences. The temptation is to compare the syntax of ordinary sentences with the syntax of dreams and to make the connection that way, to argue, as Lacan and his followers have, "that the unconscious is structured like a language" (Ricoeur, p. 38). But, as Ricoeur rightly notes, "although the technique of analysis moves entirely within the element of language" so that "speech events ... are devoted to bringing to light 'another discourse' ... belonging to the unconscious," it is necessary then to ask whether "properly speaking ... the laws of that other discourse [are] linguistic laws" (pp. 396–397).

Benveniste (1971), addressing the same issue independently from Ricoeur, argues that a comparison between the two domains of discourse is precisely what will *not* work, for dreams and other manifestations of the unconscious form "a 'language' so special that it is of the greatest importance to distinguish it from what we normally call language" (p. 74). "Everything seems to take us farther and farther away from an experiential correlation between the logic of dreams and the logic of an actual language" (Benveniste quoted in Ricoeur, 1970, p. 397). Taken as two languages, the syntax of dreams is too compressed, too discontinuous to be viewed as operating analogously to the syntax of natural language. To speak of the "language" of dreams or the "language" of the unconscious is like speaking of the "language" of flowers. The metaphor (not unlike "reading someone's mind") is intended to suggest that these are systems, interpretable calculuses, with their own laws and regularities. There is no harm in using "language" in this extended sense. What is misleading is the Lacanian claim to be doing something more rigorous, and, interestingly, one looks in vain for any development of the assertion, any serious attempt on the part of the Lacanians to specify precisely the nature of these languages or the syntax they might share. What is dangerous about the implied connection is the tendency for "language" or "discourse" or "syntax" to become totemic words which close rather than open investigation. This, no doubt, was the evil Benveniste was reacting to when he argued so vociferously for

6. THE GRAMMAR OF REPRESENTATION   113

the discontinuity between the structure of language and the structure of dreams.

To go back to my original question, How then does language, as discourse, operate in psychoanalysis and in literature? It is not so easy to return to Freud in this instance. Although he understood that what is available to the analyst is, in fact, a narrative – the patient's narrative – and although he understood that in this sense all therapy begins with the language by which the patient represents him or herself, Freud did not turn his attention to the style of that representation except in a very general way. He did notice it, however, as " 'A Child Is Being Beaten' " (1919) demonstrates. In that essay he points out the distancing effect of the particular grammatical form, "a child is being beaten." Not only is the subject, "a child," generic rather than person-specific, but the whole utterance is transposed into the passive so that neither the subject of the sentence nor the agent (whoever is doing the beating) need be specified. Freud notes that far more women than men reported this dream or fantasy, and he speculates on whether this particular construction corresponds in some way to something profound in the female psyche. Putting aside the connection with women (a point which we need not argue here, if indeed sufficient evidence exists to argue it at all), what is of interest for us is Freud's recognition of the significance of the grammatical form. Freud's attention is not strictly on the double or the symbolic meaning of the utterance. Certainly, the locution was used, as Freud observed, to conceal a quite different sentence, sometimes "I am being beaten," or "My father is beating me," or "My father is beating another child." But the place to begin, he senses, is with the sentence as given, with its omissions and transpositions, and the question to ask is not what is this sentence replacing but what is peculiar about this grammatical representation of the event?

Events, after all, have no necessary linguistic structure; they can be realized in language in many different ways. Why, then, this construction? Why is the event represented as ongoing ("is being beaten") rather than as finite, since presumably no one can beat indefinitely? Why the choice of a construction which allows the agent to be omitted? Why the impersonal "a child?" Very likely, these whys can never be definitely answered. Nevertheless, it is the significance of such linguistic choices – the assumption that grammatical forms can have meaning and that the use of a particular form is to some degree a discretionary choice about how this event is to be represented and where the speaker is to be placed in relation to it—that Benveniste had in mind when he spoke of the rhetoric of discourse as the connecting link between language and the unconscious.

Benveniste (1956/1971) makes the point that the symbolism of dreams and of the unconscious "makes use of extremely condensed signs which, in organized language, would correspond more to large units of discourse than to minimal units" (p. 74). In other words, the linguistic corollary of the dream symbol is not the word but the sentence at the very least. Perhaps not surprisingly, at precisely the moment that Benveniste was arguing for an analysis of discourse as necessary to interpretation, the very area he was aiming to revive came into prominence both in linguistics and in English ordinary language philosophy. Of course, it came under different names. It was called discourse analysis, or the interplay between "la langue" and "la parole" (Saussure's terms), or philosophy of action, or speech act theory. Different as these fields of inquiry are, they all share Benveniste's interest in the manifest structure of language as opposed to the search for what lies beneath. As with the psychoanalytic awareness that, whatever else one looks for, the immediate matter for analysis is the patient's narrative, his or her linguistic representation of events, so in ordinary language philosophy there was a similar realization that any discussion of concepts is, finally, a discussion of sentences. Thus, more recently, psychology and philosophy (and literature, as we shall see) have indeed come together, as Ricoeur said, in language; not, however, in a concern for its symbolic aspect so much as in a renewed attention to the syntax and semantics of sentences, the language of representation.

Scahfer's (1976) *A New Language for Psychoanalysis* marks the shift in focus in psychoanalysis from smaller units of language to larger ones. Borrowing some of the terms and categories of English ordinary language philosophy (action, agent, happening, cause vs. reason), he asks psychoanalyst and patient alike to look closely at how language is being used to claim or disclaim responsibility. He argues that the grammar of constructions like "the impulse seized me," "the words poured out of my mouth," "my conscience torments me" (p. 143) needs to be taken seriously as dramatizing the disavowal of agency, and that abstractions like "rigid defense" or "libidinal energy" similarly reinforce a deterministic, non-agentive view of human behavior (p. 9).

The intricacies of Schafer's discussion are not immediately relevant to our purposes. What is important is his concern with the sentences as given, with what is said rather than what is symbolized. He asserts that much of the language of psychology has worked to underscore the view of the patient as patient (that is, as acted upon, suffering, undergoing) as against the view of the patient as agent (as intending, choosing, doing) (pp. 103–104). No "impulse seizes" one, nothing "slips out," nor does one's mind "play tricks" (pp. 131–132), although the grammar certainly permits such representations. Schafer reminds us that these *are* representations, and as such simply constitute one way of describing an event for which there are also other representations with enormously different impact. In his examples, for instance, there is a central "I" which is being omitted, with the event represented instead as something other than the subject's doing: "What, after all, did Freud show in the *Studies on Hysteria* ... but that a neurotic symptom is something a person *does* rather than *has* or has inflicted upon him or her?" (p. 153).

Schafer's demand for a totally "action-oriented" language is certainly questionable, both theoretically and practically; it is not clear that such a therapeutic language would be desirable, accurate, or possible. All the same, in refocusing discussion about the language of psychoanalysis in the direction of grammar, and particularly in drawing attention to those elements in the grammar that we tend to notice least (like the relations that hold between subject and verb), Schafer has performed an invaluable service. Furthermore, he has gone to the right sources, philosophers like Wittgenstein, Ryle, Anthony Kenny, Elizabeth Anscombe, and David Pears, whose work with language, fascinating though it is, has not yet much penetrated into either psychoanalytic or literary critical thinking.

Even Schafer's mistakes are useful. English offers many ways of avoiding agency besides the passive construction. Consider Schafer's own example, "the impulse seized me," which reverses the conceptual agent through metaphor, or consider sentences like "the twig snapped," "the water boiled," which are neither passives nor conventional actor/action sentences but happenings, i.e., events represented without reference to an agent or cause. Yet Schafer tends to speak as if the passive were the only form for avoidance and, furthermore, as if everything that looked like a passive had the same underlying structure. There are other errors. For example, emotion is not, either grammatically or conceptually, "an action or mode of action" (p. 365). Nor is " 'His intentions were honorable' ... a way of saying 'He acted honorably' " (p. 199). Nor are "I am pleased," "He was sad," "They'll be sorry" (p. 292) a consonant series. It is arguably wrong even to put the first two together since "I am pleased" is either a report or an exclamation and "He was sad" is an inference, but "They'll be sorry" is absolutely different. It is, in fact, a threat and works grammatically not at all like the other two sentences cited but like a promise ("You shall have your money") in which the grammatical subject is "they" or "you" but the conceptual subject, the person who undertakes to bring it about, can be none other than the speaker.

It is not that Schafer is unaware of shades of difference; the problem is that he does not have fine enough control of the subtleties of grammar to work out the details. In this, he is hardly alone. Beginnings are always faltering. Nevertheless, the sort of conceptual/grammatical analysis Schafer has in mind is crucial to psychoanalysis or to literary criticism or to any of the disciplines concerned with the interpretation of texts. How events are represented linguistically – where human action is placed in a general scheme of occurrences, the degree of agency that is claimed or disclaimed, whether events are described from the point of view of their beginning, middle, or end – all such data can help map that unconscious territory Freud was looking for when he turned to language for information about how the mind works.

Schafer understands that the same event – the movement of an arm, to use Wittgenstein's example – is open to alternate descriptions. "His arm rose" invokes a very different set of assumptions from "He raised his arm." The first regards the arm as a part of physics, the second defines the event as humanly willed. Generally, we slip from one mode to another so easily that no commitment to a particular vision seems involved. From time to time, however, one finds so consistent (insistent?) a grammatical pattern that no investigation of meaning can make sense without taking it into account. This appears to have been the case with the sentence Freud reports hearing in " 'A Child Is Being Beaten.' " It is often the case in literature, where the critic is similarly attuned to listen for repetitions.

Beginning where Schafer leaves off, with the idea that *"it is all a question of the rules of language being used, not of facts"* (pp. 226-227), I want to look at some instances in which the grammar of the representation is not only meaningful but also supplies the very texture of the work. That my examples are drawm from literature is partly accident – it is the field I know best – and partly a matter of choice, for literature provides wonderful and provocative data, as psychoanalysts from Freud on have recognized. At the same time, one could theoretically find one's text anywhere – for example, the psychoanalytic "text" developed between patient and analyst, where it is perhaps more important even than it is in literature to distinguish the language by which events are represented from the facts themselves. To do this, we need to make fairly detailed grammatical discriminations. In what follows, I am going to suggest some possible directions for how to proceed.

Let us begin with the question of aspect – where the subject stands in relation to an event or the point of view from which an event is described, outside or inside, at the beginning, middle, or end. Aspect is difficult to recognize in English because we think of verbs as marked primarily for tense, in contrast to languages like Russian which have aspect obligatorily built into the very ending. Nevertheless, aspect is fairly easy to recognize in a form like the present perfect which partakes of both tense and aspect. For example, as the 19th-century grammarian Henry Sweet pointed out, the sentence "I have shopped all afternoon" implies that it is still afternoon, that the speaker is still involved in the time frame of the event. "I have come early," while a less clear instance, still implies something carried over into the present ("and I am now here") in contrast to the simple past, "I came early," which conveys no sense of present result. The most elusive of the present perfects are perhaps the most interesting. Zandvoort calls these the "perfect of experience," where the event, while it is clearly in the past, unlike the shopping example, has some residual effect which lingers as experience. To take some examples from literature, consider how the meaning would change if Keats's sonnet "Much Have I Travelled in the World of Men" began "Much did I travel." What would then be emphasized is the pastness of the event and the speaker's isolation from it in the present. Instead, the actual line, "Much have I travelled," prepares us to hear how that past event still affects the speaker and what he still retains from it. To turn to another poet much preoccupied with the presence of the past, consider the difference in Wordsworth between the opening of "Tintern Abbey," "Five years have past ... and I have come," where the past experience continues to be alive and available to him, and the finality and sense of separation of the following from one of the Lucy poems, "She died, and left to me....The memory of what has been/ And never more will be." Or, in contrast to Keats's "Much have I travelled," here is the opening of a Wordsworth poem which underscores separation: "I travelled among unknown men.... 'Tis past, that melancholy dream."

Aspect involves not only inclusion and exclusion, presence and absence; it also segments events in relation to the beginning, the duration, or the conclusion. "I began to eat," "I ate for hours," and "I finished eating" are not marked for aspect in English as they are in languages which require specific grammatical forms, so we express the differences lexically without being aware that these are, in fact, grammatical distinctions. Certain of our verb forms, like the progressive – "I am reading," "I was running" – preserve the durative sense, although as with the perfect, this often shades into what looks like a simple tense. However elusive, such aspectual distinctions are often significant. Tennyson, for example, uses a high proportion of inceptive acts, like setting sail, or duratives (activities), like weaving and wandering, while he seems to avoid completed acts. He will rarely describe an event retrospectively from the point of view of its outcome: More often, he represents beginnings – Sir Bedivere casting the dying Arthur's sword into the lake without being able to foresee the arm rising out of the water to grasp it – or he sets figures in the middle of the process where again the result is not clear – Merlin following "the gleam," Sir Galahad searching for the Holy Grail without knowing exactly what it is he is looking for. Perhaps this pattern is best clarified when contrasted with someone like Hemingway, whose representation of the world is the reverse of Tennyson's.

If the aspectual world Tennyson realizes in language is full of the ambiguities and doubts attendant upon inconclusiveness, Hemingway's is a world linguistically overdetermined by delimiting modifiers and overmarked for ends. In "The Big Two-Hearted River" events are consistently presented from the perspective of their goal, retrospectively, with the modifiers adding specificity as a hedge against the unforeseen. Consider the following typically Hemingway sentence: "He stood ... looking out across the country toward the distant river." These modifiers are not merely the specifics of vivid writing; they are not randomly distributed over different parts of speech; they describe neither Nick (was he not? sweaty? lost? dark-haired?), nor the day, nor the terrain. Instead, they are consistently adverbial; they focus on the act of standing looking and restrict the direction of gaze. Consider how different the effect would be with the open-ended "Nick looked around." Or consider the aspect (point of view) of the following, also from "The Big Two-Hearted River": "While he waited for the coffee to boil he opened a small can of apricots. He liked to open cans. He emptied the can of apricots out into a tin cup." Not only does almost everything center around the verbs, some verbs are in fact doubly marked, to specify and even overspecify the end. We find not "he waited," which is absolutely open, nor "he waited for the coffee," which fixes an endpoint, but "he waited for the coffee to boil." Again, Nick "empties the can," with "empty" telescoping the process and the result into one word. Furthermore, he doesn't simply empty the can, he empties it "out" and "into a tin cup." It is with grammatical details like these that Hemingway builds into Part I of the story the sense of control that Nick so desperately needs. There is enormous satisfaction in viewing tasks as finite, easily accomplished, and clear as to what constitutes completion, and in describing events, Hemingway carefully preserves Nick and the reader from the frustration of dull can openers and recalcitrant lids. This perspective is also conveyed grammatically by marking the verbs not once but twice as to end as if to foreclose them against the untoward. The end of Part II of "The Big Two-Hearted River" is different in mood. There are many more modals (which are marked as a class for uncertainty) when Nick approaches the swamp—"woulds" and "mights" which hint at "tragic" consequences if one chances the unforeseen.

If we move to the problem of agency—which brings into question the relation of the subject to the verb—we find that that too can be grammatically represented in complicated ways. While we are familiar in English almost exclusively with active and passive sentences, philosophy of action has provided useful and subtle subcategories which alter our very conception of the active/passive distinction. In philosophy of action, the fundamental cut is between sentences which involve a human agent ("I ate dinner," "I smoked") and those which do not specify or even require a human agent ("The butter melted," "The door opened"). In the world there are no doubt agents and causes behind the latter events, but in English it is linguistically possible to have sentences which focus on what happened rather than on who or what brought it about.

What philosophy of action offers for all fields interested in human behavior and human language is a more discriminating vocabulary than "active" and "passive" for describing the way events can be represented in language. It is stylistically significant, for example, that the heroine in *The Mysteries of Udolpho* is consistently cast as the grammatically object. A breeze makes Emily shudder, a noise frightens her, a strange fear fills her with dread, until finally the represented world in the novel becomes one in which cause is piled upon cause while Emily merely reacts or is acted upon. While we may not realize it, the Gothicism itself is created in large part by the grammar. The sense of looming and unnameable dangers, the heroine's excessive susceptibility are generated out of the transposition of the heroine from subject to object.

Since active and passive are sentence types we readily recognize, it is presumably not necessary to borrow the paraphernalia of other fields to characterize them. But frequently—in Tennyson, for example—one finds a different and somwhat more complex pattern, one which avoids both active and passive. In Tennyson, agency is minimized and hence activities occur where we might expect purposive acts, and even these activities are eventually transposed into agentless happenings. For these discriminations we do need a new vocabulary of precisely the sort Schafer wants in order to explain the language of the psychoanalytic process. Usually Tennyson has been described as torn be-

6. THE GRAMMAR OF REPRESENTATION

tween action and inaction, but the linguistic representation of that dilemma has not been fully examined because the intermediate resolutions he chooses—inceptive acts, ongoing activity, durative happenings, continuous movement—have not been available to us as categories. Yet, think of how many Tennyson poems end with the speaker committing him or herself to exactly these options. The Lady of Shallott sets herself afloat, Ulysses does too, or at least seems about to, so does Merlin in "Merlin and the Gleam," so do the sailors in "The Voyage." The speaker in "Locksley Hall" implies the same commitment to wind and wave: "For the mightly wind arises, roaring seaward, and I go," he announces in the last line of the poem. These choices are more than motifs; they are grammatically grounded in non-agentive ("the mighty wind arises") and open-ended ("and I go") constructions.

Sometimes, however, it takes a very close reading to recognize the grammatical basis of the atmosphere of Tennyson's poems because he invests his language with such great conviction that it is hard to notice that some of his agentive sentences are grammatically deviant and some of his non-agentive ones ambiguous. For example, the last line of "Ulysses" has been much commented on but no one has remarked that it is linguistically peculiar. The poem ends with Ulysses determined "To strive, to seek, to find and not to yield." Now, none of thes verbs can stand without an object, although that is how Tennyson leaves them. One can say "I strive to escape" or "I seek a newer world"—some object of goal or result is needed. And, of course, "I find" by itself makes even less sense. Not even an object of result or good will help here because finding is, in fact, a happening, not something one can do intentionally. On the surface, the grammar of "I find" looks conventionally like that of "I seek" or "I yield" and yet "I seek a newer world" is radically different from "I found a penny" in the relation of the subject to the verb. In the first case, I, as the agent, brought something about; in the second, something fortuitous happened to me. It appears then that looking at the form alone can mislead us and that we need to revise our grammar to include a semantic dimension in order to give an adequate account of the subtlety and complexity of real language.

Tennyson himself knew well enough how to exploit the potential ambiguity in the semantics of acts and happenings, whatever the deficiencies of the grammar we use to discuss his work. For example, in "The Eagle," left unfinished and published as a fragment, the powerful bird reigns majestic and apart in his mountain aerie, watching closely the sea that "crawls" beneath him. Suddenly, "like a thunderbolt, he falls" and the poem is over. Is his falling an act or a happening? Is he choosing to swoop down or is he falling in retribution for his grandeur? We cannot tell and the poem, unconcluded, intentionally fragmentary, reveals no more, leaving the reader "teased out of thought" by alternative and opposing readings that cannot be reconciled.

Hemingway offers a curious parallel to Tennyson in his use of happenings. The much commented on beginning of "The Killers" will serve as an example: "The door of Henry's lunch-room opened and two men came in" (p. 279). Although the reader assumes that the two parts of the sentence, conjoined by "and," imply agency—that one of the two men opened the door—the grammar is carefully noncommital. All we actually have is a happening, "the door opened," followed by an act, "two men came in." The "and" disavows any connection but sequence, one event following another. The disconnectedness of events, the abdication of agency, is not accidental; it underscores the position, literal and figurative, of everyone in the story. Nick watches, the two countermen watch, Ole Andreson lies immobile, even the killers irrelevantly sitting and eating, lack intelligible purpose. It is a world of happenings set in motion by some unnamed and perhaps unknowable power and events follow in mindless succession with a terrible depersonalized inevitability. Nick's attempts to "do something" only emphasize the futility of human efforts to control events (even the opening of the door). Here again the grammatical forms—sentences without actor/action relations—create the sense, or rather, non-sense, of it all.

How refreshing it is, in contrast, to return to "The Big Two-Hearted River" where intention and act are paramount, where Nick truly can do something, where the grammar is consistently that of act and accomplishment: "There had been this to do. Now it was done" (p. 215). Nick sits for one precarious moment surveying what he has achieved, but then there are all those disquieting modals connected with the swamp in Part II to remind us of the fleeting nature of such satisfactions.

I could provide more examples, but perhaps this is enough to illustrate the way in which grammatical constructions carry with them a world view, the way in which a language is indeed, as Whorf said, a philosophy. The number of literary works that repay this sort of grammatical analysis is far larger than I have indicated here. I hope my examples will serve to suggest that the text, either the patient's or the writer's, is susceptible of more grammatical investigation than we have accorded to it. None of this emphasis on the linguistic structure is meant to exclude the exploration of symbols, word play, or any other feature which seems significant. What I do want to argue is that we need to broaden the range of language analysis to include a semantic/syntactic dimension, for the text is a text as well as a subtext and the surface can also yield insights.

In this respect, I believe that Schafer's instincts are absolutely right in turning to philosophy of action, and I believe psychoanalysis and literature alike can benefit from looking more closely at the work that has been done in linguistic philosophy on the interconnection of semantics and grammar. Although I have tried to demonstrate how the examination of generally unremarked details can open up rich areas for interpretation, I have not tried to outline what specific use psychoanalysis might make of such grammatical data; indeed, it would be hard for me even in literature to say exactly what one might make of all this. But I do know that introducing a new set of questions, like those about agency or aspect, provides new perspectives on language and on the representation of the self in language. And that self – the self which is projected in language – is what literature and psychoanalysis finally have to work with.

REFERENCES

Benveniste, E. (1971). Remarks on the function of language in Freudian theory. In: *Problems in General Linguistics*, trans. M. E. Meek. Coral Gables, FL: University of Miami Press. (Original work published 1956).
Freud, S. (1910). The antithetical sense of primal words. *S.E.*, Vol. XI, p. 153-163.
―――― (1913). *The theme of the three caskets. S.E.*, Vol. XII, p. 289-303.
―――― (1919). 'A Child Is Being Beaten.' Vol. XVII, p. 175-205.

Hemingway, E. (1953). "Big Two-Hearted River: Parts I & II" in *The Short Stories of Ernest Hemingway*. New York: Charles Scribner's Sons.

―――― (1953). "The Killer's in *The Short Stories of Ernest Hemin gway*. New York: Charles Scribner's Sons.

Lacan, J. (1977). "The Agency of the Letter in the Unconscious or Reason since Freud". *Ecrits*. New York: W. W. Norton, 178.

Lacan, J. (1977). Desire and the Interpretation of desire in *Hamlet, Yale French Studies*, 55/56: (1977), 11–52.

Ricoeur, P. (1970). *Freud and Philosophy: An Essay on Interpretation*, trans. D. Savage. New Haven: Yale University Press.

Schafer, R. (1976). *A New Language for Psychoanalysis*. New Haven: Yale University Press.

Zandvoort, R. W. (1960). *A Handbook of English Grammar*. London: Longmans.

IV PSYCHOCULTURAL STUDIES OF INDIVIDUAL TEXTS AND AUTHORS

7 Fantasy Work and the Crux of the Literal in Samuel Butler's *The Authoress of the Odyssey*

Margaret Ganz, Ph.D.

Samuel Butler's theory in *The Authoress of The Odyssey* (1897) that the epic was written by a woman, a West Sicilian poetess of Ionian origin who made the Sicilian coast the setting of the poem and cast herself as the Phaeacean princess Nausicaa, seemed to some, he tells us, "a mere *mauvaise plaisanterie*" (p. 123). His friend and biographer Festing Jones informs us in his introduction to the book that Butler was accused of "incurable flippancy" and that Jones had to tell his own friends who suspected that the work "had been got up as a joke" that Butler "was serious" (p. xxviii). "I have nothing extenuated, but neither have I set down aught in malice" (p. 14), Butler contends, but that is not the half of it in a writer of so complex an ironic bent and one so attuned to the workings of the unconscious. In pursuing what Jones cálls the "perpetual preoccupation – I may even say obsession – of a decade" (p. xxvi), Butler was, as two earlier essays ("The Humour of Homer" [1892/1925] and "Was the Odyssey Written by a Woman?" [1893/1925]) already suggest, perpetrating a textual analysis of a proto-psychoanalytic kind.

Indeed, any reader of the *Odyssey* who has avoided Butler's translation of the work – already complete when he wrote *The Authoress* – can find in the latter a psychological justification for almost every sense of lacunae in the epic – of elusive descriptions and dim explanations, of unmotivated decisions and actions by characters, of logistical absurdities, and of that brutality bordering on the grotesque perhaps best epitomized by Butler's comment that in this poem "women may be hanged but they must not be laughed at" (p. 120). Moreover, if Butler's insights do not name the psychical patterns with which Freud and Jung have familiarized us, they are markers pointing in the appropriate direction. Most important of all, what may at times read like a vast if subtle jest—even the title itself is, after all, good for a laugh—has ultimately so much to say about the self-indulgent, arbitrary, and yet strategic workings of fantasy in the creative process that we not only suspend simple disbelief but, while affirming the mysteries of the literal, declare any pedestrian concern about Butler's literal intentions irrelevant.

A writer who suggests that Penelope may have "picked out her web, not so much in order to delay a hateful marriage as to prolong a very agreeable courtship" (p. 136), that "over-minuteness of description" can be "evidence of unfamiliarity" (p. 10), and that the savage destruction of Penelope's suitors is no presumption against female authorship because "a woman can kill a man on paper as well as a man can" (p. 279)—such a writer is engaged in the kind of probing enterprise that Jones evokes when he says that Butler "had dived below and was . . . trying to fathom the psychology of the author" (p. xxiv). As Butler, assisted throughout by his playful whimsy, points to the possibilities of "a screw loose somewhere" (p. 136) in the *Odyssey*—be it the effect of denial, overcompensation, or, more specifically, condensation and displacement in the Freudian sense—he is raising intriguing questions about the interaction of conscious intention and submerged desire, not only in the *processes* of art but, because he is himself fulfilling a deep psychic need in his conjuring act, in the very *interpretation* of an achieved artwork.

Even if we knew nothing of the fate of this 19th-century essayist, novelist, and translator, who, in his challenges to biblical exegetes and Darwinian scientists, had already found his brilliant insights condemned, dismissed, or worse yet ignored (only Bernard Shaw proclaimed him "a man of genius"), we could not fail to detect clues to that fate in a concluding paragraph of *The Authoress*. Butler's preoccupation with the fate of genius is evident in other works (e.g., *Erewhon* [1923, p. 165] and *The Notebooks* [1926, pp.

7. FANTASY WORK IN THE AUTHORESS OF THE ODYSSEY

173-179]), but takes a particularly suggestive form here. Brooding over the fate of a presumed Authoress denied identity and fame, the "sleeping beauty hidden behind [an] . . . impenetrable hedge of a scholasticism" (p. 277), Butler may be externalizing an intimate grievance, exorcizing a personal rejection significantly dramatized in terms of Odyssean obstacles:

> Genius is an offence; like all other offences it must needs come, but woe to that man or woman through whom it comes, for he or she must pass through the Scylla or Charybdis of being either torn in pieces on the one hand, or so misunderstood on the other as to make the slipping through with life in virtue of such misrepresentation more mortifying than death itself [p. 275].

If we rightly read "mortifying" as both "ignominious" and "killing," Butler's theory of a female author–Muse and poetess at once–comes to seem the impetus for a life-giving and life-restoring enterprise. (It is hardly his first, however, since *The Fair Haven* [1873]–an ironic psychocritical reading of the Four Gospels–rescues Christ from the twin fates of death and ressurection.) *The Authoress of the Odyssey*, giving Butler's initial theory a greater focus and amplitude, is a work of creation, revivification, and reparation. To conjure a beloved *other*, whose presence in an admired work critical assumptions about the *Odyssey*'s provenance have ignored, is also to console the desolated self whose identification with an unacknowledged artist has been fed by childhood wonder. That Butler had the classics thrashed into him by a brutal father might complicate matters intolerably did we not know of Butler's lifelong despairing attempt to win paternal approbation. Freud of course has vouchsafed us many large insights into the ambiguous effects of paternal severity upon a child (even when he did not acknowledge it as such in "The Case of Schreber"), especially its fostering of a "feminine attitude." Traces of such an identification are not hard to come by in Butler as, pursuing his challenge to academic assumptions about sexual identity and intentions in an artwork, he brings to birth a special kind of feminine other.

The narcissistic aspects of this process are undeniable if one has some sense of Butler's own nature and temperament. For he detects in his Authoress's emotions the characteristic ambivalence of his own. He not only affirms his feeling "that the writer was one half laughing and the other half serious," but also comments – confirmed ironist that he is – that she "would sometimes have been hard put to it to know whether she was more in the one vein than in the other" (p. 270). He suggests in her work an "undercurrent of melancholy" and "an inarticulate indefinable half pathos, half baffled fury" (p. 279), demonstrating as he does so a remarkable critical intuition (Grene, 1967, p. xi) but also adumbrating impulses of his own. He hastens to assure us with characteristic ambiguity that "she was often, at any rate let us hope so, supremely happy" (p. 279). He uses an approximate portrait of the work itself – "so mysterious, so imperfect, and yet so divinely beyond all perfection" (p. 280) – and, by implication or at times near-assertion, as an image of its creator, an exquisite young woman's face and bust from a work in the Cortona Museum (frontispiece, p. xxxvii). Perhaps like the Gradiva, "La Musa Polinnia" has effected a deflection from the love of "a living woman" that creates a "delusion;" her alluring beauty surely equals if it does not better that of the sculpted figure now illustrating Freud's essay (1907, p. 46). Yet Butler notes at one point: "I think it highly probable that the writer of the Odyssey was both short and plain [like Butler], and was laughing at herself, and intending to make her audience laugh also, by describing herself [in the person of Nausicaa] as tall and beautiful" (p. 218). Finally, in what seems an unconscious plea for self-acknowledgment, for a naming of the feminine in himself, he voices his pervasive preoccupation at the very moment he contends that each sex is essentially more interested in discovering its own kind:

> ... had I to choose a number of shades whom I would meet, I should include Sappho, Jane Austen, and the authoress of the Odyssey in my list, but I should probably ask first for Homer, Shakespeare, Handel, Schubert, Arcangelo Corelli, Purcell, Giovanni Bellini, Rembrandt, Holbein, De Hooghe, Donatello, Jean de Wespin, and many another man – yet the writer of the Odyssey *interests me so profoundly that I am not sure I should not ask to see her before any of the others.* [p. 116; italics added]

7. FANTASY WORK IN *THE AUTHORESS OF THE ODYSSEY*

By so centrally if unconsciously pursuing that fantasy of retrieving the beloved feminine which Freud's "Leonardo da Vinci" so movingly elaborates (1910, pp. 111-118), Butler's theory would challenge our psychological consciousness even if we were unfamiliar with Greenacre's suggestion in *The Quest for the Father* (1963) that both Darwin and his antagonist Butler evinced a "feminine identification" in the oedipal struggle. Yet, though Butler's theory may have been spawned by desire, it was buttressed by critical acumen, thorough textual knowledge (by one who had distinguished himself as a classics student at Cambridge and had already translated the *Iliad* as well as the *Odyssey*), and a wide acquaintance with critical theories and historical references to the Odyssean material. (It is no small matter that Robert Graves, as he himself says in the introduction to his novel *Homer's Daughter* [1955] inspired by *The Authoress*, "found Butler's arguments for a Western Sicilian setting and a female authorship irrefutable," (p. 9) and affirms his support in his notes to *The Greek Myths* [1955, pp. 365-366].) What we confront then is a critical study of the most famous voyage home in Western literature that looks remarkably like a journey into psychic fulfillment – as close as Butler came to celebrating the ambiguous *ewig weibliche* – but one that functions simultaneously as a serious literary enterprise, an iconoclastic challenge to classicists and geographers, a probing of comedy's intentions and effect, and ultimately a quest for balance in the Charybdian maelstrom of being "misunderstood" as an artist.

The moment we affirm the need to take Butler's thesis seriously by acknowledging the overdetermined nature of his enterprise, we find ourselves in difficulties. His straightforward arguments – that "famous poetesses abounded" in "the earliest historic literature" (1897, p. 11) and hence are likely presences earlier, and that there is a prevalence, "by universal consent," of "the domestic and female interest" (1893, p. 306) in the epic – are not troublesome. Moreover, some facile distinctions between the behavior of men and women seem all too clearly earnest. The real problem lies elsewhere, as we sense that his theory is essentially inimical to academic sobriety, the playfulness of its justification perhaps more overt in the *Humor* . . . and *Was the Odyssey* . . .

but also evident in much of *The Authoress*. Yet even more than professional solemnity is left tottering by Butler's approach. Even as Grene (1967) speaks of "a kind of spoofing" in Butler's "funny ... absurd" questions, he suggests that Butler's literary sense of the work allows them "to bear on certain genuine problems of authorship and meaning" (p. 6). The only solution that presents itself to us—furnishing new complexities—is that Butler's comic adumbration of so many Odyssean elements, going beyond a very suggestive spoof, is his key to unlocking the role the unconscious plays in the creative undertaking. To be at once laughing *with* and if lovingly, *at* the ostensibly feminine handling of character and events—often by collapsing the heroic into the prosaic (Ulysses, like Telemachus, is the victim of "a number of young men who have been eating him out of house and home" [p. 278], King Alcinous "is out at elbows" [1892, p. 268]) or by emphasizing pedestrian concerns (Telemachus awakes from Minerva's warning dream "in great distress, but ... about his property, not about his mother" [p. 141])—is to be backtracking the creative road and retrieving illuminating news about unconscious maneuvers in the processes of art.

We begin to think as much when Butler's playful hunches reverberate psychologically, when they do not seem more facile deflations of grand attitudes. As he decides that "poor Mentor" is forever saddled by Minerva—when she adopts his identity to lecture Telemachus—with a "grandmotherly reputation which [he] is never likely to lose" (p. 126), Butler is not merely poking fun at a venerable figure. He is alerting us to the ubiquity of the motif of the "fairy godmother"—his own words about Minerva (1892, p. 252)—and to its dubious felicity if the intent is to celebrate heroic manhood. Having all actions subject to magic tutoring and quasi-parental management—Minerva is "omnipresent at the elbows of Ulysses and Telemachus to keep them straight and alternately scold and flatter them" (p. 111)—erodes the psychological authenticity of the heroic intention. Again, when Butler questions whether Ulysses' father, Laertes, would be "likely to continue calling" (p. 136) on Penelope while she was weaving and unravelling his funeral pall to keep suitors at bay, he comically trivializes the mortal terrors of aged authority but also suggests

7. FANTASY WORK IN *THE AUTHORESS OF THE ODYSSEY*

that Penelope's unconscious impulses, not so much regarding the fate of her father-in-law as that of her absent husband, may not be as irreproachable as her obeisance to burial rites. As for Ulysses himself, even as Butler tells us that he had been quite unresourceful on Ogygia, since "a man of his sagacity might have subtracted Calypso's axe and auger"–tools she "can hardly have wanted . . . very often" (p. 149)–to build himself the necessary raft, his whimsical view of inertia as a mode of psychic denial favors an inference of "easy infidelity" (1892, p. 254) in the conspicuously married hero.

In such playful exercises, at once comically reductive and psychologically exploratory, Butler demonstrates that flair for probing textual authenticity which deduced the strategies of Darwin's unconscious from an analysis of his style, as in *Luck, or Cunning?* (1886). Here, as he retrieves from beneath the representation of heroic stances the baroque machinations of the wish-fulfilling unconscious, his amused perception signals fantasy configurations, not least what Freud (1908) and Rank (1909/1932) would explore as the "family romance." An estranged grandfather and ambiguously devoted parents are relatively predictable figures in Butler's comic yet psychologically viable scenario of the disappointing family circle that the fantasy seeks to transcend. So of course is Minerva, the hectoring if helpful "godmother" and Magic Nurse, evocative in her Mentor guise of "a very dear kind old aunt" of Butler given to lecturing (p. 126). But, as his central figure, Butler will not choose "the leading young gentleman" already past struggles of individuation, the "canny, well-principled, and discreet" (1892, p. 254) Telemachus. It is the sprightly Nausicaa-character in and creator of the *Odyssey*–whom Butler casts as the disabused, questing, half-merciless and half-amused child in the household who at once denies, judges, and reprieves through the elusive approximations of art–fantasy weaving romance out of disillusioning realities. To rescue Ulysses, as Nausicaa does, is to recast a paternal figure along the more romantic lines Minerva has evoked by beautifying his features. Yet Nausicaa desists, a relationship between them being the psychical impossibility that it is. (That is not, of course, how Butler puts it at his most skeptical: "How characteristic . . . of the manhatress," he notes, "is Nausicaa's attempt to make out that in Ulysses she had found a man to whom she might become attached—if there were no obstacle to their union" [p. 153].)

Only the comic vision may triumph over any such impasse to allow the fantasy a certain gratification—protection and satisfaction at once—in the dubious familial love struggles. To see Butler evoke, as he does in the following passage, Nausicaa's presumable relation to her own father, Alcinous, is to be clued in to the role of the comic in Butler's psychological preoccupation with the ubiquitous figure of authority in the text—father, husband, and king at once. Only one strategy can mitigate the capacity of the paternal figure to overawe the all too observant child—*a perception of him as absurd*:

> Indeed Ulysses, Alcinous, Menelaus, and Nestor are all so like one another that I do not doubt they were drawn from the same person, just as Ithaca and Scheria are from the same place. Who that person was we shall never know; nevertheless I would point out that unless a girl adores her father, he is generally, to her, *a mysterious powerful being whose ways are not as her ways. He is feared as a dark room is feared by children*; and if his wife is at all given to laughing at him, his daughter will not spare him, however much she may cajole and *in a way* love him [p. 120; italics added].

Butler's psychological presence in this ambiguous reading (has he not transmuted the terrors of his childhood "dark room" with an ironic portrayal of his father in *The Way of All Flesh* [1903]?) must be given place in an enterprise such as his devoted to retrieving textual implications through a comic rendering of characterization and intentions. "Incurable flippancy" is not the problem, but rather the extent to which Butler is projecting, in the psychoanalytic sense, his own humorous and ironic skepticism upon his Authoress, amplifying signs of comic perception perhaps few classicists would deny into a vision of life. (Butler himself admits that "people find what they bring" but wonders whether "eminent Homeric scholars have found so much seriousness in the more humorous parts because they brought it there" [p. 270]). Is the Authoress laughing at "men's little ways and weaknesses" (p. 110), the Authoress who lives in the text as the charmingly willful daughter of the Phaeacean king, an evolved variation of the "*enfant terrible* of literature and science" that Butler ironically claims himself to be in the *Notebooks* (1912/1925, p. 182). He does speak of the skepticism in this epic being like "the occasional mild irreverence of the Vicar's daughter" (p. 259), a subject on which a canon's son might understandably be well-informed. Is his intuition about the youth of the writer—certainly at the inception of her work—informed by his assumption that a relatively undifferentiated ego can be brash, thoughtlessly cruel, erratic, greedy, mendacious, playful, and, not least, capable of idealization? Finally, is he investing the Authoress, "prehistoric Jane Austen" (1892, p. 261) that she is, with the astuteness, searing yet humane wit, and rueful humor of his crippled friend and literary advisor, the like him "short and plain" Eliza Mary Ann Savage whom he had felt guilty for not loving physically? (Jones suggests in his *Memoir* [1919, p. 106] that "in forming [his theory] he was influenced by [this] friendship.")

Accepting such possibilities hardly precludes, as was said earlier, the existence of some comic intentions in the work itself. But even for those who know classical Greek the text apparently keeps many mysteries, and comparing translations is a lesson in the elusiveness of tone as time and distance compound the disguises of the speaking psyche. So Fitzgerald (1961, p. 1) has Calypso keeping Ulysses "in her sea-hollowed caves" because "she craved him for her own"; Lattimore (1965, p. 27) has her detaining him in her "hollowed caverns," "desiring that he should be her husband"; while Butler (1925, p. 1) tells us that Calypso "had got him into a large cave and wanted to marry him." The challenging if unanswerable question in this and other instances remains whether the creator was amused. True, Butler's whimsical readings receive some support from modern classicists, who note that "Homer smiles" at Ulysses' plight when he has to meet the Scherian girls naked, a "worn lion . . . absurdly cast" (Finley, 1978, p. 80), that Alcinous is "a bit of a fool" (Kirk, 1962, p. 370), a "genial old king [who] seems to have been of the kind to welcome, like Nestor, any new victim of his garrulity" (Stanford, 1963, p. 63), and that there is "a curious undertow of satire . . . in the Penelope part of the poem" (Grene, 1967, p. xvi). But such passing comments, like the reference to a "crafty, amused, deeply feminine amity" in Minerva's relation to Ulysses (Steiner, 1962, p. 11), hardly suggest a pervasive comic vision that informs and sustains the world of the text.

All we can hope to explore where language in the *Odyssey* is concerned is the significance of Butler's preference for the "Tottenham Court Road" style of translation (p. 6) that determines his critical approach. Butler's choice fits his lifelong suspicion of stylistic obfuscation as a mode of denying reality and his concomitant emphasis on simplicity and directness, if of a very subtle sort. Here, the rejection of high-flown emotions, rhetorical elaboration, and tonal formality in his renditions, intimately tied to comic effects, since a bald style deflates incongruously in this heroic context, seems to make more easily accessible to consciousness material a grandiloquent translation could veil or a stodgy one deface. (Comically yoking in Calypso primitive claim and institutional prerogative through plain statement certainly bares the visceral impulses socialization has repressed—as no reference to "crav[ing] him for her own" ever will.) Butler's discussions of theme, character, and action achieve the same effect. His airy paraphrases and restatements not only reduce the heroic to pedestrian proportions—a standard comic technique—but force us to consider the checkered career of denial, repression, and sublimation in the attempted transfigurations of art. Even when Butler is being most mischievous at the expense of a character, he remains the psychologist alert to underlying intentions; he senses and makes us feel that the absurdities of Menelaus are diverting not as fact but as signature:

> We know from Il. vii, 470–475, [*Iliad*, which Butler posits his Authoress knew so well that her use of it is at times "unconscious cerebration" (p. 229)], that Menelaus used to sell wine when he was before Troy, as also did Agamemnon, but there is a frank *bourgeoisie* about this invitation [to Telemachus and Pisistratus] which a male writer would have avoided. Still franker, however, is the offer of Menelaus to take them on a personally conducted tour round the Peloponnesus. It will be very profitable, for no one will send them away empty-handed. . . . As for the refreshments which they are to have immediately, the king explains that they will have to take pot-luck, but says he will tell the women to see that there is enough for them, of what there might happen to be in the house.

7. FANTASY WORK IN *THE AUTHORESS OF THE ODYSSEY* 137

> That is just like Menelaus' usual fussiness. Why could he not have left it all to Helen? After reading the Odyssey I am not surprised at her running away with Paris; the only wonder is that a second great war did not become necessary shortly after the Trojan matter had been ended [p. 145].

As Butler's whimsical rethinkings project for us Alcinous failing to deliver on his promise to Ulysses of a gold goblet and a talent of gold, Ulysses rushing to protect his chest of gifts with a Circean knot, and Pisistratus complaining that "he cannot attend properly to his dinner and cry at the same time" (1892, pp. 265, 254), he is repeating the verdict passed on the silliness of Menelaus with only minor differences. All three versions of the fallible male sustain Butler's playful contention that the inspiration of the *Odyssey* is a form of feminine protest by the child in the house:

> Fancy what the position of a young, ardent, brilliant woman must have been in a small Sicilian sea-port, say some eight or nine hundred years before the birth of Christ. It makes one shudder to think of it. Night after night she hears the dreary blind old bard Demodocus drawl out his interminable recitals taken from our present Iliad, or from some other of the many poems now lost that dealt with the adventures of the Greeks before Troy or on their homeward journey. Man and his doings! always the same story, and woman always to be treated either as a toy or as a beast of burden, or at any rate as an incubus. Why not sing of woman also as she is when she is unattached and free from the trammels and persecutions of this tiresome tyrant, this insufferably self-conceited bore and booby, man? [1892, p. 256].

Yet the very *embourgeoisement* of the text that Butler's comic readings almost inevitably induce—the drop downward in social status serving as a step backward in a history of psychic sublimation—is the manifestation of a reductive strategy not limited to pointing up masculine absurdity. Butler's amusement, sparing neither masculine nor feminine foibles, is thus more widely strategic than it may seem. As it punctures Penelope's aloofness with the following rebuke for not discouraging her suitors, it asks us to probe the elusive desires that underlie the role of disconsolate wife:

> Sending pretty little messages to her admirers was not exactly the way to get rid of them. Did she ever try snubbing? Nothing of the kind is placed on record.... Then there was boring—did she ever try that? Did she ever read them any of her grandfather's letters? Did she ever sing them her own songs, or play them music of her own composition? I have always found these courses successful when I wanted to get rid of people.... Did she set them by the ears by repeating with embellishments what they had said to her about one another? Did she ask Antinous or Eurymachus to sit to her for web—give them a good stiff pose, make them stick to it, and talk to them all the time? Did she find errands for them to run, and then scold them, and say she did not want them?... or keep on sending them back to the shop to change things, and they had given ever so much too much money and she wished she had gone and done it herself? [p. 135].

Thus Butler's alertness to comic implications, far from justifying a presumption that he is foisting on us a practical joke regarding the text itself and the identity of the Authoress, may well be a warrant that he is taking us for a very different kind of ride, his aliveness to certain psychic truths about the working fantasy allowing us vicariously to travel back and forth the devious road that it navigates, Ulysses-like, to reach its desires. Indeed, whether Butler's brief for the authenticity of a female writer takes a comic turn or not, it celebrates the complex attributes Freud has taught us to associate with the unconscious: its capacity for change, displacement, disguise, and reversal; its versatility; its unpredictability. Butler's psychological instincts, like Freud's, intimately related not only to a sense of the comic but to a complex imagination and a philosophical bent, are sharply attuned to the improvisational talent, the sheer gumption evident in what, since childhood, Butler had thought of as "the Iliad's wife." A passing whimsical verdict on the destruction Ulysses nearly endures at sea—"I have such a shipwreck at Drury Lane" (1892, p. 253)—indirectly pays tribute to the artifices of the creative unconscious; more sweeping is the affirmation: "Such kingdoms of heaven as the Odyssey never do come by observation" (1893, p. 276).

7. FANTASY WORK IN *THE AUTHORESS OF THE ODYSSEY*

But beyond praising the resourceful fabrication of details, Butler contends that unconscious creativity has performed the miracle of turning an unpromising subject into one of the greatest literary achievements. A work devoid of "amatory" concerns (the "mixture of perfect sponger and perfect lover" in the suitors "is grotesquely impossible" [p. 133] and whose "interest" ostensibly turns mainly on the revenge taken by a bald middle-age gentleman, whose little remaining hair is red" (p. 278), is probably the second greatest poem ever written. Butler never claims, as Freud might have, that the very fascination of the work inheres in the limitations of its subject and treatment, even if he is intent on emphasizing its "carelessness in respect of consistency and plausibility," "ignorance of commonly known details," and "disregard of ordinary canons" (p. 278). He does not assert the primacy of the unconscious. Yet, by alerting us throughout to the existence of certain strategies—nugatory and compensatory—he justifies his sense and our own that the work's fascination does not hinge on heroic and romantic considerations. And, while contemplating the paradoxical renown of so ungainly a subject, he affirms the necessity for creator and reader alike to lead a depth existence, the artist submerged beneath the surface realm of "rules and canons," the reader looking through "clothes and grammar" to a distant though not inaccessible psyche, the still living mind of the artist, that is at once ideal and mirror image of the best self:

> If the Odyssey enforces one artistic truth more than another, it is that living permanent work in literature (and the same holds good for art and music) can only be done by those who are either above, or below, conscious reference to any rules or canons whatsoever—and in spite of Shakespeare, Handel, and Rembrandt, I should say that on the whole *it is more blessed to be below than above*. For after all . . . what really stirs us is the communion with the still living mind of the man or woman to whom we owe it, [the work], and the conviction that that mind is as we would have our own to be. All else is mere clothes and grammar [pp. 278–279; italics added].

The writer who had so brilliantly hypothesized the working of unconscious memory in *Life and Habit* (1877), coming independently to the same conclusions as Ewald Hering (Breuer's mentor admired by Freud), is here once again dealing with the unconscious, even if his concern takes the different form of drawing an analogy between its attributes and the manifestations of a feminine temperament. For Butler connects the work's female authorship not only with a pervasive resiliency but with an imaginative arbitrariness suggestive of unconscious processes: "a kind of art for art's sake love of a small lie" and a liking for "flimsy disguises and mystifications that stultify themselves, and mystify nobody" (p. 124). Even as he shrewdly points to details suggesting the kind of ignorance ascribable to a woman (e.g., a misapprehension about a rudder's placement on a ship, the structure of an axe, the milking of ewes), Butler emphasizes that these objects and actions are nonetheless being depicted with noticeable aplomb by one who, like many "young people," will "not let the native hue of resolution be balked by thought" (p. 180), is "not going to stick at trifles when she mean[s] having her own way," (1893, p. 294), is intent on "flogging us uphill" (p. 163) as long as it suits her wish-fulfilling purpose.

The force of Butler's analogy between a not fully sublimated instinctual life and the feminine temperament is heightened in *The Authoress* by a central Butlerian stance which may seem somewhat eccentric at first. For his examination of the *Odyssey* often takes the form of those deceptively simple questions with which shrewd children bag unwary adults, forcing them to unravel the work of repression. Directly and circuitously Butler is raising questions that, on the surface, seem pedestrian exercises by the most literal of minds, especially regarding the behavior of Penelope and her suitors: Why do they stay around for years courting a reluctant fortyish widow? Why are there no rivalries for "their middle-aged paragon?" Why does she not simply close the door of her house when the suitors go home to sleep? Why does she seem ready to choose after she has strong evidence of Ulysses' return? (pp. 130–132, 160). Butler's whimsically phrased doubts, while confirming the psychic breeziness in his Authoress's craft, also affirm that the logistical absurdities, if artistically dubious, are psychologically viable in their satisfaction of complex desires. The sense that there is a "screw loose somewhere" is really a sign that an elaborate enterprise of psychic camouflage is taking place.

Arbitrariness in the handling of the Odyssean material is, Butler suggests, the clue to a major effort at *negation*, which, in

7. FANTASY WORK IN *THE AUTHORESS OF THE ODYSSEY*

rescuing the reputation of a feminine character, champions femininity itself. The shadow of Clytemnestra's atrocious crime hovers, as critics note, over the work; "another woman's guilt," Butler tells us, "was only not extenuated because it is absolutely denied in the face of overwhelming evidence—I mean Penelope's" (p. 122). Though he does next to nothing with the "scandalous version of [her] conduct . . . curent among the ancients" (p. 130), his stress on an effort of repression by the Authoress attests to his psychoanalytic prescience. Even a comment such as "the amount of caution with which [Penelope] is credited is to some extent a gauge of the thickness of the coat of whitewash which the writer considers necessary" (p. 130) tells us much about Butler's psychological acumen. Even if we choose to read a specific "whitewash" as a more general denial of sexuality or of the potential for adultery in a maternal figure, Butler's intuition that in unconscious processes an affirmation may signal its opposite remains valid.

Whether Butler is posing serious or mischievous questions or voicing complaints (Ulysses should have "hugged" his old dog, "fleas or no fleas" [p. 159]), he evokes the childish inquisitions adult storytellers endure, gauntlets thrown down before the conscious world by those still at home in the unconscious. Such challenges reflect an ignorance of the craft of repression—a knowledge that the emperor has no clothes, without an awareness that an adult conspiracy denies his nakedness. Tempered and controlled by adult self-consciousness, Butler's childlike literalness has a way of collapsing the facades repression has erected that is much more insidious than a child's. The question of why "poor Pisistratus," who, Butler slyly tells us, "has been very good and amiable all through" (p. 157), is not getting any presents at Menelaus' court, while his friend Telemachus is being showered with them, is just the kind a child might ask. But Butler's whimsical assertion that "a male writer would have given something" suggests that the feminine poetic justice in this work, rooted in unconscious desires, reflects more devious objectives than the conventional distribution of prizes that obtains in a self-satisfiedly masculine world.

To make literal demands in that equivocal sense when examining an artwork is to draw attention to the ambiguous position of artist and critic alike, who no longer possess the innocent cunning of childhood yet cannot settle for the compromised vision of maturity. Travelling the road between these two states makes them vastly knowledgeable about obstacles and oases; though they can only name putatively, every question is a diagnosis regarding the nature of the world or the intentions of the artwork. The term "man" in Butler's comment that "if the truth were known, we might very likely find that it was man rather than woman who has been the interloper in the domain of literature" (p. 13) may be read as a metaphor for achieved worldliness. By indirection children, women, and artists are in the—if the pun is allowed—no man's land in which traffic with the unconscious is the central reality. In children that traffic is ubiquitous; in the woman-artist Butler has conjured here it is more controlled, allowing for some comic distancing but also producing some baroquely unreal effects; in the critic-artist, Butler himself, it liberates the kind of hindsight about artistic intentions and strategies that also probes their success or failure, and connects unconscious desires with the larger "complexes"—the patterns that psychology has named and that art has consecrated.

Intuitions of the oedipal struggle, the Electra complex, the Mother archetype (has Queen Arete provoked a "mother complex" in Nausicaa?) might come naturally to a reader of the *Odyssey* attuned to the psychological reverberations of mythic material. But Butler's emphases and questions and his conjuring of a creator who is playful child and feminine artist heighten our consciousness of fantasy elements. His awareness of the romantic limitations of the poem from one vantage point signals us to seek out its appeal elsewhere, in the romance with a difference that the oedipal *family* drama here provides. What on the surface seems a story of middle-age reunion and obstacles overcome proves—if we take our cue from Butler's indirect but inspired probings—the ultimate fantasy scenario of paternal return and revenge for childhood misbehavior. Penelope's ambiguous dream of the eagle destroying the "favourite geese . . . eating mash out of a tub" (p. 86) and the concern of some of the suitors that Ulysses may be "one of the gods who go about the world in disguise to redress wrong, and chastise the insolence of mankind" (p. 77) are fasincating clues to that connection between the divine and the

7. FANTASY WORK IN *THE AUTHORESS OF THE ODYSSEY*

paternal so subtly explored by Freud (e.g., in "Leonardo da Vinci" [1910, p. 123] and *Totem and Taboo* [1913, p. 147]) and clearly anticipated by Butler in the "Memoir" section of *The Fair Haven* (1873).

If we keep in mind that the motif of the return-revenge of the paternal figure, so dramatically explored in later centuries through the Don Juan legend, is central to the appeal of the *Odyssey*, then Butler's questions about the grotesque behavior of the suitors vying for an older woman's attention with a curiously unimpassioned perseverance are as psychologically pertinent at his rebuke to Penelope for not exasperating her suitors out of existence. Such Butlerian challenges, refined by his comic vision, unearth for us the fantasy content of the material, especially when we apply to them Rank's (1925/1975) imaginative suggestions in *The Don Juan Legend* (pp. 74-96). Rank contends that the feminine band conquered seriatim by Don Juan is "a wish-fulfilling transformation of the harrassing clan of brothers" in the primal struggle, involving a multiplication of "the one conquered woman in the heroic myths" into "thousand and three." Just as, in Rank's version, Don Juan's very compulsion to repeat suggests a dissatisfaction that can only be assuaged by a single triumph elsewhere – the total possession of the mother – from our viewpoint the ambiguous behavior of Penelope toward the hundred odd suitors (the "favourite geese" who "feed" while the husband is conveniently delayed or destroyed) may likewise camouflage search for an alternate satisfaction – the possession of the son.

As the Statue of the Commander will, in a later century, issue from the Mausoleum to punish the dissolute yearnings and brash challenge of the son-figure at a deadly banquet, so Ulysses returns from strange realms (including that of the dead) to wreak atrocious vengeance on the insolent suitors whom a terrible warning has likewise not deterred from feasting. Butler's often comic views of Telemachus' ostentatious propriety and his perfunctoriness amounting to rudeness where his mother is concerned, perhaps signal a shift in emphasis to the "horde" of tolerated suitors who, through the fantasy's strategic operation of denial, function as stand-ins for Telemachus where Penelope is concerned. Butler's stress on Nausicaa's ambiguous impatience with her own young suitors, confided, significantly, to Ulysses, implies a reverse identification with Penelope. Nausicaa seems less interested in prospective spouses than in the paternal figure of the wanderer-hero – beautified by Minerva – whom she has rescued. (Circe and Calypso, Butler tells us, behave "as the writer thinks Nausicaa would do if she were a goddess and had an establishment of her own" [p. 215].) Penelope, however, seems by her own encouraging messages, and by the suspicions Minerva casts on her, even if only to get Telemachus home, to be more interested in the prospective spouse than in the long-absent husband. ("Penelope, Helen [of Troy], and Arete [Nausicaa's mother] are only one person" [p. 215], Butler notes.) Defending Penelope's virtue, which in Butler's terms is denying Penelope's sexual guilt, can be read, however, not as the Authoress's championing of a character on whose fidelity tradition has already cast some fascinating doubts (Apollodorus, translated by Frazer, 1921, pp. 301-307; Graves, 1955, pp. 375-376), but as a major enterprise in negating a different kind of *shared* guilt – the excursion of fantasy into the realm of proscribed desires, where gender and generational obstacles are lifted.

Exorcising that psychic guilt, Butler will again suggest, if only indirectly, is made possible by the grotesque killing of the female servants who, in their sexual promiscuity with the suitors – a betrayal of their master – have actualized the fantasy. Butler's awareness that the logistics of the actual hanging are incomprehensible, that there is something peculiarly "fierce" in having the guilty female servants clear out the suitors' dead bodies and clean the blood from the tables and seats before they are themselves summarily strung up, and that the ruthlessness of the destruction is in proportion to the desire to avenge "female honour ... violated by those of woman's own sex" (p. 123-124) suggests a possible intuition that the punishment has a special psychic value. Just like the killing of the suitors, the unreality of which Butler stresses by calling it "aggressive in its want of plausibility," so this destruction fulfills deep unconscious needs and hence can have neither the concreteness nor the relative dignity that a moral judgment of sexual misbehavior in the staff of a household might possess. In the realms of fantasy, arbitrary decisons and curiously dehumanized actions obtain.

7. FANTASY WORK IN *THE AUTHORESS OF THE ODYSSEY*

Butler's central claim to be taken seriously is, other considerations aside, surely justified by the psychological validity of his reading of the text. It is truly an interpretation—in the unlocking of the fantasy it suggests by positing an unconventional artificer and by rethinking, questioning, and rephrasing the material, often in comic terms. But the accusation that Butler was all too literal in his attempt to document Ulysses' voyages as a circular trip around the coast of Sicily (although Apollodorus speaks of such a possibility, Graves points out that Butler "came independently to the same view" [1955, p. 365]) must also be reconsidered, his seriousness needing qualification to be correctly estimated. The very impulse to map, mentally and actually, may after all reflect a psychological intensity alien to the matter of taking an imaginative work at face value. (Butler's tracing out of the voyages—the fantasy voyages that Ulysses' adventures so often seem to be—by the light of Admiralty charts may not be so distant from Freud's mapping out the territory of the unconscious in sketches, cartoons, and drawings.)

Butler's compulsion to account literally for place, behavior, and physical phenomena—with a feel for historical hints and a flair for topographical clues close to inspiration—has a special psychological dimension and a complexity of intention that transcend questions of geographical accuracy. His search for place as well as woman functions simultaneously as an attempt to best scholarly convictions, as a wish-fulfilling impulse to give his beloved work not only a special Muse but a local habitation, and, not least, as defense mechanism against the very lures of fantasy work, whose waywardness might cast the psyche adrift if the mind were not held to the solidity of place. Butler's compensatory tilt to the safety of enclosure and stasis is surely a significant element in his thesis that the Authoress relies on the circumscribed Sicilian world she knows, indeed uses Trapani (Drepanum) both for the land of the Phaeaceans and for Ithaca. As every physical place is given a geographical identity by Butler (e.g., the Aegadian Isles replacing the Ionian ones), it is as it were psychically *held in place*. Aeolus, we are told, is not an island that "floated about, and thus changed its place" but is "as fixed as any island" (p. 193); hints, emendations, identifications all affirm that any excursions from the relative "terra firma" of Sicily (p. 193n.) involve some nearby island (pp. 192–209). Most important of all, every scene of Ulysses' wanderings is in the vicinity of Butler's land of the heart's desire. It is after all Italy, first loved when he was a young boy, and not Greece that is identified as the creative realm, and he takes special pleasure in "bringing back the Odyssey and its writer to their own home and people" (quoted by Jones, 1919, p. 173).

At once compromise and defense, Butler's geographical theory reflects a nature compounded of the singleminded perseverance of the resourceful Ulysses and the free-wheeling inventiveness of his Authoress. To such a temperament a sane coexistence of fantasy with dogged rationality might seem at times as proscribed a union as that between Nausicaa and Ulysses. (In this context Butler's experiences of a dizziness while working on this material – which made him "get instinctively as near palings and walls as I can" [quoted by Jones, 1919, p. 225] while out of doors – is very suggestive.) The setting of geographical boundaries would then be an essential part of the conjuring act which has brought the Muse back to life. That the wandering fantasy – of which Ulysses is the mere creature – can not only repel whirlwind and storm, siren song and devouring mouth, but be returned from nightmare wandering to the daytime safety of familiar ground is indirectly affirmed by Butler's pondering of maps and charts, his consultation with the Greenwich Astronomer Royal, his excursions to Sicilian caves, his examination of Cyclopean walls, his own mapping out of the circular voyage home from Trapani to Trapani (p. 191).

Because Butler's mind so markedly encompassed, indeed straddled, different modes of apprehending reality, conscious and unconscious, literal and figurative, masculine and feminine (it seems most appropriate that the *Odyssey* should give him a "half Bayeux tapestry, half Botticelli's Venus rising from the Sea, or Primavera, feeling" [p. 11]), the reverberations of his ambiguous seriousness threatened his audience much more strongly than jesting or scholarly eccentricity of a conventional sort. In an academic and worldly sense Butler was not serious but in every other sense he was. The crux, of course, lies in the assumption of what constitutes seriousness, and, by implication, the literal itself. Remembering the ambiguous connotations Butler exploits in naming his hero Ernest in *The Way of All Flesh* and his use of the term "earnest" (quoted by Jones, 1919, p. 273) regarding his work on *The Authoress*, one must grant that, as Jones said, he "was serious," but acknowledge in him that qualified solemnity regarding truth that is the perquisite of children, clowns, poets, and ironists. The playful renderings Butler invites us to entertain must be measured against sobering intimations of an obsessive attachment to the work that seems an erotic playing for keeps:

> As soon as I began to talk [Jones tells us], he was silent, but he was not listening; he was miles away, helping Nausicaa to wash her clothes at the salt-works of S. Cusumano; or sitting with Eumaeus in his hut on slopes of Monte Erice; or he would be going in and out of the house of Ulysses and seeing how like it was to the stabilimento at Selinunte, where he had had lunch, and how unlike a house in Gower street. . . . [1919, p. 208].

But such evidence of earnestness is also inevitably modified by the work of probing unconscious impulses through a comic vision. Even as he is "reading the riddle that had so long baffled [him]" (p. 8), Butler, the critic-detective in his dubious role of interpreter and sage, is challenging us to jettison received ideas on truth, seriousness, and the literal. More particularly, *The Authoress of the Odyssey* incites us to acknowledge the ubiquitous activities of fantasy as elements in the artwork, as clues to the creator's presence, and as inescapable prejudices and prerogatives in the reader's ultimate interpretation.

REFERENCES

Apollodorus. (1921). *The Library* ("Epitome"), Vol. 2, trans. J. Frazer. London: William Heinemann.

Butler, S. (1923). *Erewhon*. In H. F. Jones & A. T. Bartholomew (Eds.), *The Shrewsbury edition of the works of Samuel Butler, Vol. 2*. (Original work published 1872) London: Cape.

⎯⎯⎯ 1923. *The Fair Haven. Shrewsbury Edition*, 3, (Original work published 1873)

⎯⎯⎯ (1925). The Authoress of the Odyssey. *Shrewsbury Edition*, 12. (Original work published 1897)

⎯⎯⎯ Trans. *The Odyssey. Shrewsbury Edition*, 15, 1925. (Original work published 1900)

⎯⎯⎯ (1925). The Humour of Homer. Was the Odyssey Written by a Woman?

Collected essays. Shrewsbury Edition, 19. (Original works published 1892 & 1983)

_____ ( ). *The Notebooks. Shrewsbury Edition*, 20, 1925. (Original work published 1912)

Finley, J. H. (1978). *Homer's Odyssey.* Cambridge, MA: Harvard University Press.

Fitzgerald, R. Trans. (1963). *The Odyssey.* Garden City, NY: Anchor.

Freud, S. (1959). Delusions and dreams in Jensen's *Gradiva.* Family romances: *The Standard Edition of the Complete Psychological Works of Sigmund Freud*, 9 (1906-1908). Ed. James Strachey. London: Hogarth, 1959.

_____ (1910). Leonardo Da Vinci and a Memory of His Childhood. *S. E.*, 11.

_____ (1913). *Totem and Taboo. S. E.*, 13.

Graves, R. (1955). *Homer's Daughter.* Chicago: Academy Chicago, 1982.

_____ (1955). *The Greek Myths*, Vol. 2. Baltimore: Penguin.

Greenacre, P. (1963). *The Quest for the Father.* New York: International Universities Press.

Grene, D., Ed. (1967). *The Authoress of the Odyssey* by Samuel Butler. Chicago: University of Chicago Press.

Jones, H. F. (1919). *Samuel Butler: A Memoir*, Vol. 2. New York: Octagon Books, 1968.

Kirk, G. S. (1962). *The Songs of Homer.* Cambridge, MA: Harvard University Press.

Lattimore, R. Trans. (1965). *The Odyssey of Homer.* New York: Harper.

Rank, O. (1932). *The Myth of the Birth of the Hero.* New York: Vintage. (Original work published 1909)

_____ (1975). *The Don Juan Legend*, ed. & trans. D. G. Winter. Princeton: Princeton University Press. (Original work published 1925)

Stanford, W. B. (1963). *the Ulysses Theme.* Oxford: Blackwell.

Steiner, G. (1962). Introduction: Homer and the scholars. In: *Homer: A Collection of Critical Essays*, eds. G. Steiner & R. Fagles. Englewood Cliffs, N.J.: Prentice-Hall.

8 The Symbol as Symptom: Romance and Repression in Hawthorne's *The Scarlet Letter*

Elissa Greenwald, Ph.D.

The idea that "The Custom-House," Hawthorne's long autobiographical essay "prefatory to" *The Scarlet Letter* (1850), is integral to the work it precedes has been increasingly documented by critics in the past twenty years. The preface has been seen variously as a rehearsal of the themes of *The Scarlet Letter,* a version of the story in miniature, and an exposition of the right way to read the tale (Bales, 1977; Eakin, 1971; Stouck, 1971). The revival of psychological and linguistic interpretations of *The Scarlet Letter* in the past few years (Baym, 1982; Bell, 1982; Duncan, 1981; Franzosa, 1978, 1981; Jordan, 1981; Ragussis, 1982) suggests the timeliness of applying psychoanalytic criticism to the relation between the preface and the tale. In this paper, I shall try to show that "The Custom-House" is not only thematically appropriate but psychically necessary to the story it introduces. It not only sets up Hawthorne's literary method—the way of writing and reading he calls "romance"—but makes that method the necessary condition for the writer's and reader's entry into the world of *The Scarlet Letter.* As Hawthorne makes clear in the preface, the writing of romance freed him from the stifling despair he experienced in the Custom-House; the recovery of his literary creativity solved the personal crisis he encountered in public office. Thus Hawthorne proposes romance as a cure, not just of creative difficulties but psychological conflicts, for himself and potentially for his readers as well.

In "The Custom-House," Hawthorne's stultification is the result of a conflict between private urges – the desire to exercise his creative "gift" – and the demands of the public role as officer of the custom. The conflict is also expressed as one between instinct and authority: Hawthorne's creative instincts are stifled by the harsh judgment of the condemning Puritan ancestors whom he evokes in memory. These ancestors, he feels, would consider his artistic work "worthless, if not positively disgraceful" (p. 10). Instincts are so entirely suppressed in the Custom-House that they are reduced to those of involuntary reverence for one's birthplace (Hawthorne's "mere sensuous sympathy of dust for dust" [p. 9]) and appetite for food (on the part of the Inspector, whose "few commonplace instincts ... did duty ... in lieu of a heart" [p. 17]). In *The Scarlet Letter* itself, Hawthorne's experience of the conflict between instinct and authority, private self and professional role, is acted out dramatically in the sphere of private passion, where instinct takes the form of the powerful urgings of antisocial sexuality, and authority is embodied in the presence of Puritan judges.

The tale, then, dramatizes the conflict that led to the impasse of feeling Hawthorne reached in the Custom-House, and in a larger sense, the empty, unnatural world of the 19th century. This representation, or repetition, of Hawthorne's dilemma gives the romance a function like that of the transference in psychoanalysis; Hawthorne's description of the realm of romance is very close to Freud's definition of the protected realm of the transference. Hawthorne's romance is a space between two worlds, "somewhere between the real world and fairy-land, where the Actual and the Imaginary may meet, and each imbue itself with the nature of the other" (p. 36). The realm of romance is like the province of creative activity itself as Freud describes it. In noting the relation between the poet and daydreaming, Freud (1908) states that the poet's created world, like the play of children, at once uses reality and escapes from it:

> ... the child distinguishes it...his play-world...quite well from reality; and he likes to link his imagined objects and situations to the tangible and visible things of the real world. ... Every child at play behaves like a creative writer, in that he creates a world of his

8. ROMANCE AND REPRESSION IN *THE SCARLET LETTER*

own, or, rather re-arranges the things of his world in a new way which pleases him better [pp. 143–144].

So Hawthorne (1850) emphasizes that while the moonlight of romance transforms things of "substance" into "things of intellect" (p. 36), the materials of romance remain actual objects. The tie to reality is never cut; indeed, Hawthorne implies that romance makes us see reality more clearly or deeply, for moonlight "makes every object so minutely visible" (p. 35). Romance as Hawthorne defines it is analogous to the realm of the transference, which Freud (1914) calls an "intermediate region between illness and real life through which the transition from the one to the other is made" (p. 154). Freud says that in the transference what has been repressed is repeated or represented rather than remembered. The basis of present disorders is found in the buried experience of the past. The transference repeats or represents the past in the guise of a present experience, and so constitutes an "artificial illness" subject to treatment. But, as Freud notes, it is at the same time "a piece of real experience" (p. 154).

Though "artificial," then, the transference has reality, as Hawthorne claims that the romance he creates constitutes "more real life" than that of the Custom-House (p. 23, pp. 44–45). The real life to which transference gives existence is the buried life of the past. The "constructions" of the analyst make this past content conscious and so "recover a fragment of lost experience" (1937, p. 268). Hawthorne's discovery of the scarlet letter is also a "construction," because it recovers a "fragment" of the past that has been long buried and would otherwise have been lost entirely (the letter is found amidst a heap of abandoned paper, "Custom-House lumber" [p. 30]). Hawthorne here identifies the "lost experience" of his own personal past with the "historic truth" of public history, the "authorized ... facts" (p. 32) of Puritan Salem, in a story which is both part of the public record and of his personal history (for women like Hester Prynne were condemned by Hawthorne's ancestors, the Puritan judges). In Hawthorne's case, Freud's use of the term "historical truth" to refer to the past of the individual becomes quite literally historical truth, as Hawthorne seeks escape from his impoverished present in history itself. Hawthorne's task is to uncover the "historical truth ... brought up from the repression of the forgotten and primaeval past" (Freud, 1937, p. 268) which is both his own and that of an entire society (the manuscript containing the scarlet letter is found amidst private papers that have been mixed up with official historical records).

Hawthorne seems to find his route back to the past of the 17th century through a series of "delusions": the viewing of the scarlet letter itself, which he imagines can burn him; the vision of the ghost of Surveyor Pue, who exhorts him to write the story; the ghosts who haunt his moonlit chamber of romance. Delusions, Freud (1937) notes, are analogous to constructions in analysis. For, like constructions, they restore and represent the past: "The delusion owes its convincing power to the element of historical truth which it inserts in the place of the rejected reality" (p. 268). Hawthorne rejects the present-day reality of the Custom-House and substitutes for it the "historical truth" of the past. Hawthorne turns delusions into constructions in "The Custom-House." The delusions are the most palpably fictive elements in what otherwise seems a factual narrative (realistic enough to enable contemporary readers to identify most of the figures portrayed). Hawthorne does not so much have as create or construct delusions. Thus he can turn ghosts, visions, dreams—almost hallucinatory "symptoms"—into "attempts at explanation and cure" (Freud, 1937, p. 268).

Hawthorne's romance is a form of self-cure, for, as he implies, writing *The Scarlet Letter* released him from the death instinct that had led him to confinement in the Custom-House, "the mere sensuous sympathy of dust for dust" (p. 9). The cure, Hawthorne feels, must be completed by the reader, who will "find out the divided segment of the writer's own nature, and complete his circle of existence by bringing him into communion with it" (pp. 3-4). In analysis, the cure is performed by transforming the "representation" of the transference into interpretation through the mutual work of analyst and patient. So Hawthorne depends on the reader's interpretation, which is incorporated into the work in the multiple interpretations among which the reader must choose.

Hawthorne sees himself as engaged in a discourse or interchange with the reader made possible by their meeting in the "neutral territory" of romance (p. 36). He posits the reader as a lis-

8. ROMANCE AND REPRESSION IN *THE SCARLET LETTER*

tening presence, in a role like that of the analyst, from the opening of the book:

> ... as thoughts are frozen and utterance benumbed, unless the speaker stand in some true relation with his audience – it may be pardonable to imagine that a friend, a kind and apprehensive, though not the closest friend, is listening to our talk; and then, a native reserve being thawed by this genial consciousness, we may prate of the circumstances that lie around us, and even of ourself [p. 4].

Hawthorne's success in inducing readers to enter into this transference is attested to by the responses of such readers as Henry James, who reacted to *The Scarlet Letter* by transferring to it, enchanted by the book as Hawthorne was by the fictitious letter itself (James, 1879, pp. 87–88). By inducing readers to enter into a transference with him, Hawthorne can achieve his goal of producing a community of "human hearts" outside as well as within his work, widening romance's sphere, that of "the truth of the human heart."

Hawthorne enters into the world of romance, between actuality and imagination, by means of the scarlet letter itself, for Hawthorne as for his heroine Hester Prynne the "passport" (p. 199) from one realm to another. In going from the colorless present of the preface to the vividly colored past of the tale, moreover, Hawthorne discovers behind "the present disavowal" (the ban, self-imposed or otherwise, on literary creativity) "the original repression" (the ban on sexuality) (Freud, 1937, p. 268). For by uncovering the scarlet letter, Hawthorne not only reawakens his creative gift, but seems to reawaken sexual instincts as well – the "A" represents the inextricable mixture of language and sexuality, as sexuality is inscribed into language at its beginning. But whereas the Puritan ancestors (the representation of an excessively strong superego) may be braved on the literary front, their authority in condemning sexual affairs is apparently not to be challenged. It seems, then, that when Hawthorne views the scarlet letter, his superego clamps down on the original, sexual instinct, placing it in a state of repression that lasts throughout the book.

Hawthorne's response to the letter, when he first discovers and beholds it in "The Custom-House," seems indeed to be a "primal repression," for it "consists in the psychical (ideational) representative of the instinct being denied entrance into the conscious. With this a fixation is established..." (Freud, 1915, p. 148). In the scarlet letter "A" Hawthorne is confronted with the origin of his own creativity, the beginning of language itself. But he is further faced with the sexual instinct to which, as a son of the Puritans, he assuredly knows the "A" refers—"A" for adultery. That throughout the work, neither the word nor the idea "adultery" ever appears is evidence of Hawthorne's strong repression of the meaning of the letter when he first confronts it. That its sexual connotations have been evoked, nevertheless, is shown by his extreme reaction to it when he places the letter on his breast, which it burns with a "sensation not altogether physical":

> My eyes fastened themselves upon the old scarlet letter, and would not be turned aside. Certainly, there was some deep meaning in it, most worthy of interpretation, and which, as it were, streamed forth from the mystic symbol, subtly communicating itself to my sensibilities, but evading the analysis of my mind.
>
> ... While thus perplexed ... I happened to place it on my breast. It seemed to me ... then, that I experienced a sensation not altogether physical, yet almost so, as of burning heat; and as if the letter were not of red cloth, but red-hot iron. I shuddered, and involuntarily let it fall upon the floor [pp. 31–32].

Hawthorne's intense reaction can be viewed as a result of repression's capacity to preserve the affect of the thing repressed even as the mental presentation is banished. According to Freud (1894), when the ego attempts to prevent an undesirable idea from entering consciousness ("treating the incompatible idea as *non arrivée*" [p. 48]), the idea is split off from its affect. Though the ego may succeed in divorcing a powerful idea from its affect and so turn "this powerful idea into a weak one" (p. 48), the affect of which it has been "robbed" will persist elsewhere: "The sum of excitation which has been detached from [the idea] must be put to another use" (p. 49). In Hawthorne's case, then, the excitation produced by the idea "adultery" is no longer attached to the idea,

8. ROMANCE AND REPRESSION IN *THE SCARLET LETTER*

but continues to exist: Hawthorne feels strong "heat" when he places the letter on his breast, and excess meaning continues to "stream forth" from it.

With Hawthorne's refusal to admit the word or idea "adultery" into consciousness comes fixation on the letter, the feeling of being entranced by it. Even in the book's last chapter Hawthorne is unable to remove the imprint of the letter, although now it is engraved on his brain rather than his breast, perhaps signifying the sublimation of sexuality in creativity: "We have thrown all the light we could acquire upon the portent, and would gladly, now that it has done its office, erase its deep print out of our own brain; where long meditation has fixed it in very undesirable distinctness" (p. 259).

Hawthorne's transformation of the stimulus of the letter into a physical sensation is identical with the process of "conversion" that Freud (1894) describes as a form of hysteria, by which "the incompatible idea is rendered innocuous by its sum of excitation being transformed into something somatic" (p. 49). The conversion here is the transformation of the sexual excitation provoked by the idea "adultery" into the physical sensation of "burning heat." As Freud notes, such a conversion is difficult to eradicate:

> ... by this means the ego succeeds in freeing itself from the contradiction with which it is confronted; but instead, it has burdened itself with a mnemic symbol which finds a lodgement in consciousness, like a sort of parasite, either in the form of an unresolvable motor innervation or as a constantly recurring hallucinatory sensation, and which persists until a conversion in the opposite direction takes place [1894, p. 49].

An act of repression, then, is the *reason* for the symbolism of *The Scarlet Letter*. The confrontation with the "A" in "The Custom-House" transforms the letter into a "mystic symbol" for the duration of the book—indeed, on the last page the letter appears as an emblem. Throughout the work, the symbol finds an almost universal "lodgement in consciousness," in the hearts of the major characters as well as those of almost every member of the Puritan community, the "host" for this "parasite." The "unresolvable motor innervation" and "recurring hallucinatory sensation" resulting from conversion may both be seen in Arthur Dimmesdale, in, respectively, his gesture of placing his hand over his heart and his hallucinatory vision of the scarlet letter in the sky.

In turning the letter into a symbol, Hawthorne evades its linguistic meaning. This level of signification briefly occurs to him when he first views the "A": "This rag of scarlet cloth ... on careful examination, assumed the shape of a letter. It was the capital letter A" (p. 31). But in the paragraph following that in which Hawthorne places the "A" on his breast, its linguistic meaning has already been repressed—the letter has been transformed into a "mystic symbol." Hawthorne evades the significance of the "A" as the first letter of the alphabet, the beginning of a sequence, or the first letter of a word, "adultery." If the "A" were allowed to assume its level of meaning as letter, it would point unequivocally to the hidden sin or its originator, the unrevealed father Arthur Dimmesdale whose initial the "A" is.

Hawthorne's repression of sexuality is also a repression of language, which, like sexual instincts, can be generative but can also swerve from morality (in the "lies" of fiction). As the transformation of the "A" into a symbol conceals the identity of the author of the "crime," Hawthorne conceals his role as author, the person who has "fathered" the scarlet letter in a different sense. For, through the fiction of the discovery of the letter, Hawthorne disclaims authority or authorship while claiming the "authority" of historical fact. The "A" as symbol, then, is a symptom not only of the disease of sexual repression universal in the Puritan community but of a dis-ease with language, a fear that the literal would be as anarchic as the sexual. Hawthorne's task is to recover not only a buried past but language as well: to make symbolism into the language of the heart, to use the vehicle of repression to undo repression. Hawthorne must reclaim his own authority by acknowledging his instincts, rather than by depending on an external authority. In this sense, *The Scarlet Letter* is a cure of, as well as by, language.

Hawthorne's romance must provide an interpretation, like that of analysis, which will deliver both sexuality and language from their imprisonment by repression. According to Lacan (1968), the symptoms of repression constitute a fractured language within

8. ROMANCE AND REPRESSION IN *THE SCARLET LETTER*

which the healing Word is hidden: "The symptom resolves itself entirely in a Language analysis, because the symptom itself is structured like a Language, because it is language from which the Word must be delivered" (p. 32). Lacan's point is particularly appropriate to *The Scarlet Letter*, where the symptom—the red "A"—is quite clearly an element of language. As Lacan suggests, the healing language of analytic interpretation releases the symbol, the inscription of the symptom on the subject's flesh, from that flesh: "[The analyst] interprets the symbol, and lo and behold, the symptom, which inscribes the symbol in letters of suffering in the subject's flesh, disappears" (p. 70). So Hawthorne searches for a curative interpretation to counter the punitive inscription of the fathers. His letter is "most worthy of interpretation" because by means of that interpretation it may be transformed from a means of punishment to a generative force, the first letter of a new language.

Lacan differentiates the blocked language of the symptom from the Word to which the analyst's interpretation gives utterance. Hawthorne also tries to distinguish two kinds of language—that of his romance and the word of the fathers, which "inscribes the symbol in letters of suffering" directly on Hester and, through internalized repression, on Dimmesdale. While the Puritans use writing to separate, to impose hierarchies and division, romance writing dissolves divisions, between fancy and actuality, light and darkness. Romance's "neutral territory," under the veil of a picturesque or moonlit atmosphere, gives the freedom to act out the drama of instinctual feelings. Whether Hawthorne successfully opposes Puritan repression—whether a "conversion in the opposite direction" ever occurs—is hard to determine. For certainly the letter has not been delivered from its symbolic status by the end of the book, where it appears on an "engraved escutcheon."

"The Custom-House," then, sets up the psychic patterns within which *The Scarlet Letter* is confined: the conflict between instinct and authority, the preexisting repression which has already made the "A" a symbol. Within the story, language's alternate capacities to punish or redeem are embodied in the characters of Arthur Dimmesdale and his unacknowledged child Pearl. Dimmesdale is the most extreme case in the story of the consequences of repression. He is depicted as a false romancer, whose preaching heightens his "disease" of repression rather than curing it. By contrast, Pearl represents the capacity of language to make anew. Hawthorne presents the possibility that for a child who is not a daughter of the Puritans, neither sexuality nor language need be equated with sin. Only Dimmesdale's ultimate acknowledgment of Pearl and the possibilities she represents can constitute the "cure" of romance.

According to Freud, conversion begins when the ego is "confronted with a contradiction." The contradictory claims of instinct and authority, private impulse and public role, which Hawthorne faced in the Custom-House are brought to an irresolvable impasse for Arthur Dimmesdale in the opening dramatic scene of *The Scarlet Letter*. In this scene, as Hester Prynne is placed on trial on the scaffold, Arthur Dimmesdale finds the contradiction between his ungoverned sexual instincts and his "office" as minister made inescapable when he is asked to exhort Hester to reveal her "partner in crime," and so become at the same time judger and judged. This is the moment that turns the scarlet "A" into a "mnemic symbol" for Dimmesdale. In this scene, for the first time, in a gesture ambiguously signifying either concealment or pledging of troth, Dimmesdale places his hand on his heart (p. 68). Henceforth, while suppression has been imposed on Hester from without and enables her to "work out" (p. 80) her "sin," Dimmesdale must repress his instincts himself. Freud says that "acts of innervation" in conversion hysteria address the part of the body with which the instinct is associated. Though Dimmesdale's gesture is an attempt to conceal his sexual impulses, its effect is to reveal them, for Pearl recognizes the shared experience of her mother and the minister by associating the gesture with the scarlet letter. As Hester stands on the scaffold wearing the scarlet letter, then, Arthur Dimmesdale is affixed with another symbol, the gesture of placing his hand over his heart. In the course of the story, this gesture becomes "a custom," involuntary at that, and finally "a constant habit" (pp. 113, 120, 122).

In Dimmesdale, repression "ramifies like a fungus ... proliferates in the dark" and "takes on extreme forms of expression" (Freud, 1915, p. 149). Freud notes that repressed material exercises a magnetic effect, drawing other material into the unconscious. Dimmesdale's neurosis is indeed an extreme "form of expression," for his nightly self-scourgings resemble other instances of punitive "writing," from the symbolic inscriptions of the Puritans to the writings in blood with the "iron pen" of the Black Man.

Dimmesdale's self-scourging acts out the unresolvable contradiction he faces in the scaffold scene when he is asked to act as both judger and judged. As Crews (1966) notes, "the original sexual desire has been granted recognition on the condition of being punished, and the punishment itself is a form of gratification. Not only the overt masochism of fasts, vigils, and self-scourging ... but also Dimmesdale's emaciation and weariness attest to the spending of his energy against himself" (p. 142). The impoverishment of the ego resulting from repression makes his body a battleground for opposing forces. Dimmesdale eventually is at the mercy of his unconscious, tortured by the vicious cycle of a punitive superego and excessively strong and ungovernable instincts.

The loss of the middle ground of the ego makes Dimmesdale's "form of expression" incapable of the integration of Hawthorne's romance. Hawthorne looks into a mirror to spiritualize reality (p. 36); Dimmesdale to enter further into the maze of self (p. 145). Hawthorne's moonlit room makes possible "intercourse" between the mind and its objects: Dimmesdale's introspection actualizes his own fears and guilt (as a "herd of diabolic shapes") and turns people (Hester) into ghosts. Hawthorne's moonlight of romance integrates fancy and reality; Dimmesdale splits the world into the irreconcilable opposites of "utter darkness" and "the most powerful light" (p. 145).

Dimmesdale's vigil indicates that he has reached an impasse, for this description is followed by another form of "The Minister's Vigil," in which he attempts to release himself from torment. In this chapter, in a second scaffold scene, the minister attempts to reconcile the conflict between his roles as Puritan and literal father. As he stands on the scaffold and clasps hands with Hester and Pearl, a surge of feeling, "a tumultuous rush of new life," reanimates him. "The three formed an electric chain" (p. 153)—the energy clearly has a "charge" for Dimmesdale, as repressed sexual feelings return. The return of the repressed is manifested by the appearance of the scarlet letter in the sky, which Hawthorne clearly identifies here as a "symptom." Renewed contact with Hester has reawakened Dimmesdale's sexual desire; the return of the repressed makes him see its symbol now in a "hallucinatory sensation." The unconscious writing that emblazoned the symbol on his flesh now engraves it in bloody letters on the "page" of the "firmament" (p. 155).

Dimmesdale's hallucination, strangely enough, is seen by others. He is approached the next morning by a sexton who reports that the symbol has been seen and already incorporated into Puritan typology, interpreted "to stand for Angel ... as our good Governor Winthrop was made an angel this past night..." (p. 158). Since the sexton's interpretation is preceded by Dimmesdale's vision, which Hawthorne "impute[s] ... solely to the disease in his own eye and heart" (p. 155), Puritan interpretation is seen to be another form of neurotic projection. Hawthorne suggests that Dimmesdale's "disease" is universal in the Puritan community; his delusion is shared because of the burden of repression on the entire society: "One might . . . describe that neurosis as an individual religiosity and religion as a universal obsessional neurosis" (Freud, 1907, pp. 126–127). The discrediting of Puritan typological interpretations invites a liberating interpretation which would release the symbol from the flesh of the sufferer rather than engraving it everywhere in letters of blood. How is "conversion in the opposite directon" to occur? How can "universal obsessional neurosis" be translated into "the truth of the human heart?"

The vehicle for this translation is Pearl, identified with libido, for her wildness reflects the "impassioned state" (p. 91) of her mother during her conception and birth. Conversion or cure in *The Scarlet Letter* requires her parents' acceptance of Pearl. For Pearl is the "scarlet letter endowed with life," an analogy which Hester has carefully "wrought out" (p. 102). As the scarlet letter "capable of being loved" (p. 113), Pearl, as Dimmesdale himself surmises, can redeem her parents (p. 115). By acknowledging Pearl as their creation, her parents can escape the doom which is the consequence less of Original Sin than of guilt.

Though Pearl is free of Puritan moral standards, she has a strong affinity for "truth" in the sense of sincerity. In a way, Pearl learns the language anew. She does not know the "outward form"

8. ROMANCE AND REPRESSION IN *THE SCARLET LETTER* 161

(p. 112) of the New England Primer, in which the letter "A" commonly appeared with the legend "In Adam's fall, we sinned all"; she does not automatically associate the birth of language with Original Sin. No child of the Puritans, she is not aware that children are considered sinful, and so escapes "the disease of sadness, which almost all children ... inherit ... from the troubles of their ancestors" (p. 184). Rather than inheriting Dimmesdale's "disease," Pearl may cure it; the child may redeem the father.

Unlike everyone else in the book, Pearl refuses to see the "A" as a symbol. For her, simply, "it is the great letter A" (p. 178). She sees its meaning as linguistic *and* communal: She associates her mother's "A" with Dimmesdale's gesture and so sees the tie of intimacy between them. Pearl is an infant preacher of the word that links human hearts rather than the punitive letter of Puritan punishment. When Hester asks Pearl if she knows the meaning of the letter, Hester soon becomes the questioner and Pearl the interpreter (p. 179). Pearl's role is to establish a new, saving interpretation; like Hawthorne himself, "the one only thing for which she had been sent into the world was to make out [the letter's] hidden import" (p. 178). Pearl creates a natural language, disencumbered of social constraint and associated with innocence, when she devises "the letter A ... freshly green, instead of scarlet" (p. 178).

Pearl's "mission" toward her mother is "to soothe away the sorrow that lay cold in her mother's heart, and converted it into a tomb"(p. 180). This possible "conversion in the opposite direction" is preceded by a premature attempt to undo rather than work out repression, when Hester and Dimmesdale meet in the forest. Freud (1926) describes the effort to free oneself of something painful through the simple act or gesture of banishing as an attempt at magical "undoing." Such acts, according to Freud, are usually accompanied by a gesture of literally casting off something (1926, p. 119). Hester, in the false "conversion" of the forest scene, attempts to undo the past, to make it as if it never were, by casting off the scarlet letter. Dimmesdale sees this moment as a true "conversion" in religious terms: " 'I seem to have flung myself—sick, sin-stained, and sorrow-blackened—down upon these forest-leaves, and to have risen up all made anew.... This is already the better life!' " But Hester's gesture of flinging off the letter reveals that this is not true conversion—release from repression—but mere undoing—wishing the painful conflict away: " 'The past is gone!... With this symbol, I undo it all, and make it as it had never been!' " (pp. 201–202).

Pearl prevents this undoing, in a scene in which she seems to reinstate repression, like the Puritan fathers (she even looks like a Puritan judge here, with her "frown ... pointed finger, and imperious gesture" [p. 209]). But she insists that Hester reassume the letter, rather, because the letter provides the only way to work out repression. Discarding the letter would mean denying the being of Pearl, the means to legitimize the bond between Hester and Dimmesdale. To discard her would be to discard their connection to language: Pearl is the oneness of their being as embodied in a "living hieroglyphic" (p. 206). By acknowledging and interpreting this living symbol, Hester and Dimmesdale can be released from the stigmatizing symbols of their concealment. Indeed, as Pearl is here described as "the character of flame" (p. 207), she raises the possibility of the "A" becoming a purely natural language or apocalyptic writing, one in no need of interpretation because it speaks directly. In the last part of the book, the vision of an unmediated language finds expression in two ways, in the supernatural revelation of Dimmesdale and the modulation of language into action for Hester.

After the forest scene, in the chapter entitled "The Minister in a Maze," we see a further vicissitude of Dimmesdale's instincts. In the forest, Dimmesdale finds no freedom from repression; rather, his instincts break through the dam of repression to find expression in perversity. The instincts' search for expression finds its outlet in Dimmesdale's writing, a displacement of the sexual feelings aroused in his forest encounter with Hester. Sitting down to eat "with a ravenous appetite," Dimmesdale exercises, in his writing, only another appetite, in a nightlong effort hardly distinguishable from sexual activity: "He wrote with such an impulsive flow of thought and emotion, that he fancied himself inspired.... He drove his task onward, with earnest haste and ecstasy. Thus the night fled away, as if it were a winged steed, and he careering on it" (p. 225). This is the language of sexuality rather than the more humane and disciplined "truth of the human heart." The mention of "appetite" here recalls Hawthorne's criticism of the Inspector in "The Custom-House," whose "few commonplace instincts ... did duty .. in lieu of a heart." It is hard to see sublimation in this effort, as Crews does; rather, Dimmesdale's instincts are simply confused with "inspiration" (p. 148).

The description of Dimmesdale's writing echoes not Hawthorne's description of his romance in the preface but his view of his role as decapitated surveyor, after he has been expelled from the Custom-House, "careering though the public prints" (p. 42). Hawthorne feels he has achieved a "crown of martyrdom," the end Dimmesdale also reaches. Rather than achieving the lifegiving solution of romance, Dimmesdale can resolve the conflict between his role and his instincts only through death, as Hawthorne found no solution to the oppressiveness of the Custom-House except to "die" out of it.

For Dimmesdale, repression is never undone. In his Election Sermon, his instinct finds a voice, to Hester's ears, in an "undertone." But its voice is no voice; pure instinct can be expressed only as a "shriek," "a cry of pain." The question remains – can instinct be integrated with language, find communicable expression, and perhaps change a cry of pain to one of joy?

Dimmesdale's final scene, his revelation of the letter on his chest, is almost supernatural, like the earlier scene on the scaffold. Hawthorne there attributed supernaturalism to the guilty projections of a repressed individual and society. Yet Hawthorne notes that apocalyptic truth can be attained in a different way. When the "multitude ... forms its judgment ... on the intuitions of its great and warm heart, the conclusions thus attained are often so profound and so unerring, as to possess the character of truths supernaturally revealed" (p. 127). With Dimmesdale's death, the supernaturalism of the book subsides. But the language and revelation expressed unconsciously in Dimmesdale's Election Sermon – the "tongue native to the human heart, wherever educated" (p. 243) – in the last chapter of *The Scarlet Letter* becomes conscious and active. Language gives way to activity, as the quest with which Hawthorne entered the Custom-House – to "share in the united effort of mankind" (p. 38) – is fulfilled in Hester's life after Dimmesdale's death. As minister to women in their troubles, Hester becomes an example of the sublimation of wayward instinct into striving for a public good. Hester communicates through "comfort and counsel" (p. 263), the unmediated language of the human heart. Here words are used for an active purpose, resolving the split in the preface between literary and practical life. As Hester has been cured of the "stigma" of the letter, she provides the "remedy" for others, a healing language which relieves the manifold inscriptions which deface both men and women. Hester's sublimation doubles Hawthorne's own, his capacity to turn repression into sublimated activity in the writing of romance.

I began by comparing romance to the transference; the necessary cooperation of the reader might imply that Hawthorne is the patient, the reader the analyst. But the relation may be reversed. Note, for example, Hawthorne's gesture at the end of the first chapter when he offers the reader a blossom from the rose bush which stands "so directly on the threshold of our narrative"; "We could hardly do otherwise than pluck one of its flowers and present it to the reader. It may serve, let us hope, to symbolize some sweet moral blossom, that may be found along the track, or relieve the darkening close of a tale of human frailty and sorrow" (p. 48). Freud notes that when the analyst gives the patient a gift, he can watch it evoke "storms of transference." Hawthorne's gift may be intended to evoke such transference, placing the reader in the role of patient. The completion of the romance, then, would represent a cure for reader as well as writer.

Does the rose blossom indeed "relieve the darkening close" of the tale? What we find at the end of the work is the encapsulation of the scarlet "A" into an emblem, a red letter against darkness. Here what "relieves" the darkness of the device is the scarlet letter itself, "one ever-glowing point of light" (p. 264). The rose bush, the symbol of nature, hope, and love, has been transformed into the scarlet letter; implicitly, the "A" has been transformed from a symbol of repression into a symbol of love. Such a change was implicit throughout in the figure of Pearl, whom others identify as the "scarlet letter endowed with life," but who describes herself as a blossom plucked off the rose bush. Hawthorne embodies in the final emblem ("On a field, sable, the letter A, gules") the irresolvable conflict between individual desire and social constraint. He acknowledges the conflict and affirms the essentially tragic nature of human life in the duality of the emblem, in which even the "one ever-glowing point of light" is "gloomier than the shadow." But that conflict, which originally stifled Hawthorne's creativity, has now been brought into his artistic work and contained within it; the letter has become a validating stamp which seals off the story to which it originally gave access.

ACKNOWLEDGMENTS

I would like to thank Richard Millington for suggesting the analogy between romance and the transference, in an unpublished paper, "Romance as Cure: The Story of Hawthorne's Prefaces." I would also like to thank Maurice Charney and David Leverenz for their comments on earlier versions of this essay.

REFERENCES

Bales, K. (1977). Hawthorne's prefaces and romantic perspectivism. *ESQ: A Journal of the American Renaissance, 23*, 69–88.
Baym, N. (1982). Hawthorne and his mother: A biographical speculation. *American Literature, 54*, 1–27.
Bell, M. (1982). The obliquity of signs: *The Scarlet Letter. Massachusetts Review, 23*, 9–26.
Crews, F. (1966). *The sins of the fathers: Hawthorne's psychological themes.* New York: Oxford University Press.
Duncan, J. L. (1981). The design of Hawthorne's fabrications. *Yale Review, 71*, 51–71.
Eakin, P. J. (1971). Hawthorne's imagination and the structure of "The Custom-House." *American Literature, 43*, 346–358.
Franzosa, J. (1978). The Custom-House, the Scarlet Letter, and Hawthorne's separation from Salem. *ESQ: A Journal of the American Renaissance, 91*, 57–71.
Franzosa, J. (1981). A psychoanalysis of Hawthorne's style. *Genre, 14*, 383–409.
Freud, S. (1974). The neuro-psychoses of defence. In J. Strachey (Ed. and Trans.), *The standard edition of the complete psychological works of Sigmund Freud (Vol. 3, p. 43–68).* London: Hogarth Press. (Original work published 1894)
_____ (1959). Creative writers and day-dreaming. In J. Strachey (Ed. and Trans.), *The standard edition of the complete psychological works of Sigmund Freud (Vol. 9, p. 143–153).* London: Hogarth Press. (Original work published 1908)
_____ (1959). Obsessive actions and religious practices. In J. Strachey (Ed. and Trans.), *The standard edition of the complete psychological works of*

Sigmund Freud (Vol. 9, p. 117-127). London: Hogarth Press. (Original work published 1907)

──────── (1958). Remembering, repeating and working-through: Further recommendations on the technique of psycho-analysis II. In J. Strachey (Ed. and Trans.), *The standard edition of the complete psychological works of Sigmund Freud* (Vol. 12, p. 147-156). London: Hogarth Press. (Original work published 1914)

──────── (1957). Repression. In J. Strachey (Ed. and Trans.), *The standard edition of the complete psychological works of Sigmund Freud* (Vol. 14, p. 143-158). London: Hogarth Press. (Original work published 1915)

──────── (1959). Inhibitions, symptoms, and anxiety. In J. Strachey (Ed. and Trans.), *The standard edition of the complete psychological works of Sigmund Freud* (Vol. 20, p. 77-172). London: Hogarth Press. (Original work published 1926)

──────── (1963). Constructions in analysis. In J. Strachey (Ed. and Trans.), *The standard edition of the complete psychological works of Sigmund Freud* (Vol. 23, p. 257-269). London: Hogarth Press. (Original work published 1937)

Hawthorne, N. (1962). The scarlet letter. In W. Chanat et al. (Eds.), *The scarlet letter: The centenary edition of the works of Nathaniel Hawthorne* (Vol. 1). Columbus, OH: Ohio State University Press. (Original work published 1850)

James, H. (1956). *Hawthorne*. Ithaca, NY: Cornell University Press. (Original work published 1879)

Jordan, G. G. (1981). Adultery and its fruits in *The Scarlet Letter* and *The Power and the Glory:* The relation of meaning and form. *Yale Review, 71*, 72-87.

Lacan, J. (1968). *The Language of the Self* (A. Wilden Ed. and Trans.). Baltimore: Johns Hopkins University Press.

Ragussis, M. (1982). Family discourse and fiction in *The Scarlet Letter*. *English Literary History, 49*, 863-888.

Stouck, D. (1971). The surveyor of the Custom-House: A narrator for *The Scarlet Letter*. *Centennial Review, 15*, 309-329.

V PSYCHOANALYSIS AND SHAKESPEARE

9 The Purloined Handkerchief in *Othello*[1]

Peter L. Rudnytsky, Ph.D.

> *The letter as a signifier is thus not a thing or the absence of a thing, nor a word or the absence of a word, nor an organ or the absence of an organ, but a knot in a structure where words, things and organs can neither be definably separated nor compatibly combined.*
> —Barbara Johnson (1977)

I

Implicitly or explicitly, every attempt to interpret a specific literary text is a thematization of the problem of reading. Every interpretation must situate itself within the context of previous readings of the same text as well as within the crosscurrents of diverse trends in contemporary thought. It is, as Gadamer (1975) has shown, not necessary for an interpreter to be aware of the "history of effects" (*Wirkungsgeschichte*) of a work for him or her to be subjected to its power. On the other hand, a successful interpretation depends on a recognition of one's embeddedness in history and on "the achievement of the right horizon of enquiry for the questions evoked by the encounter with tradition."

---

[1]An earlier version of this paper was read before the Columbia University Seminar on the Theory of Literature.

The significance of the handkerchief in *Othello* is one of the most time-honored cruxes of interpretation in the play. Indeed, the first major critical commentary on *Othello*, that of Thomas Rymer in 1692, sets the terms for subsequent discussion by attacking Shakespeare for allowing the plot of his tragedy to depend upon something so trivial as a lost handkerchief:

> So much ado, so much stress, so much passion and repetition about an Handkerchief! Why was not this call'd the *Tragedy of the Handkerchief?* ... Had it been *Desdemona*'s Garter, the Sagacious Moor might have smelt a Rat: but the Handkerchief is so remote a trifle, no Booby, on this side *Mauritania,* cou'd make any consequence from it.

As so often, the strictures of an intelligent neoclassical critic go directly to the central issues of a work of art. Rymer's sense of the incongruity between the cause and the effects of Othello's downfall is wholly justified, and must be attended to by any reader who seeks to gain insight into Shakespeare's artistry in *Othello*.

In speaking of the handkerchief as "purloined," I mean to suggest a relation between this traditional problem of Shakespearean exegesis and a cluster of writings in contemporary literary theory. Edgar Allan Poe's short story "The Purloined Letter" (1845) has given rise to a series of influential commentaries, intrinsically interesting in their own right but possessing ramifications extending far beyond their immediate occasion. Lacan (1972), in his "Seminar on 'The Purloined Letter,'" offers a reading of Poe's story that is in effect also a meditation on Freud's *Beyond the Pleasure Principle* and an elaboration of his own contention that "it is the symbolic order [i.e., language] which is constitutive for the subject." Lacan's "Seminar" provoked a polemical reply from Derrida (1975), who reanalyzes Poe's story to argue that Lacan's psychoanalysis, seemingly so radical, is actually based on a metaphysical belief in truth and presence Derrida names "phallogocentric transcendentalism," which must be rejected in favor of his own insistence on "dissemination" or the priority of writing over speech. Finally, Johnson (1977), in a masterful subversion of the possibility of mastery, takes on all three of her illustrious predecessors and shows convincingly how

9. THE PURLOINED HANDKERCHIEF IN *OTHELLO*   171

"Derrida's own reading of Lacan's text reproduces precisely the crimes of which he accuses it"–i.e., oversimplification and distortion–to the point where it becomes impossible to know "whether Lacan and Derrida are really saying the same thing or only enacting their own differences from themselves."

This series of interpretations of Poe bears directly on *Othello* because, as I shall try to show, the handkerchief in Shakespeare's play, like the letter in Poe's story, functions as a "floating signifier," the circulation of which, in Lacan's words, "determines the subjects in their acts, in their destiny." The controversy between Derrida and Lacan is likewise exemplary of a tension we shall encounter in examining *Othello* between "deconstructive" and "psychoanalytic" readings. This contrast is itself illustrated by the commentary of de Man (1979) on yet another purloined object, the ribbon stolen by Rousseau in Book II of the *Confessions*:

> Once it is removed from its legitimate owner, the ribbon, being in itself devoid of meaning and function, can circulate symbolically as a pure signifier and become the articulating hinge in a chain of exchanges and possessions. As the ribbon changes hands it traces a circuit leading to the exposure of a hidden, censored desire.

To the psychoanalytically oriented critic, de Man's reference to the "hidden, censored desire" revealed by the circulation of the ribbon–or handkerchief–cannot fail to point to the repressed desire for incest which lurks in the Oedipus complex. Exactly this insistence on imposing oedipal paradigms, however, is at the heart of the objections to psychoanalysis of deconstructionists such as Derrida and de Man, the latter of whom interprets the ribbon as "substituting for a desire which is itself a desire for substitution." In analyzing the function of the handkerchief in *Othello*, we shall find ourselves confronted by the simultaneous necessity and impossibility of choosing between a view of it as representing the "desire for substitution" and the Oedipus complex.

There has been much distinguished work done on *Othello* in recent years, almost all of it informed to some degree by psychoanalysis and some of it touching on the handkerchief. The essays of Snow (1980), Kirsch (1978), Boose (1975), and Cavell (1979), and the chapters in books by Green (1979) and Greenblatt (1980) have been of the greatest value to me, along with the earlier study by Heilman (1956). The "horizon of enquiry" in this paper is thus constituted by a triangulation: the tradition of interpretations of *Othello*, the issues in contemporary theory evoked by my title, and the text of Shakespeare's play itself. But if it is the lesson of hermeneutics that every interpretation is governed by the "history of effects," it must also be recognized that every text is structured by repetition and consequently is a composite and not an isolated entity.

These self-conscious reflections about the nature of interpretation have been prompted by the ostentatiousness of the handkerchief as an emblem of the procedures of literary analysis. Although he does not allude to *Othello*, perhaps the best reply to Rymer's objections concerning the handkerchief is contained in Hartman's (1981) remarks on the use of images or metaphors in philosophical discourse:

> Something in appearance marginal, supplementary, accidental (a "case" cited by chance, an illustrative metaphor) tells us that the essence or thing itself is missing. The thing instanced becomes, as it were, a disgruntled representative of the absent (perhaps always absent) thing, and paradoxically gains more authority than the argument it was intended to supplement. And here is where literary study sees *its* chance.... It seizes on the images and metaphors that slip, deliberately or not, into pure or scientific discourse, and reflects on whether this allowance of dream or icon may not be closer to the real subject.

The handkerchief may indeed seem too "remote a trifle" to serve as the occasion for tragedy, but this "marginal, supplementary, accidental" object, which "tells us that the essence or thing itself is missing," nonetheless comes as close as anything to being "the real subject" of *Othello*.

II

Shakespeare himself draws attention to the tension between the marginality and centrality of the handkerchief by contriving to introduce it into the play at the midpoint of the action, at the culmi-

9. THE PURLOINED HANDKERCHIEF IN *OTHELLO* 173

nation of the Temptation Scene in Act III, Scene iii, after Iago has implanted the seeds of jealousy in Othello. Desdemona enters, and the following exchange ensues:

> *Oth.* I have a pain upon my forehead, here.
> *Des.* Faith, that's with watching, 'twill away again.
>   Let me but bind it hard, within this hour
>   It will be well.
> *Oth.* Your napkin is too little [3.1.284-87].

Shakespeare's language functions at once on a naturalistic and an allegorical level. Othello's "pain upon my forehead" alludes to the traditional horns of cuckoldry, but also suggests that his headache may be a psychosomatic symptom of jealousy.[2] Desdemona's reply, that his agitation is the result of "watching," while it has the literal meaning of "not sleeping," simultaneously evokes the prurient voyeurism that is so prominent a feature of his conduct. Her offer to "bind" his head with her handkerchief, beyond being an attempt to minister to his physical needs, is a metaphorical expression of Desdemona's love, which Othello rejects by branding the handkerchief "too little."

After being brushed aside by Othello, the handkerchief embarks upon what proves to be a symbolic itinerary in the second half of the play. It is immediately picked up by Emilia, Desdemona's lady-in-waiting and wife to Iago, who surrenders it to her husband. Iago uses the handkerchief to further his schemes of revenge by planting it in the chamber of the disgraced Cassio and informing Othello that he has seen it in Cassio's possession. Cassio brings the handkerchief to his paramour, the courtesan Bianca, and requests her to copy the pattern, as Emilia had earlier thought of doing. Bianca accepts it, though she suspects the handkerchief was given to Cassio by "a newer friend" (3.4.181). Subsequently, she angrily returns the handkerchief to him, and at the worst moment possible—when Iago has hidden

---

2. Subsequently, when Othello falls into a trance, Iago refers to his condition as "an epilepsy" (4.1.50), but when he asks Othello upon his recovery "Have you not hurt your head?" (59), the latter interprets his question as a mocking allusion to cuckoldry. The entire play partakes simultaneously of naturalism and allegory.

Othello and arranged for him to spy upon a conversation between himself and Cassio. It is the appearance of Bianca with the handkerchief in Act IV, Scene i that causes Othello to resolve to murder both Cassio and Desdemona. After this exchange, the handkerchief is not mentioned again until the last scene of the play. Both during and after the murder of Desdemona, Othello appeals to Cassio's possession of the handkerchief as his justification, until Emilia reveals the truth about its disappearance: "O thou dull Moor, that handkerchief thou speak'st of/ I found by fortune, and did give my husband" (5.2.225-26). Thus, as Heilman (1956) has noted, in this final twist to the "court metaphor" that pervades the drama "the handkerchief does have evidential value—but the reverse of what Othello had supposed," for Emilia's words establish at one stroke the innocence of Desdemona and the guilt of Iago.

Beginning with Desdemona, the handkerchief comes into contact with all three of the female characters and their male counterparts. It thus becomes evident how pertinent are Lacan's (1972) formulations. The symbolic itinerary of the handkerchief is the itinerary of the signifier, and "it is not only the subject [i.e., Othello], but the subjects [i.e., the other characters], grasped in their intersubjectivity, who . . . model their very being on the moment of the signifying chain which traverses them." But if the subjects are defined by their place in the "signifying chain," it is also true that the handkerchief acquires something of the qualities of each of the characters through whom it passes. It has experienced the purity of Desdemona, the realism of Emilia, and the sexual frankness of Bianca; it has also been touched by the absolutism of Othello, the cynicism of Iago, and the cupidity of Cassio. Had the handkerchief returned to Desdemona, its circle completed, Iago's plot could not have succeeded. But the circuit it traces is an open one, and hence does not save the life of Desdemona, though it does expose the machinations that are the cause of her death.

Just as the meaning of the handkerchief is different for each character, so Shakespeare presents multiple views of love in *Othello*, none of which may be regarded as normative. It is tempting, for example, to regard the love of Desdemona and Othello as wholly "good," a "marriage of true minds," and that of Emilia and

Iago or Bianca and Cassio as superficial or "bad." But though there is considerable truth in this view – as exemplified in the desires of Emilia and Bianca to copy Desdemona's handkerchief (see Levin, 1978) – it is also the case that the love of Othello and Desdemona ends tragically because it lacks the sense of balance that would be provided by the attributes found in the two other couples. The naïveté of Desdemona, who cannot bring herself to pronounce the word "whore," is qualified by Emilia's justified protest against the double standard of sexual conduct adhered to by men: "What is it they do/ When they change us for others? Is it sport?" (4.3.96-97). Emilia's own self-righteous respectability in turn finds a counterweight in Bianca, who, when Emilia brands her a "strumpet," tellingly replies: "I am no strumpet, but of life as honest/ As you that thus abuse me" (5.1.122-23). No character speaks more than a partial truth; only the handkerchief, which traverses them all and is itself lost, embodies the possibility of a marriage that would integrate the qualities distributed among the three couples in the play.

III

For Lacan (1972), the signifier is "by nature symbol only of an absence." Hartman (1981), similarly, writes that the "illustrative metaphor" serves as "a disgruntled representative of the absent (perhaps always absent) thing." In *Othello*, the "absent thing" is in one very concrete sense the sight of Desdemona engaged in intercourse with Cassio. "Would you, the supervisor, grossly gape on?/ Behold her topp'd?" (3.3.95-96), Iago tormentingly inquires of Othello. But because Desdemona is not guilty of adultery, such a sight is inherently unattainable, and the handkerchief "gains more authority than the argument it was intended to supplement." Othello cries out for the "ocular proof" (3.3.360) of his wife's infidelity, but it is in his own fantasies of betrayal that Iago's power lies. Upon being shown the "thing instanced" – Cassio with the handkerchief – Othello is consequently persuaded that he has seen the nonexistent "thing itself."

If the handkerchief comes to stand in Othello's mind for Desdemona's adultery, it is because he has previously been led to equate the handkerchief with Desdemona's love. But just as Othello is mistaken in believing that the loss of the handkerchief is proof of the loss of Desdemona's love, so he is mistaken in his initial assumption that love is a matter susceptible to empirical verification. Honor, Iago admits, "is an essence that's not seen;/ They have it very oft that have it not"; but he diverts Othello's attention to the fallacious physical evidence: "But if I give my wife a handkerchief—" (4.1.10-16). The impossibility of obtaining certain knowledge of Desdemona's fidelity *or* her infidelity is what torments Othello, and leads him to replace what is "not seen" with the "ocular proof" of the handkerchief.

The handkerchief participates simultaneously in the realms of appearance and reality. It serves, as Othello states in the last scene, as a "recognizance and pledge of love" (5.2.214) between himself and Desdemona. But it also, through the manipulations of Iago, comes to represent Desdemona's *reputation* for love and chastity, which is a matter of perception and not invisible essence. After she discovers the loss of her handkerchief, Desdemona declares to Emilia: "Believe me, I had rather have lost my purse/ Full of crusadoes" (3.4.25-26). The same imagery is used earlier by Iago when he tortures Othello with the contrast between the insignificance of being robbed of his money, "Who steals my purse steals trash; 'tis something, nothing," and the permanent damage to the "immediate jewel" of his "good name" (3.3.155-57) that would follow from being cuckolded by Desdemona. As the success of Iago's plotting against both Othello and Cassio goes to show, moreover, the loss of one's "good name" or reputation can have fatal consequences. It is not enough to possess the essence of love unless one can also survive in the world of appearances. Boose (1975), who entitles her article " 'The Recognizance and Pledge of Love,' " views the handkerchief as a "symbolic token" and claims that Desdemona "cannot actually lose it." Hodgson (1977), on the other hand, denies that the handkerchief is a "symbol of love," suggesting instead that it "is an emblem of Desdemona's reputation." Surely, however, the handkerchief may connote both the reality of Desdemona's love and its appearance, just as Othello himself is torn between the visions of life held by Desdemona and Iago.

9. THE PURLOINED HANDKERCHIEF IN *OTHELLO*

Othello's obsessive and perpetually frustrated quest to behold Desdemona in the act of adultery duplicates the fears of her father Brabantio. In the opening scene, Iago taunts Brabantio with graphic descriptions of Desdemona engaged in sex with Othello: "Even now, now, very now, an old black ram/ Is tupping your white ewe" (1.1.90-91). To the psychoanalyst, any such voyeuristic preoccupations must have infantile roots, and be derived from early thoughts or memories of spying on parental intercourse. When, in Act IV, Scene i, Othello covertly watches Iago and Cassio engaged in bantering conversation, ostensibly about Desdemona though in reality about Bianca, and Bianca then enters with the handkerchief, the very staging of Iago's plot is calculated to revive in Othello unconscious fantasies of the primal scene.

Shakespeare's characters are not, of course, real people, and in a literal sense possess neither childhoods nor unconscious fantasies. But there is compelling evidence to suggest that Shakespeare anticipated Freud's discoveries about the importance of early experiences and the unconscious. In *Othello*, much of this evidence is provided by Shakespeare's modifications of the 16th-century *novella* by the Italian Giraldi Cinthio that is his principal source for the play. For example, Shakespeare, but not Cinthio, has Othello ascribe to the handkerchief a magical power derived from its function as a talisman of the marital bond between his own parents. When Desdemona is unable to produce the handkerchief, Othello warns her that it was given to his mother by an Egyptian "charmer":

> She told her, while she kept it,
> 'Twould make her amiable, and subdue my father
> Entirely to her love; but if she lost it,
> Or made a gift of it, my father's eye
> Should hold her loathed, and his spirits should hunt
> After new fancies [3.4.58-63].

As Kirsch (1978) has noted, in this passage depicting "the primitive world of a child's merger with his mother, there is already implicit in what Othello says the sense of his own primal betrayal."

Thus, by evoking the world of Othello's childhood, and linking it specifically with the handkerchief, Shakespeare shows the origin of Othello's jealousy of Desdemona in his reaction to the traumatic knowledge of parental sexuality.

Just as Shakespeare provides Othello with a childhood, he does so as well with Desdemona. There is a close parallel to Othello's story about the handkerchief in Desdemona's "Willow Song," which she sings at the close of Act IV as she ominously anticipates her own death. She prefaces it by telling Emilia:

> My mother had a maid call'd Barbary;
> She was in love, and he she lov'd prov'd mad,
> And did forsake her. She had a song of "Willow,"
> An old thing 'twas, but it express'd her fortune,
> And she died singing it. That song to-night
> Will not go from my mind [4.3.26-31].

The same "primitive world of a child's merger with his mother" recalled for Othello by the handkerchief is here summoned up by Desdemona, and her speech likewise contains "the sense of her own primal betrayal." The tragic outcome of the love between Othello and Desdemona, therefore, is played out against the backdrop of these representative screen memories of early childhood attributed to both characters.

Othello, with a black man as its hero, is a play evidently concerned with the experience of forbidden love. Another of Shakespeare's departures from Cinthio, which heightens this motif, is his invention of the character of Brabantio. In addition to being black, Othello is considerably older than Desdemona, and it is plausible to explain the attractions of these two features to her in terms of an unconscious incestuous fixation. By supplying Desdemona not only with an imaginary childhood but also an actual father, Shakespeare is able to show how the working out of her choice of object obeys the principle of the repetition compulsion. Indeed, as in *Oedipus Rex*, where Jocasta is both wife and mother to Oedipus, so the tragedy in *Othello* stems from the fact that Othello, initially so open and generous, proves to be all too exact a replica of Brabantio. Othello, as I have suggested, imitates Brabantio's voyeuristic obsession with Desdemona's sexuality;

9. THE PURLOINED HANDKERCHIEF IN *OTHELLO*   179

and when in Act V, Scene ii, Othello enters to murder Desdemona, he carries a lighted taper as Brabantio had done upon being roused by Iago in Act I, Scene i. Similarly, the judicial hearing into Desdemona's alleged sexual misconduct which Othello conducts parallels that demanded by Brabantio following her marriage to Othello (see Heilman, 1956).

The pivotal and fateful scene for the course of the marriage between Othello and Desdemona is that in which she appeals to Brabantio to sanction her passage from the role of daughter to wife. Pleading with her father before the Venetian Senate, Desdemona reminds him of the inevitable transition of generations and says that she perceives a "divided duty":

you are the lord of duty;
I am hitherto your daughter. But here's my husband;
And so much duty as my mother show'd
To you, preferring you before her father,
So much I challenge that I may profess
Due to the Moor, my lord [1.3.184-89].

Desdemona, as Greenblatt (1980) has pointed out, "does not question the woman's obligation to obey, invoking instead only the traditional right to transfer her duty." Yet even this assertion of limited freedom proves intolerable to Brabantio, who, upon hearing Desdemona's declaration, immediately disowns her, "I had rather to adopt a child than get it" (191), and departs from the scene with his prophetic curse against Othello: "Look to her, Moor, if thou hast eyes to see;/ She has deceiv'd her father, and may thee" (292-93).

Brabantio's hostility toward Othello is an extension of that which he feels toward any suitor for his daughter's hand. Desdemona's first wooer in the play is in fact not Othello but Roderigo, Iago's gull, another addition by Shakespeare to his source. When, in the opening scene, Brabantio is awakened by the clamors of Iago and Roderigo, his first reaction is one of annoyance: "In honest plainness thou has heard me say/ My daughter is not for thee" (1.1.97-98). But after learning that Desdemona has eloped with Othello, Brabantio makes common cause with Roderigo in his enmity against the Moor: "O would you had had her!" (175).

Brabantio, it is clear, is an incestuously fixated father, unable to acknowledge his daughter's sexuality. Her choice of Othello, a black man and a foreigner, thus becomes a confirmation of his worst fears, as is evinced by his reaction to the news of her marriage: "This accident is not unlike my dream,/ Belief of it oppresses me already" (1.2.142-43). By blocking instead of facilitating Desdemona's coming of age, Brabantio bequeaths to her an exaggerated version of "the Oedipal curse every sexual relationship undergoes in the process of being assimilated by the patriarchal order of things" (Snow, 1980).

By marrying Desdemona, Othello places himself in the proprietary position formerly occupied by Brabantio. No less than Brabantio, moreover, Othello is unable to tolerate even the slightest waverings in Desdemona's loyalties. "To be once in doubt/ Is once to be resolved," Othello assures Iago, "And on the proof, there is no more but this –/ Away at once with love or jealousy!" (3.3.179-82). Othello's undoing, as Snow (1980) remarks, comes when Iago "is able to make Othello look at himself and Desdemona in terms of Brabantio's warning." Iago reminds him: "She did deceive her father, marrying you" (3.2.206), and Othello, having acceded to the role of Brabantio, can only see in Cassio a version of himself.

Brabantio's curse, the law of the betrayed father, therefore functions as "the equivalent in *Othello* of the oracle" (Green, 1979) in Greek tragedy. As if in illustration of the teachings of psychoanalysis, Shakespeare shows how the existence of genuine chance in human life is not incompatible with the ineluctable workings of the repetition compulsion. *Othello* is notable for its cruel twists of sheer accident (see Stockholder, 1973). Both Emilia's initial finding of the handkerchief and Bianca's entrance as Othello is spying on the conversation between Iago and Cassio are strokes of fortune which Iago, being a masterful improvisator (see Greenblatt, 1980), is able to turn to his advantage. But the outcome of these random events, as far as Othello and Desdemona are concerned, is the fulfillment of Brabantio's curse, that is, their destruction by the infernal machine of tragedy.

So closely is the fate of Othello tied to that of Brabantio that the news of Brabantio's death is only brought by Gratiano in the final scene, after Othello has slain Desdemona:

9. THE PURLOINED HANDKERCHIEF IN *OTHELLO* 181

Poor Desdemon! I am glad thy father's dead.
Thy match was mortal to him, and pure grief
Shore his old thread in twain [5.2.204-06].

Desdemona's marriage was "mortal" to Brabantio, but no less so to her and Othello; and by delaying the announcement of Brabantio's death until the interval between Desdemona's murder and Othello's suicide, Shakespeare repeats the collision between father and husband for a final time over the lifeless body of Desdemona.

IV

The same primal scene fantasies animating Othello as a character are aroused in the audience or readers of Shakespeare's play. Like Othello, who desires to obtain the "ocular proof" of his wife's adultery, we long to pry into the secrets of the matrimonial bedchamber. But just as Othello's quest to look upon the "thing itself" is condemned to deferral and displacement, so too we must content ourselves with no more than the partial gratifications of the "thing instanced."

If, moreover, Othello's sight of Desdemona in Cassio's arms is "always absent" because it does not exist, there are grounds for suspecting a similar problem with regard to the marital relations between Othello and Desdemona. For on every occasion when Othello might be expected to consummate his marriage with Desdemona—at the outset, when they are both at the Sagittary, and subsequently on Cyprus—the lovers are interrupted by alarms raised by Iago. "The purchase made, the fruits are to ensue;/ That profit's yet to come 'tween me and you" (2.3.9-10), Othello says to Desdemona after their reunion on Cyprus. This speech strongly implies that the marriage has not as yet been consummated, and the uproar attendant on the brawl involving Cassio and others, which rouses both Othello and Desdemona, leaves the audience unsure whether they are, in Iago's words, "fast married" (1.2.11) even on Cyprus. I do not claim that the marriage is definitely not consummated, only that Shakespeare deliberately shrouds the matter in uncertainty, and that this ambiguity is of crucial thematic importance to *Othello* (see Cavell, 1979).

Because of the disturbances staged by Iago, the wedding night, on which the play opens, is indefinitely prolonged, and Othello and Desdemona appear to be engaged in a perpetual act of *coitus interruptus* (see Heilman, 1956). The scene of Desdemona's murder, therefore, also becomes that of the consummation of her marriage to Othello. Only in "the final scene, the scene of murder," writes Cavell (1979), is "the thing *denied our sight* throughout the opening scene" acted out before the audience. Desdemona herself is conscious that her death bed is also her marriage bed, since she requests of Emilia, "Prithee to-night/ Lay on my bed my wedding sheets" (4.2.104-05), and further enjoins her prior to singing the "Willow Song": "If I do die before thee, prithee shroud me/ In one of these same sheets" (4.3.24-25).

But the pattern of "imperfect consummation" (Heilman, 1956) established earlier in the play is not resolved even at the moment of Desdemona's murder. Considerable attention is given to the question of how exactly Desdemona is to be murdered. Upon seeing Cassio with the handkerchief, Othello first asks Iago to procure poison; but the latter—speaking with the voice of Othello's own unconscious (see Rogers,1969)—urges: "Do it not with poison; strangle her in her bed, even the bed she hath contaminated" (4.1.207-08), to which Othello responds: "Good, good; the justice of it pleases" (209). When Othello utters his last words before the murder scene, however, a different specter is raised: "'Thy bed, lust-stain'd, shall with lust's blood be spotted" (5.1.36). This imprecation suggests that Othello intends to stab Desdemona, in retaliation for a sexual transgression in which her loss of virginity—whether inside or outside of marriage—becomes indistinguishable from the act of adultery (see Greenblatt, 1980).

But in the murder scene itself, Othello reverts to his plan of smothering or strangulation. Indeed, he places great emphasis precisely on *not* spilling Desdemona's blood:

> Yet I'll not shed her blood,
> Nor scar that whiter skin of hers than snow,
> And smooth as monumental alablaster [5.2.3-5].

Both before and after the murder, Othello uses language that underscores Desdemona's chastity, speaking of the "chaste stars" (2) and expostulating to her dead body: "Cold, cold, my girl?/ Even like thy chastity" (275-76). These references, combined with his refusal to "shed" Desdemona's blood or to "scar" her white skin, reveal Othello's preoccupation with his wife's virginity, which he desires to restore or preserve intact even in death.

Throughout the play, Othello displays an extreme reluctance to accept the passage of time that is inevitable in human life. His ideal seems rather to be to escape from the world of time and change into an infinitely prolonged moment of static perfection. Upon being reunited with Desdemona in Cyprus, his summit of happiness in the play, Othello declares:

If it were now to die,
'Twere now to be most happy; for I fear
My soul hath her content so absolute
That not another comfort like to this
Succeeds in unknown fate [2.1.189-93].

Desdemona, realizing the dangers of equating happiness with death, replies: "The heavens forbid/ But that our loves and comforts should increase/ Even as our days do grow!" (193-95). Desdemona's murder, in addition to sanctifying her virginity, becomes for Othello the means of acting out the necrophilic fantasy that underlies his inability to accept Desdemona as an independent sexual being. "Be thus when thou art dead," he says as he kisses her as she sleeps, "and I will kill thee/ And love thee after" (5.2.18-19). The collapse of the distinction between Desdemona's marriage bed and death bed, grounded in the incestuous curse that transforms Othello into a replica of Brabantio, culminates in Othello's fusion of murder with a still imperfect sexual consummation.

Because even the final scene does not grant us certain knowledge of the status of marital relations between Othello and Desdemona, our own desire for the "ocular proof" remains no less frustrated than that of Othello. This deprivation, as I have indicated, leads not only to prolongation of the wedding night for the duration of the play but also to what psychoanalysts would call "displacements of affect." For example, following the brawl on Cyprus, Iago describes the momentary concord that had reigned among the participants "in terms like bride and groom/ Devesting themselves for bed" (2.3.180-81). In addition to reminding Othello of the interruption of his own sexual activity, Iago's simile cannot fail to pique the curiosity of the audience to learn what is taking place in the bridal chamber. Similarly, the fictitious dream of Cassio's which Iago recounts to Othello, in which Cassio "laid his leg" (3.3.424) across Iago's thigh and cursed Othello's possession of Desdemona, shocks both Othello and the audience with its sexual explicitness, while in reality proving nothing. But just as it is the sight of Cassio with the handkerchief that serves as the exemplary "thing instanced" for Othello, so the handkerchief must replace for the audience what is permanently *"denied our sight."*

That the handkerchief possesses this function also for the audience is illustrated by a further modification of his source made by Shakespeare. In Cinthio (Bullough, 1973), the handkerchief is described in general terms as "embroidered most delicately in the Moorish fashion." But Shakespeare is considerably more specific. In the course of the Temptation Scene, Iago inquires of Othello: "Have you not sometimes seen a handkerchief/ Spotted with strawberries in your wive's hand?" (3.3.434-35). As a signifier, the significance of the handkerchief must reside ultimately in its function and not in its contents. For this reason, impressionistic attempts to ascertain the meaning of the strawberries—such as Wangh's (1950) association to nipples—are likely to remain unconvincing. Nonetheless, some purpose in Shakespeare's innovation must be found, and the key resides in the word "spotted," which links the strawberries embroidered on the handkerchief with the "lust's blood" by which Othello believes his bed to have been "spotted." Thus, as Boose (1975) has argued, in the handkerchief "Shakespeare was representing a visually recognizable reduction of Othello and Desdemona's wedding-bed sheets," though it is not necessary to draw Boose's conclusion that the marriage was therefore consummated.[3] Rather, just as for Othello,

---

3. Ross (1960) discusses the emblematic meanings given to strawberries in the Renaissance, and shows their connection to the ideas of both true and deceitful and good and to the figure of the Virgin Mary.

through its connection with parental sexuality, the handkerchief becomes the substitute for the "primal scene" of Desdemona engaged in intercourse with Cassio, so for the spectator it becomes a symbol of all the "displacements of affect" in the tragedy.

For Rymer, the handkerchief was, specifically, insufficiently *intimate* an article to provide reasonable grounds for Othello's suspicions: "Had it been *Desdemona's* Garter, the Sagacious Moor might have smelt a Rat." But through the identification between the handkerchief and the wedding sheets, Shakespeare shows that precisely the reverse is the case. Indeed, being "spotted" with strawberries as if with blood, the handkerchief may be taken as a "feminine napkin," a symbol of the mysteries of female sexuality.

Othello is unable to love Desdemona without the handkerchief. But it is only the loss of the handkerchief that causes it to acquire value in his eyes. Thus, Rymer's comparison of the handkerchief to a "Garter" comes to seem particularly inspired, because the handkerchief acquires, in a clinical psychoanalytic sense, the status of a fetish, without which Othello is incapable of experiencing sexual attraction to Desdemona (see Green, 1979). As Freud (1927) argued, the explanation of fetishism resides in the male's need to deny that women lack a penis and, therefore, are castrated. It is, of course, in relation to the mother that this fear of castration is first instilled, and the object chosen as a fetish is consequently a substitute ultimately for the absent maternal phallus. That the handkerchief belonged to Othello's mother before being given to Desdemona, and that his father likewise "would hold her loathed" without it, reinforces this interpretation. In addition to all the other optical illusions for which the handkerchief provides a "disgruntled representative"—the "primal scenes" withheld from both Othello and the audience—the maternal penis is perhaps the most disturbing "always absent thing."

When Desdemona reports to Emilia the mistreatment she has received from Othello and pleads, "Alas the day, I never gave him cause," the latter replies:

> But jealous souls will not be answer'd so;
> They are not ever jealous for the cause,
> But jealous for they're jealous. It is a monster
> Begot upon itself, born on itself [3.4.158-62].

This exchange continues to resonate in our minds during the opening lines of Othello's soliloquy as he prepares to murder Desdemona:

> It is the cause, it is the cause, my soul;
> Let me not name it to you, you chaste stars,
> It is the cause [5.2.1-3].

For Othello, the "cause" is the abstract principle of justice, by which he believes his actions to be motivated (see Nowottny, 1952). But his speech is difficult to construe because the word "it" has no antecedent, and thus the "cause" in fact remains unspecified (see Money, 1953). This impersonal construction, however, perfectly conveys the way that Othello's jealousy is itself without a "cause," except insofar as it is a "monster" incestuously arising out of his own mind. The word "cause," derived etymologically from the Latin *causa*, is cognate with the French *chose*, and thus returns us to that Freudian "thing," the absent yet indispensable phallus Othello refuses even to "name."

V

But with this discovery of the meaning of the handkerchief as a fetish, we arrive at the most predictable of psychoanalytic conclusions, which calls forth a Derridean critique. For once we have found the purloined letter or handkerchief "between the legs of the woman," have we not committed ourselves to accepting "the *transcendental* position of the phallus," that is, to a doctrine of "castration as truth," in which something indeed "is missing from its place, but the lack itself is never missing"? (Derrida, 1975).

Just as he lends himself to psychoanalytic interpretation, Shakespeare provides the evidence that makes possible the "deconstruction" of psychoanalysis. Most notably, in the final scene of the play, after Desdemona's murder, Othello follows his description of the handkerchief as a "recognizance and pledge of love" with a *second* account of its origin: "It was a handkerchief, an antique token/ My father gave my mother" (5.2.216-17). From a psychoanalytic perspective, the possibility of reconciling the two

9. THE PURLOINED HANDKERCHIEF IN *OTHELLO*

stories Othello tells is a tempting one. It might plausibly be argued that the later, simpler version is the "true" one, and that the earlier fable concerning the Egyptian "charmer" is a jealous fantasy, invented by Othello on the spur of the moment to test Desdemona's love for him. But to the deconstructive critic, any such attempt to assign priority to one story over the other is wholly misguided, the point of their juxtaposition being the impossibility of arriving at any "unity of the signifier, that is, of the phallus" (Derrida, 1975).

Here, what I have termed the "open" circuit traversed by the handkerchief also comes into play. Lacan (1972) writes in the final sentence of his "Seminar" that "what the 'purloined letter' . . . means is that a letter always arrives at its destination." To this, Derrida (1975) counters that "a letter does *not always* arrive at its destination, and since this belongs to its structure, it can be said that it never really arrives there." The failure of the handkerchief to return to Desdemona gives Derrida's reply to Lacan considerable force. How, then, are we to mediate between the competing views of the handkerchief as representing the "desire for substitution" and all the psychoanalytic tenets summed up in the Oedipus complex?

Johnson (1977) points the way to some answers with her brilliant deconstrution of Derrida's "Disseminar." "When Derrida says that a letter *can* miss its destination," she observes, "he reads 'destination' as a place which preexists the letter's movement." But to hypostatize the notion of "destination" in this manner is to miss Lacan's point, which is that "the letter's destination is not its literal addressee, nor even who possesses it, but whoever is possessed *by* it." Thus, "the very rhetoric of Derrida's differentiation of his own point of view from Lacan's" bears out what Lacan is saying, and "Derrida's remarks *against* psychoanalysis . . . are not *objections* to psychoanalysis but in fact a profound insight into its very essence." Even the discrepancy between Othello's two narratives concerning the handkerchief, which I have cited as an argument for deconstruction, is not so clear-cut, for it is the Lacanian psychoanalyst Green (1979) who insists that "the mystery of this double origin" must not be attenuated by "any simplistic explanation such as, for example, that the Moor made it all up in order to frighten Desdemona."

From the wooing of Desdemona to Othello's suicide speech, *Othello* is a play preoccupied with "narrative self-fashioning" (Greenblatt, 1980). But if, as Lacan maintains, "it is the symbolic order which is constitutive for the subject," every attempt to tell the story of one's life leads not to integration but to self-dispossession. Procuring a hidden weapon with which to stab himself, Othello recalls an only superficially random expression of his loyalty to the Venetian state:

Set you down this;
And say besides, that in Aleppo once,
Where a malignant and a turban'd Turk
Beat a Venetian and traduc'd the state,
I took by th' throat the circumcised dog,
And smote him—thus [5.2.351–56].

At once executioner and victim, insider and outsider, Othello "imposes upon himself this suicide by the sword, inflicting upon himself the castration he abhorred in Desdemona" (Green, 1979). Othello's reference to the Turk as "circumcised"—Moslems as well as Jews being differentiated from Christians by the practice of circumcision—points to this underlying theme of castration, just as the "throat" may be taken as representing an upward displacement for the penis. Thus, even as Othello's life dissolves in his final story, the mark of castration embodied in the handkerchief reinscribes itself.

If *Othello* is illuminated by the reading I have put forward in this paper, this is not because the play in any way *endorses* a "phallogocentric" perspective, but rather because, through its exploration of the "male order of things" (Snow, 1980), it dramatizes the *consequences* of the unconscious fantasies also brought to light by Freud. In any case, as Johnson (1977) notes, "the disagreement between Lacan and Derrida arises not over the *validity* of the equation 'letter = phallus,' but over its *meaning*." Whether psychoanalysis must submit to deconstruction, or vice versa, becomes a moot point when both modes of interpretation are seen to be effects of "the purloined letter of literature" (Johnson, 1977). *Othello* is a tragedy of its jealous hero, but to understand its structure we must "follow the thread of the signifier in the unfolding of the play" (Green, 1979), and thus Rymer spoke more truly than he knew when he protested that Shakespeare ought to have called it "the *Tragedy of the Handkerchief.*"

REFERENCES

Boose, L. E. (1975). Othello's handkerchief: "The recognizance and pledge of love." *English Literary Renaissance, 5,* 360–374.
Bullough, G. (Ed.). (1973). *Narrative and dramatic sources of Shakespeare* (Vol. 7). New York: Columbia University Press.
Cavell, S. (1979). Epistemology and tragedy: A reading of *Othello. Daedalus, 108,* 27–43.
de Man, P. (1979). *Allegories of reading.* New Haven: Yale University Press.
Derrida, J. (1975). The purveyor of truth (W. Domingo et al., Trans.). *Yale French Studies, 52,* 31–113.
Freud, S. (1971). Fetishism. In J. Strachey (Ed. and Trans.), The standard edition of the complete psychological works of Sigmund Freud (Vol. 21, p. 152–157). London: Hogarth Press, 1971. (Original work published 1927)
Gadamer, H.-G. (1975). *Truth and method* (G. Borden & J. Cumming, Eds.). New York: Crossroad. (Original work published 1960)
Green, A. (1979). *The Tragic Effect* (A. Sheridan, Trans.). Cambridge: Cambridge University Press. (Original work published 1969)
Greenblatt, S. (1980). *Renaissance self-fashioning.* Chicago: University of Chicago Press.
Hartman, G. H. (1981). *Saving the text.* Baltimore: Johns Hopkins University Press.
Heilman, R. B. (1956). *Magic in the web.* Lexington: University of Kentucky Press.
Hodgson, J. A., (1977). Desdemona's hankerchief as an emblem of her reputation. *Texas Studies in Literature and Language, 19,* 313–322.
Johnson, B. (1977). The frame of reference: Poe, Lacan, Derrida. *Yale French Studies, 55–56,* 457–505.
Kirsch, A. (1978). The polarization of erotic love in *Othello. Modern Language Review, 73,* 721–740.
Lacan, J. (1972). Seminar on *The Purloined Letter* (J. Mehlman, Trans.), *Yale French Studies, 48,* 38–72. (Original work published 1966)
Levin, H. (1978). *Shakespeare and the revolution of the times.* Oxford: Oxford University Press.
Money, J. (1953). Othello's *It is the cause . . .*: An analysis. *Shakespeare Survey, 6,* 94–105.
Nowottny, W. M. T. (1952). Justice and love in *Othello. University of Toronto Quarterly, 21,* 330–344.

Rogers, R. (1969). Endopsychic drama in *Othello*. *Shakespeare Quarterly, 20*, 205-215.

Ross, L. J. (1960). The meaning of strawberries in Shakespeare. *Studies in the Renaissance, 7*, 225-240.

Rymer, T. (1956). A short view of tragedy. In C. A. Zimansky, (Ed.), *The Critical Works of Thomas Rymer*. New Haven: Yale University Press. (Original work published 1692)

Shakespeare, W. (1974). *Othello*. In G. B. Evans et al., (Eds.), *The Riverside Shakespeare*. Boston: Houghton Mifflin. (Original work performed 1604)

Snow, E. A. (1980). Sexual anxiety and the male order of things in *Othello*. *English Literary Renaissance, 10*, 384-412.

Stockholder, K. S. (1973). Egregiously an ass: Chance and accident in *Othello*. *Studies in English Literature 1500-1900, 13*, 256-272.

Wangh, M. (1950). *Othello*, the tragedy of Iago. *Psychoanalytic Quarterly, 19*, 202-212.

VI LACANIAN INTERPETATION AND THE FRENCH FREUD

10 The Graphic Unconscious

Tom Conley, Ph.D.

Under this title I shall not argue for a specifically psychoanalytic theory of literature. Already the notions of the unconscious, *l'inconscient*, and *Das Unbewusste* are varied and blurred enough to become, when superimposed, the unconscious itself. That the unconscious knows no definition of its essence could allow us to debate for and against anything in the paragraphs to follow. Suffice it to remember that the unconscious has been marshalled to allow myriad interpretations of literature, history, politics, and the human sciences; that it appears to be both a precious and dangerous armament of psychoanalytic rhetoric; that, like *desire*, *Trieb*, *dénégation*, or other concepts of Freudian stamp, it cuts with a double edge. Rather than documenting work done on the unconscious in psychoanalysis and literature in Franco-American schools of the last two decades (roughly, since Lacan's pronouncement that the unconscious is patterned according to principles of classical rhetoric in 1957 to Lacoste's (1981) summation that *Il écrit*, that is, that the unconscious is bound as much to sight and perspective as to transfer of words), I shall sketch the lines of a program of reading and writing literature in terms hypothesizing that the unconscious has been the object of most Western speculation since the early Renaissance. In this tradition the unconscious figures as an absence, a sense of loss, an unattainable but pervasive current of unchannelled force knowing neither time, history, contradiction, or sexual difference. We need only frame our discussion according to the limits that a writer such as de Certeau (1975, 1982) has assigned to it.

> As the seen object can be written, homogeneous with the linearities of the spoken meaning and constructed space, then the *voice* creates an aparté, opens a breach in the text, restores a struggle and a clinch. *Voice off* [p. 246].

More to the point is what we can make of the unconscious not "in" or "of" literature and art, but as their very crux, their essence. Psychoanalysts have already informed critics and historians that the unspoken dimension of a work is absolutely indispensable for its aesthetic articulation, assuring us that an inauthentic work has no unconscious; which is to say, a piece of artistic rubbish—what generally circulates in theaters, galleries, and print, and is passed through most major media—reeks simply because it offers no insoluble problems nor solutions to any of the dilemmas that are intrinsic to its workings (Abraham, 1978). Since criticism generally regulates codes and dispositions of the reading and interpretation of the arts, we find ourselves searching for what cannot be found. Yet since higher education is generally in intimate rapport with the media (one undertakes four years of study in the liberal arts in order to learn how to beware of the ways of the media and how to implement a critique of them—which the media encourages in recognizing that a negative relation with its forms and means will increase its consumption), too often the unconscious becomes an easily discerned effect. With its disappearance comes the end of all literature and art as well as psychoanalysis.[1] Its presence is falsified by an *obvious* presence in words that accord sublimity to everyday life.

---

[1] I am thinking here of Fredric Jameson's "Periodizing the '60's," a lecture delivered in 1980 (in Minneapolis, in a colloquy entitled "Writing Literary History"), in which he argues that late-capital strives to remove every trace of the unconscious from everyday life. It turns events traumatizing subjects into media fictions. On this reading, the Vietnam war was undertaken to mollify the effects of genocide that persisted nightmarishly in our memory of Hiroshima and the concentration camps. The fiction of the war—including television coverage, glossy films such as *The Deer Hunter,* and *Apocalypse Now,* and novels such as

10. THE GRAPHIC UNCONSCIOUS   195

This is why most of the works studied in curricula of literature are difficult, boring, hermetic, sometimes obvious, and often (we hope) of no consequence outside of their own conditions, discourses, and bizarre patterning of their elements. They refuse to make any conciliation with an unconscious, and they deny that they can conjure up its presence through any form of artifice, narrative technique, or other literary maneuver. What we must do is emphasize that the unconscious has invariably to do with the graphic webbings of traits and inscriptions. Today, writers undertake the mystical task of transcribing the rhythms of a language whose voices they see. They script meaning through the visible substance of words and generate fictions from their physical inscription. The sense of literature derives, then, from the play of its unconscious graphics and the content of its voices.

No doubt the advent of silent film concretized the hidden mechanisms of the institution of literature. Its division of images from intertitles dismantled the double unity of linearity and tabularity (or "mimesis" and "diegesis" as Aristotle had cast them) at the basis of most aesthetic expression. For a first time written texts were transported from a surface below our eyes, displaced ninety degrees upward, translated from scripts into moving images—through retinal suspension—in variously modulated frames and projected in continual motion above us. Their hieratic position and unbroken narrative continuity conferred authority upon them and invited the spectator to absorb passively what they offered. For film makers, the ease with which cadences of images and words would control entire masses of viewers was immediately evident; like a new Pantocrator staring down on masses from the ocular hemicycle of a Romanesque church, the film could profess and dictate the workings of the unconscious through differential use of its pictures and words. Here the strength of the medium—its ease in producing ideology—could be subverted from within. Thanks to exemplary countereffects worked by some Cubists and Surrealists, a spectator might view the

---

Dispatches—was written to glorify murder so that its reality, half-awake in our memories of photographs of matchstick corpses piled up like cords of wood at Belsen, would remain dormant or be forgotten, thereby to enable larger production of genocide in the future.

alternate "tracks" producing meaning in ways disarticulating – or theorizing – the production that had put them in parallel line in the first place. Simply by inverting the roles of intellection that the film asks us to play, by *reading* an image where we are told to see it, and by *seing* words and letters as abstract forms in planar relation to the aspect ratio of the frame or in respect to their visible persistence mixing with past (and even forthcoming) shots, we essay the modes producing the narrative layers of meaning.

Here we touch on the production of the unconscious as sedimented surfaces and begin to understand how the history of literature might easily be summed up in the workings of image and sound tracks of cinema. With film, almost every known literary technique is concretized to the point of caricature. Hidden voices of texts are discerned as *off; voice-over* accounts for self-translation; *lap-dissolves* recount, establish, and congeal transitions as virtual rebuses of dream scripts; *fade-ins* denote the accession of the subject to his unconscious; *closed montage* achieves the contrapuntal art that Flaubert had initiated in the *comices agricoles* of *Madame Bovary*, or that Hugo scripted in the visible plan of *La Légende des siècles*, while *open montage* – like much of Vertov's *Man with a Movie Camera* – visualizes the scatter of time in *Le Temps retrouvé*. The medium owes much to the differential pattern of an image to a word either as script or voice adjacent to a picture. In a broad way we can suggest that film immediately summed up what literature had been composing in its graphic strategies for over more than a millenium.[2]

For when we observe words no longer as semantic units whose relations provide coherence or catalyze our desire to comprehend more meaning as we move in a linear course from one sentence to the next, we begin to engage in the writing of literature. We arrest on fragments of style and discover other meanings passing through the letters and figures. This occurs when we ascertain their tabular placement in rapport to themselves as objects in tension with the frame of the page (or paragraph). On another but equally decisive level, our eyes turn to the typographical spacings, the square units marked by a letter or left blank as a gap

---

[2]The cinematography of poetic language is studied exhaustively by Ropars (1981) in the first section of *Le Texte divisé* and "The Erratic Alphabet" (1982).

10. THE GRAPHIC UNCONSCIOUS

among others. With a graphic view of the printed page, we discover that words can be separated into new figures or estranged into bizarre ciphers. A literary text can be tested to see if, at a strictly visual level, its meanings in the grammatical articulations are confirmed, denied, or supplemented. If a relation can be drawn between the figural play of the lettering and the tracing of its meaning, then conditions of allegory—or the graphic unconscious—are provided. The monolithic aspect of a word merely symbolizing a thing is turned into a dynamism of transfer by which an unsettling movement accelerates between the sign of a word and its various configurations in a nexus of currents of other fragmentary signs. Our attention to these other patterns invokes the process of inscription, tracing, erasure, and marking—all originally scenes of the production of signs. Other, new, formerly unknown and unmarked forces come to the fore and circulate between the voices (*off*) of the text and the figural patternings of its characters. When an overload of meaning is produced, or when either a short-circuiting or *mise en abyme* results from tabular and linear readings folded over each other, we begin to discern the unconscious workings of a text. When they are cast, as they are in major media, to produce predictably framed double binds, then we leave the domain of literature and the unconscious. To this I shall return below.

Here some of the mechanics of the unconscious become specific. They are not an amorphous state capitulated by *lack*, *béance*, *trou*, hole, crevasse, enigma, *faille*, or any other metaphor of absence. Rather, they are always attached to a mode of framing and suspension and are directed according to principles by which, we might suggest, the visual arts can be seen determining the networks of most literary texts. Schematically outlined: Unconscious dimensions are glimpsed when we see words as a function of Albertian perspective on the printed page. At certain crucial junctures, words or letters having no specific value in the writing acquire overdeterminate status when viewed (1) as part of the surround, border, or edge of a text; (2) as the mark occluding a vanishing point or spotting an axis in dialectical relation between center and circumference of a page or block of words; (3) as a hidden cipher, signature, or apothegm placed at the illusion of the origin of the frame, in any of the corners that opens onto its extension. By virtue of these three possibilities of visual scansion, we begin to see where other recurrences and obsessional markings are placed, as it were (if an architectural metaphor can be adjoined in the pictural ones tendered so far), in the *spandrels* of the text, in the areas between the major lines of perspective defining illusory depths of the page.[3] Once the three modes of viewing disengage layers of countermeaning or transferential junctures elsewhere, their grid can be put aside for even closer readings, by which in turn the same principles will be applied to a more narrowly defined border of sentences, single words, and letters.

Early modern literature forms the basis for a simultaneously perspectival and linear feel of the page. Almost all lyric poetry of the French Renaissance is composed to body forth an evanescent frame, a series of centers or crossings, lemmas, anamorphic inscriptions, or mobile cartouches. A visual reading of these poems can be as productive as thematic or comparative ones. A first example can illustrate how, in the late 15th century, the writer's craft entailed production of an obvious unconscious along the visible configurations of words. In Jean Molinet's quodlibet, a circumstantial rhyme entitled "*Un dictier joyeux*" (that elsewhere has been called a sterile poem because it matches ciphers and script in order to have us count mechanically from one to twenty in fourteen lines—yet as far as I know, it is the earliest evidence in France of a prototypical sonnet, a good fifty years before the genre's first official recognition in the work of Marot and Melin de Saint-Gelais), the ruse of writing and reading involves substitution of figures for words:

UN DICTIER JOYEUX

Ung homme est pendu au gibet
Me dict ung tres ord quodlibet

---

[3]The angular position of the text at its cardinal extremity has been associated with the irruption of its visual dimension. Where the horizontal and vertical coordinates cross, we encounter the unstable area where voice and script converge, or where we apprehend the graphic form that generates their division, their angularities, or, further back, their *anguish*. This is what Finas (1974) determines in her reading of the incipit of Bataille's "Madame Edwarda." Lebensztejn (1981) builds much of his *Zigzag* from this concept.

10. THE GRAPHIC UNCONSCIOUS

Qu'as tu ores, quoquin, quetis
Qui les brayes secs n'as toudis
Car foire au cul as en septembre
Octobre, novembre, decembre
On se doit monstrer doux et gent
Tres aimable a toute gent
En purgatoire seront mis
Quoquins et qui hait ses amis
Toudis scet Dieu que jadis wit
De sens fut Adam et seduict
D'Eve en paradis neuf, ou vint
Sathan, par qui ce mal advint

A JOYOUS DICKER

One man is duly hanged at the gibbet
Tells me a very dirty quodlibet
What are you for, you dumb ass
You with your britches that are so crass
For you've a fiery touchhole in September
October, November [and] December
Levity we must always show in good dose
And be affable to many and to most
Purgatory will be among the ends
For fools who hate their friends
God only knows that formerly void
of reason was Adam, who could not avoid
Eve in the paradise garden where
Satan came to bring evil to our sphere

We must count the poem in its visual scheme to detect the symbolic blockages that figures obtain within the narration:

Ung (1) homme est pendu (2) au gibet,
Me dict ung tres (3) ord quodlibet.
Qu'as tu ores (4), quoquin (5), quetis,
Qui les brayes secs (6) n'as toudis,
Car foire au cul as en septembre (7),
Octobre (8), novembre (9), decembre (10).
On se (11) doit monstrer doux et (12) gent
Tres (13)aimable a toute gent;
En purgatoire se(14)ront mis
Quoquins (15)et qui hait ses (16)amis;

> Toudis scet (17) Dieu que jadis wit (18)
> De sens fut Adam et seduict
> D'Eve en paradis neuf (19), ou vint (20)
> Sathan, par qui ce mal advint (−20).

At the center of the *dictier*, set in diagonal between the upper left angle of *ung* and *vint* at the lower right-hand edge, are two lines both central and of eccentric location:

> On se doit monstrer doux et gent
> Tres amiable a toute gent.

The demonstrative figure that illustrates the poem is the verb *monstrer* at the key of its imaginary vault. Between *onze* and *douze*, *monstrer* is just beyond the midsection of the sonnet and set adjacent to an odd, monstrous sign of eleven (a truly weird number—an even of two identical integers that are mirrored or duplicated perfectly but refer to a condition opposite to their figural shape) and a sacred even of twelve, a number rich in Christian iconography. Since the rectangular frame of the verse points back and forth from axis to edge, and because the discourse has no stability—its ciphers begin to appear everywhere in the poem, both within and next to the obvious numbers—the thing, the *res* accompanying the verb *monstrer*, its verbal illustration, can be found in the nominal reading of the clause *on se doit*: We see an evanescent hand coming through the page, the hand of God or the Devil, but a hand presaged by eleven fingers. *Onze doigts monstrés*—eleven digits seem to figure a sacred form that is both covering and spotting the vanishing point of the lyric. As such, Molinet institutes an unconscious graphic dimension through modes of a third layer of writing glimpsed between the linear and tabular (or numerical) readings he superimposes on the same plane. The frame of numbers, the central mark of monstrosity, and the *other* apothegm within the central couplet—*onze doigts monstrés au lieu de dix*, a sight not at all *tres aimable a toute gent*—generate a violent undercurrent.

But a third figural level may serve to reveal another. So far the poem has written of itself, of a visible representation of the counting of its cadences. The poet taps his fingers as he scripts fourteen lines. The poem is more urgently about what it is to measure rhymes as it writes an array of Christian triusms. Hence it economizes its composition by treating its own rhythmic problems in a figural dimension, yet only to reflect—and here is the fourth layer of the text—on its economy of an economy of means. The axial position of *monstrer*, a figure struck both with *verba* and *res*, a word and a thing, points to its own iconographical saturation that refers to a mechanical timepiece at the center of the text. This would concur with the first meaning that argues for Christian goodness. "On se doit monstrer doux et gent, Tres aimable a toute gent," contends for moderation and temperance, attributes personified in the 15th century by the Goddess of Time, parsimony, and economy, Dame Attrempance or Temperantia. Praise of God is condensed with that of a goddess of a new, pragmatic ideology which appeals to archaic deities in order to promote a proto-rational view based on the ascending class of plenary invidivuals.[4] Here the play of graphics disengages a nascent political history within and beyond the poem.

It can be argued that Molinet's is a technique common to an epistemology far different from ours; that, indeed, Holbein's "Ambassadors" sums up the renascent fascination with the square of the frame and the cipher of death better than lyrics from *La Grande Rhétorique* to D'Aubigné. That an epoch involved with optical invention focuses its obsessions on words would make short shrift of the utter modernity of their compositions. We need only recall that, in general, poets read each other and recast their strategies irrespective of periods that historians have made for convenient classification. That Henry James explicitly composed and entitled *The Ambassadors* according to the mode and method of Holbein is proof enough of the timelessness of the graphic unconscious in the hands of artists.

To essay the principle in another period, we can focus attention on a page of a recent play by Marguerite Duras. We open *Savannah Bay* (1982) and fall upon a section of dialogue between an old "Madeleine" and a *Jeune Femme*. In a voice-over of sorts, the latter retells in her words the tales she remembers from the voice of

---

[4]The iconography of Temperance is documented by Miess (1976). See also White (1969).

the former. The *Jeune Femme* speaks through Madeleine's past and confuses her personal pronoun with the third person singular of the older woman at a time of love in oblivion. The monologue – or, might we ask, is it a dialogue scripted into a trace of monologue? – evokes a time of lost union reseparated in narrative. It also beckons a scene of ravishment we remember from the story of *Lol V. Stein, Le Vice-consul,* or the memory images of *India Song*. But at the center of the flashback there is an absence marked by *les eaux de la houle,* whose verbal rhythm reproduces the graphic punctuation of memory going away, losing sight of itself on a wider horizon and then returning:

... à fleur d'eau, la pierre, la houle la recouvrait d'eau fraîche puis le soleil revenait et en quelques secondes la rendait infernale, de nouveau brûlante, c'était l'été. Elle était très jeune, à peine sortie du collège. Elle nageait loin. On ne savait jamais. Jamais. On ne savait jamais si elle reviendrait. Il y avait des moments ... on aurait pu croire que non ... pendant quelques minutes ... qu'elle ne reviendrait jamais. (*Temps*). Elle revenait. (*Temps*). Ils s'étaient connus là. Il l'avait vue allongée, souriante, régulièrement recouverte par les eaux de la houle ... et puis il l'avait vue se jeter dans la mer et s'éloigner...(*Temps*). Elle a troué la mer de son corps et elle a disparu dans le trou d'eau. La mer s'est refermée. A perte de vue on n'a plus rien vu que la surface nue de la mer, elle était devenue introuvable, inventée. Alors tout à coup il s'est dressé sur la pierre blanche. Il a appelé. Un cri. Pas le nom. Un cri. (*Temps*). Et à ce cri, elle est revenue. Du fond de l'horizon un point qui se déplace, elle. (*Temps*). C'est quand il l'a vue revenir... il a souri... elle a souri, et ce sourire....

(... skimming the surface, the stone, the surf covered her with fresh water, then the sun returned and in a few seconds made her infernal, burning again, it was summer. She was very young, scarcely out of high school. She swam far. We never knew. Never. We never knew if she would return. There were moments .. we might have thought no ... for a few minutes that she'd never come back. (*Time*). She used to come back. (*Time*). They met there. He had seen her stretched out, smiling, usually covered by the waters of the surf ... and then he saw her jump in the ocean and disappear...(*Time*). She punctured the sea with her body and she disappeared in the hole of water. The ocean closed again. Beyond

10. THE GRAPHIC UNCONSCIOUS

the horizon we saw nothing more than the bare surface of the sea, she became impossible to find, even invented. Then all of a sudden he leapt up on the white stone. He called. A cry. Not her name. A cry. (*Time*). And with this cry, she returned. From the depth of the horizon she is a moving point. (*Time*). And when he saw her come back ... he smiled ... she smiled, and this smile....)

The parentheses surrounding the center are the playwright's indications about how to punctuate the monologue. They opt for long pauses between the enunciation of the sentences at the vanishing point of the revery. Three (*temps*) mark *il*'s view of *elle* in the waters; they seem to recur with the same insistance as *jamais* associated with her at the beginning of the passage. By catching (*temps*) or *jamais* as visible attributes of *elle*, Madeleine, who is an avatar of the *Jeune Femme* who swam in the surf, all of a sudden we learn that *elle* is labeled parenthetically in the proper name of *Time* (or weather, or seasonal change). The unconscious irrupting from the graphic surface of the parenthesis takes the form of the enigmatic, wizen fiigure of Madeleine. Proustian echoes from *Combray* interfer almost hilariously, as do our images remembered of Madeleine Renaud playing many roles in Duras' other plays (among *Des journées entières dans les arbres*). Madeleine is Time itself. "The unconscious knows no time," we realize in recalling Freud's dictum, but in glimpsing the graphic rendering of the passage, we discover that perhaps time, (or news, or weather) *is* the unconscious: In Duras' text, it literally emerges from a visible pattern set almost fortuitously in the script of the two voices read through each other. They meet only where they cannot, in an aside or a parenthetical silence of the characters on the printed page.

Until now I have theorized that a view of the edge, border, and axes of a text can disengage closures on the threshold of an unconscious of writing. A pictural view can loosen the grip that narratives hold upon us; it can allow us to refashion the work and to find obsessive junctures that literally write it and confer uncanny continuities upon it. But attention to the design of a frame in rapport with the mass of meaning of the words it surrounds now brings us to a second stage of theory. Here, schematically again, we can draw attention to the function (1) of single letters as copulas of various skeins of meaning that counterweave or are of a thread of a different color than those of grammatical design in the vocal layer of the text (in graphic shapes of alliteration, assonance, in presence of transitional terms such as *cependant,* therefore, *et,* so, *mais, ainsi, voilà,* etc.). These become phantasmatic marks propelling or arresting the writing; they are significant insofar as they mark the simultaneous return and repression of dimensions of which the work cannot speak. It would not be unwise to speculate that over the last two decades almost all psychoanalytic reading of literature of Lacanian inspiration in France has taken place in these areas. No better illustration of an application of tacitly Lacanian conclusions to this mode can be cited than that at the center of *S/Z,* a work confirming what elsewhere (1982) Roland Barthes noted apropos of Massin's *La Lettre et l'image*: "All poetry, all the unconscious are a return to the letter" (p. 95). Yet the relation of the hidden or embedded letter we retrieve as a point both releasing and binding the energies producing literature opens onto (2) the double relation instituted by the letters of a title (or characters of the name of an author just below it) to their recurrence in the text beneath them. Here we encounter the emblematic aspect of both poetry and prose. When we seek the inscription of the title within the contents of a work, we are of course striving to make a rebus of the figure that initiates our consciousness of a text. Seen again, it becomes a condensation—a stenographic, mnemonic summation—of the originary violence of the author's writing at the very time it displaces meaning from the head to the body of the work. Writers are always casting titles into their work or disallowing their entry. Sometimes the title becomes our production. We think of Duchamp who names a snow shovel hanging in a museum "In Advance of a Broken Arm" to deflect our anticipation of the title we would put forward in the name of mimesis—*snow shovel,* which is to read that, now in a museum, "it's *no(w)shovel."* The shift from title to object theorizes the stake of the readymade. Strong visual use of titles in and about their texts and attributes removes the statically symbolic relation of words reflecting the world; it makes of symbolism a dynamic network of vocal and visual recurrences and drives over and beyond mimesis (or causality) we associate with narrative representation.

The relation of a title to the work below it has a long visual tradition that is worth reviewing. The heading is placed in *superscription* while the text is its *subscription*. According to emblematics, between these two lines must be inscribed an image that mediates the condensed, enigmatic shape (often in a foreign language) above and its longer explanation in vulgar form below (see Klein, 1970). It might be that most literature since the Renaissance partakes of this configuration; if so, many works will require a plastic reading of their graphic mediation. The dynamics of (1) the letter and (2) the emblematic aspect of a textual object can allow us to designate a third area, (3) where, in a fashion following the emblematic tradition, the unconscious is visualized as a hidden, universal *langue* in the imaginary space between one language and another—framed by extension of single words and their spacings. When other words—whether homonyms, cognates, or completely different but identical words from a foreign language can be read coherently across (or *anamorphically*, as it were) a given text in a manner adding other logical dimensions to it, then we see the birth of a hybrid but crucially modern literature. When it was written self-consciously in the Renaissance, the name awarded to it was "macaronic." But today, when the unconscious has a ruseful presence in writing, the designation cannot hold. For languages now slip and waver, they press onto and englobe each other. Discourse can no longer obey laws of genre or analogy.

Here we must return to three or four examples. The first—and perhaps the most brutally evident—instance confirming the latency of emblems can be found in the diamond-shaped sign that makes us smile when we are driving through suburbs. We are told to decelerate since children may be playing near the road: We read a panel that emblazons SLOW over an embossed image of a boy (usually in knickers) running to the left. His feet prance over the word CHILDREN at the bottom. Our first reaction is to speed up (we would do humanity a service in ridding the world of an imbecile since *slow children* are near the road). Or do we shift gears because, by virtue of habit or for reason of an asyndeton that results from the configuration of the emblem, we infer that there is nearby a school or hospital for retarded youth? The sign elicits a violent reaction exactly where it orders us to be prudent. The double bind is not miraculous: It is generated by the contradiction between a purely limited, local meaning and the longstanding visual tradition which has dictated the triadic composition. The image of the child framed by the borders in *subscriptio* and *superscriptio* is part of a ploy that puts the viewer at a momentary loss as to how to read and see the words.

In reflecting on the effect of the emblem as we drive, we realize that more often than not the brand of car in which we are riding has been coded according to the same rules. If we are at the wheel of a recent *Dodge*, for example, we begin to read the word and letter image of the model, the *Aries K*, in a similar – but now horizontal – way. The *K* subscribes the initial superscription of *A*. We gloss *ries* as an image to discover that in the frame of the letters is not to be found the mythic figure of a phallic Aries but the homonym of the unconscious, the reading of A RISK. To buy and to drive an Aries K is to take a deadly risk.

The moment of fear and desire – of ideology – we are told to experience in the ambiguity of a text as an image and vice versa in most media is what most modern literature takes as its task to undo. In a word, contemporary literature theorizes the double binds of the type that we see everywhere in daily life. Since we have designated "modern" beginning with the later 15th century, our second example can be drawn from Montaigne. At the outset of "De trois commerces," we spot the emblematic procedure that generates the tensions of all the later essay:

CHAPITRE III: De trois commerces

Il ne faut pas se cloüer se fort à ses humeurs et complexions.
We must be nailed so strongly to our humors and complexions.

Book III and essay number three appear to inspire the topic of three modes of diversion. The order imposed by the numbers forces a tone of writerly nonchalance: "If today is the third of March, and if I was born in '33, why not write about threes this morning?" The words that assume the shape of an image are those of the title; the foreign cipher is the Roman numeral in superscription while, below, the incipit should reflect or explicate – even summarize – the two terms above because its position in subscription requires it to do so. But no, the sentence sabotages them: No sooner than Montaigne strikes triads in word and image, he writes of quadruples—four humors and four complexions are nailed to the frame of *fort* or *furca* (*ci fort*) that is a division of two. When doubled, the two jumps to four over the three. The force of the tourniquet spins from the tension of its dysymmetry in the order of the relation of the letter and figure of the text to the markings of its title. As such the beginning reflects on the spiral of logic that reproduces the turn of the screw of the printing press embossing the title where it is; and it entertains the frame of an absence of figures and figuration that dominates the project of the *Essais*. This suggests why Montaigne so often speaks of himself vaingloriously in the third person, as a writer who "faict des *Essais* qui ne sauroit faire des effets" (Paris: Gallimard-Pleiade, 1962, p. 971). He is scripting a visible homonym of *Effais* and *effect* (the *s* almost identical to the *f* in 16th-century typography): This book has no sufficient intention; its origin is an effect, an unconscious totality wrapped in the trace of its cause.

Montaigne's play of graphic and voice in the shifts of single letters, in emblematic dispositions of lines, and in the rapport of titles (as images) to their text (luring of voice) is repeated identically in modern letters, and no writer is better aware of this than Samuel Beckett. We need only glance at the visible shape of the titles in his recent work. In *Têtes mortes* (1972) he appears to translate and then encrypt pieces he wrote earlier in his career under the sign of a row of death's heads (in printers' jargon, "une tête" designated a capital letter[5]). But the work of the character and title open onto a broader issue of an unconscious *langue* written across the graphics. A final volume, *Têtes mortes*? Or an algebraic continuum of "tes-tes-mor-tes-tes-tes-mor-tes-tes-tes-mor-tes-tes-tes-mor-tes," etc.? The writing cannot logically come to completion by force of the pattern of the graphemes *tes* and *mos* across, on the one hand, English and French and, on the other, the passage from and to a referent of classical painting of still-lives.

This is not all. Beckett adds the names of the tales under the heading *Têtes mortes* in a brief parenthesis: (*D'un ouvrage*

---

[5]Montaigne explains this in "Considération sur Cicéron": "I pile up heads only to lay out others."

abandonné, bing, sans, assez). The first of the series can function either as a title that mediates *bing, sans,* and *assez*. But the sign of the *memento mori* requires the title to transliterate through itself and its former titles—"Done over age a band (un) done né." It is born dead and then when un-, done, alive, *né*. If this unbinds or unbands the name of the work, if it releases the confusion of life and death from its scansion of itself, then other titles that crown Beckett's work can be brought into play. The Band of *d'un ouvrage abandonné* refers to *a Dernière Bande* which is *donné* (done *ne*) on the same page listing the works of earlier date, and so on. Then *Bing*, the proper name, is a pervasive echo of "B-ing," a letter which is a present participle of the verb that *to be*, being, is not. "*Bing, sans, assez*": As always in Beckett's cryptography, the final term recurs like the repressed which is released when seen and heard at once. So *assez* is quite enough after begin *sans;* or it is a statis of the meditation which the titular death's head has evoked in calling for a position of *ascèse* (pronounced literally *a*-say-*z* in an Anglo-Irish gloss of *assez*, a word that englobes the beginning and end of the alphabet). This graphically reveals the entire posture of Beckett's works. They are always about scenes of meditation about writing.

We can wonder if, perhaps, we hasten too quickly to conclusions about the translinguistic unconscious of Beckett without our having made a requisitely dense or protracted—ascetic—reading. We can surmise that the graphic unconscious disallows the metaphysics of search because it recoups all of the tension of hermeneutics in the play of its surfaces in every repeated inscription. These are always of the same essence but share different tonalities in modern poetry and prose. The marking may change from author to author (every one has a different set of characters with which to write) but the process does not. We can venture positing that most literature reflects its unconscious according to the same limits of graphic chance. If this is true, we should be tempted to conclude that literature can no longer be found in the field of belles-lettres, but somewhere in derivation of the art of psychoanalysis. Texts elicit our will to cure them of their figural neuroses. Cases of sorts, modern texts force the reader to listen to their graphics and to engage in the allegorical dreamwork of latencies always present on their figural surfaces.

10. THE GRAPHIC UNCONSCIOUS

To essay these remarks, we can return to the thirty-third page of *Savannah Bay*:

> Elle était très jeune, à peine sortie du collège. Elle nageait loin. On ne savait jamais. Jamais. On ne savait jamais si elle reviendrait. Il y avait des moments ... on aurait pu croire que non ... pendant quelques minutes ... qu'elle ne reviendrait jamais.
>
> She was very young, hardly out of college. She used to swim far. They never knew. Never. They never knew if she would return. There used to be moments ... they might have believed otherwise ... for a few minutes ... that she would never return.

To repeat, time is present because it (parenthetically) suspends. Now the visible echoes of Duras' poetry, the recurrent *on ne savait jamais*, congealing from one line to the next, reflect and diffract the title in which their letters are held in both emblematic and translinguistic relation. *Savannah Bay* is an unconcious scripting of *on ne savait jamais*. The echo is masked by the seeming distance (that we usually maintain) between the English and the French. Cut between the tongues, *on ne savait jamais Savannah Bay*. Bay is B, *bée*, a *béance* opened by the immediacy of time knowing no difference of language, space, or continent. An American reader calls up images of peaches and hears a southern drawl of Savannah, Georgia, but anyone who knows the paths of figural typology and the great Hegelian migrations of script to voice in its *translatio studii* between the Orient and the West, Savannah returns to Laos, to Savannahket, a town near the bay of the Mekong delta. All the nightmare of the wars in Indochina and Vietnam are congealed in the erotic passage of the title into the topographical latency of the words *on ne savait jamais*. Ever more since, like them, the place is unnamed but rewritten to modulate the title of the play it will have become at the end of its reading. Before the text draws to a close, Madeleine tells us that Henry Fonda will play a central role in it. Upon hearing a love song, Madeleine intercedes, "C'était Henry Fonda, c'était Savannah Bay, c'était dans une pièce de théâtre: Titre: Savannah Bay. Acteur: Henry Fonda" (p. 83). The late Hollywood actor is little more than a function of his displacement into a stage drama that never took place, and through which his transliterated name *En ri Fonda* – melting into a laughter of tears – forces the *onde*, the *undus*, the where of the waters, to flow back into the voice of Time in the name of Madeleine. Here the names, titles, and mixes of language pry open a historical and political dimension through the graphics of the text.

For the most part, work of this facture defines current conditions of literature. Wherever languages are in flux because of historical and demographic shifts, literature reflects and reproduces their confusions and forces. And the more the texts are confused, the better indeed is the literature. It loses its monolingual look and therefore tampers with the ideology producing meaning. It has heteroclite garb and cannot, like difficult style, quite easily be forgotten.

We can theorize the beginning and end of this period of writing as being situated, first, on the distant end of the spectrum, in the Renaissance; its surfaces today in the many postwar eras since 1945. In the early 16th century the writing class blossomed with trade and new modes of circulation. It developed exactly from confusions of tongues in which, as Latin lost its strength as a language of Law, vulgar tongues became median languages that would stand between Rome and the thousands of dialects around them. No doubt written documents became literature in the ways that managed to make of their ruses official social forms. The play that initiated their compositions became repressed. Text and image separated in the course of the Reform and only now have converged again and slipped over each other.

It can be added that today no regional usage or national literature remains intact; each is written already translated into what it speculates to be in money or use-value. Before formulating six points characterizing the types of analysis that can release the graphic unconscious from art and literature, we alluded to the fact that many contemporary works fail because they try to impose an unconscious upon us. In their form they construct predictable double binds. The works fail because they move or enervate us, because they are pleasing, or because they sell on the basis of small doses of fear they draw from us in promoting the spectator or reader to believe in the existence of emotive depths, or to have faith in our own affective reactions to their style. (Such would be the sensuous pace and framing of films like *Bonnie and Clyde* or *The Tin Drum*; the crapulously "heroic" expressionism of Julian Schnabel; Warhol's accessible ironies; the breathtaking serenity of Irving's *Garp*.) In these the former workings of the six types of rift of word and image generate calculated effects. Nothing heterogenous to their systems of meaning interrogates them from within: They remain pure and sublime and, even worse, unified in their message.

Because many productions of modern art employ the graphic unconscious for the purpose of shackling the buyer, we must now see if our analysis can carry a political dimension. Painfully evident is the fact that the title of this essay almost plagiarizes Jameson's (1981) *Political Unconscious*. Jameson argues that all reading of modern literature is—whether readers like it or not—virtually Marxian. He writes of six arcs of a great hermeneutic circle spliced together from Auerbach's figural typology, Frye's "anatomies" of literature, Lukács' totalizing literary history, Greimas's semiotic gridding, Lévi-Strauss's anthropology of myth, and Freudian dreamwork. They all turn around an absent center of the Marxian project he puts at their axis. The configuration of the book is its own unconscious. As Jameson says with recurrent circularity in the last sentence, "That is, after all, what Marxism is all about." The unconscious Marxism of that sentence is in effect its own will to encircle or copyright everything in its own name. In doing so, it purposefully alienates everything that goes unquestioned in our daily lives, and in this fashion it cuts into the unconscious dimensions, the ideologies and nightmares of politics that are that the bottom of all representation.[6] Wrong or right, Jameson's process always has to be right because it reaches back to the "absent causes," or the gaps that open onto the unnameable march of History, a history knowing no finality or event or specific time and place. Because History and politics are the unconscious, we can frame and eventually disaggregate some of the ideologies that control us.

Throughout his analysis Jameson uses the concept of the *ideologueme* as a first step toward a process of change within the field of literary criticism. An *ideologueme* can be defined as a min-

---

[6]On this score it would be productive to trace Jameson's synthesis of the concept of *alienation* and compare it to Lacan's productive use of *séparation* in "Position de l'inconscient," in *Ecrits* (1966). This would be the topic of a longer study.

imal sign of social contradiction held within an utterance, a design, or a turn of style in any piece of modern literature. His appreciation of the concept is thematic – almost rapidly immaterial – while ours is virtually materialist – that is, grounded in the evidence of ink, image, paint, and paper. Here, in an apposite manner, as the title "The Graphic Unconscious" would suggest, the study of art as a political and historical form can be executed across the tension of image and word of more texts of the literary canon. By *viewing* literature, by alienating its words or voices into images and back and forth, we begin to politicize the field of criticism. If a Sartrean term can be dug out of the oblivion of the fifties, this sort of praxis turns reading and writing into an *act of literature.*

It does not accept sublime artifacts as given truth or stable objects to be treated according simply to the codes that inform it. This would be tantamount to stylistics and would pay little heed to the history of inscription in both the production of a text in its time and our use of it in ours. By supposing that the graphic part of a text is the bedding of much of its unconscious, we draw our attention to areas that reading often takes for granted. And, as we have shown, wrong or right, this mode of analysis has the option of disengaging in an ethical coup the ideological – that is, the beautiful, the tantalizing, the charming or attractive, even ugly – side of the arts in view of our need often to refuse to buy them. It accounts on all levels for the mediations that its figural supports provide for a work. Analysis of the graphic unconscious not only writes new works from old ones, but it also heralds conditions for the possibility of resurgent vanguards. By this I suggest that figural readings of texts can determine some degree of their mediation, degrees to which they are written to be sold, marketed, and passed off. In the areas where fragments of major media are tossed back into analysis, patterns of graphic residue can be shaped into new collages that make, finally, of interpretation, something resembling a work of art.

In a specifically psychoanalytic context the work at stake would be identical to discoveries of *symbolic blockages*, that is, areas where a text or discourse arrests and encapsulates itself in the difference of intellection that the Western tradition of reading versus seeing has maintained in its ideology over the last four centuries or at least since the advent of Alciati. Now, after having disengaged a politics of the unconscious as we have through a contrast between the project sketched next to the thematic Marxism of Jameson, by way of conclusion we can suggest that our work literally eradicates the unconscious as a viable concept.[7] For where we ascertain differences that produce ambiguity and confusion, we condense the unconscious into a rebus of image and voice, but we also unlace it from the very knots where we discovered it. When the unconscious is rendered graphic, it no longer exists. Yet since it is everywhere and nowhere, it must be arrested right here, period

REFERENCES

Abraham, N. (1978). Le temps, le rythme et l'inconscient. In: *L'Ecorce et le nayau*. Paris: Aubier-Flammarion.
Barthes, R. (1982). *L'Obvie et l'obtus; essais critiques III*. Paris: Seuil.
Beckett, S. (1972). *Têtes mortes*. Paris: Editions de Minuit.
de Certeau, M. (1975). *L'Ecriture de l'histoire*. Paris: Gallimard.
_____ (1982). *Le Fable mystique*. Paris: Gallimard.
Duras, M. (1982). *Savannah Bay*. Paris: Editions de Minuit.
Finas, L. (1974). *La Crue*. Paris: Gallimard.
Jameson, F. (1981). *The Political Unconscious*. Ithaca, NY: Cornell University Press.
Klein, R. (1970), *La Forme et l'intelligible*. Paris: Gallimard.
Lacan, J. (1966). Position de l'inconscient. In *Ecrits*. Paris: Seuil.
Lacoste, P. (1981). *Il écrit. Une mise en scène de Freud*. Paris: Galilée.
Lebensztejn, J.-C. (1981). *Zigzag*. Paris: Flammarion.
Miess, M. (1976). *French Painting in the Time of the Limbourgs*, Vol. 1. New York: Braziller.
Ropars, M.-C. (1981). *Le Texte divisé*. Paris: P.U.F.
_____ (1982). *The Erratic Alphabet*, 10–11, pp. 147–161.
White, L. (1969). *Temperantia* and the virtuousness of technology. In *Action and Commitment in Early Modern Europe*. Princeton: Princeton University Press.

---

[7]The notion of *symbolic blockage* belongs to the analytic vocabulary of Bellour, a critic of film and literature known for his work on Hitchcock and the Brontë sisters. Its psychoanalytic resonance is manifest in an exchange conducted between him and the Lacanian analyst Rosolato in *Hors cadre* (1983), 1:150–167, a publication on film theory and cultural analysis published by the University of Paris VIII, Vincennes à Saint-Denis.

11 Burying the Treasure: Forgetting as Creative Work in Freud and in Proust[1]

Jerry Aline Flieger, Ph.D.

> *And yet, even when nothing remains of the past, after the death of human beings and the disintegration of objects . . . odor and taste linger on, like souls, to recall, to wait, to hope, above the ruins of all else, in order one day to bear without faltering, on their nearly impalpable droplets, the immense edifice of memory.*
>
> *(Mais, quand d'un passé rien ne subsiste, après la mort des êtres, après la destruction des choses . . . l'odeur et la saveur restent encore plus longtemps, comme des âmes, à se rappeler, à attendre, à espérer, sur la ruine de tout le reste, à porter sans fléchir, sur leur gouttelette presque impalpable, l'édifice immense du souvenir.)*
> —Marcel Proust, A la Recherche du temps perdu, I

> *All that is to live in immortal song,*
> *Must first be submerged in life.*
> (Was unsterblich in Gesang soll Leben,
> Muss im Leben untergehn.)
> —Schiller as cited by Freud (1939), in *"Moses and Monotheism"* [p. 101]

WRITER AS WORKMAN

Much of Freud's writing is concerned with the concept of forgetting as actual psychic work—rather than the mere weakening of memory through time—a labor which entails the repression of problematic material and its storage in the unconscious. In

---

[1] This paper was first presented at the 1982 Convention of the Modern Language Association.

"Moses and Monotheism" (1939), for example, Freud characterizes the forgetting-work as a task of isolation or burial of problematic memories:

> The forgotten material is not extinguished, only repressed; its traces are extant in the memory in their original freshness, but they are isolated by "counter-cathexes." They cannot establish contact with other intellectual processes; they are unconscious, inaccessible to consciousness [p. 94].

The metaphor of motivated forgetting or repression as a kind of burial is explicit in several of Freud's earlier works, including "Civilization and its Discontents" (1930), where Freud compares the individual psyche to a great city that has been built and rebuilt on the same site, leaving traces and artifacts of former periods in the earth below. Thus all forgotten material, Freud maintains, is not only "buried" in a kind of psychic cellar storehouse, but is "somehow preserved, and in suitable circumstances may be brought to light" (p. 69).

Marcel Proust's creative *recherche* is in large part, of course, just such an effort to "bring to light" or to "establish contact with" material isolated in his unconscious store, and by so doing, undo the psychic work of forgetting. Indeed, Proust's celebrated characterization of the work of fiction as an "immense edifice of memory" (I, p. 47; all translations of Proust are mine) casts the writer in the role of contractor-architect, a workman who strives to erect a monument to lived experience through the constructive labor of remembrance. Proust's architectural metaphor emphasizes the solidity of the edifice created by the master-builder, but this same imagery also suggests that the narrative structure, however solid, has a tenuous foundation. Upheld only by ghostly pillars of sensation ("odor and tast linger on, like souls"), the work seems to rise up out of the wreckage of memory, "above the ruins of all else." The writer reconstructs the past at a demolition site, out of the rubble of memories eroded and pulverized by the inexorable progress of forgetting. Hence the destructive process of the forgetting-work—the burial and transformation of memory of lived experience—would seem to be every bit as crucial to the writer's creative effort as is the constructive activity of remembrance, the unearthing and reconstitution of forgotten experience.

Proust's writer is not only a craftsman who painstakingly builds a mnemonic edifice; he is at the same time an absent-minded worker of sorts, who must perform the "undertaking" of forgetting, the burial which allows for the transformation of persona history into a work of art. The forgetting-work, for Proust as for Freud, is an enabling labor that is an essential part of the creative act, for the burial of lived experience must precede its haunting return in the text. Indeed, for Proust, it is only by undermining the structure of personal memory that the writer is able to produce the fertile wreckage from which he may (re)construct the fictional work.

Proust's own novel seems to be generated in large part by several networks of related imagery that emphasize the role of forgetting in the creative act—clusters of metaphors that, significantly, resonate throughout Freud's writings as well. These images in the work of both writers are concentrated around four central themes or ideas: the burial and subsequent excavation of mineral or archeological treasure; geological metaphors suggesting either the formation of treasure from surface materials in the slow process of stratification and crystallization, or the sudden spewing forth of white-hot emotion in a kind of volcanic eruption; ghostly images of memories resurrected from the underworld of forgotten experience; and images of forgetting as a disguise or costume worn at the masked ball of memory. Each of these imagistic networks is richly associative, overdetermined with references to the other networks, especially since each functions finally as a metaphor for writing or creation itself, understood as a dialectical play of memory and forgetting.

A superimposition of these recurring image networks in Proust and in Freud solicits a kind of parallel reading, requiring a critical double vision, a simultaneous reading of both writers as artists and as theoriticians. This symmetrical reading of Freud and Proust, it should be noted, is a departure from the usual procedure of psychoanalytic literary criticism, which not only grants Freud a theoretical or clinical authority of reference, but also often brings to bear the rich body of psychoanalytic theory after

Freud.[2] In this essay, by comparison, the focus is on Freud's highly speculative writings on the aesthetic process—writings rich in suggestive imagery—rather than on his authority as analyst. Such a procedure has the advantage of permitting us to read Freud as a creative writer, and the corollary advantage of granting Proust a certain authority as "analyst" of the creative process. Ultimately, this poetic/theoretical collaboration between Freud and Proust—read as *aestheticians* who speculate metaphorically about the role of the forgetting-work in the creation of the work of art—should suggest a way of thinking of the role of obstacle (understood as obstruction of the writer's "wish" or desire) in the generation of the literary text. In other words, a Proustian reading of Freud, through the network of images sketched above, when coupled with a somewhat more customary Freudian reading of Proust as producer of a textual symptom, may serve to reveal how a certain artistic absent-mindedness function as generative obstacle, enabling the writer to transform the work of forgetting into the play of the text.

NOVEL AS GHOST STORY

> *Now fills the air so many a haunting shape,*
> *That no one knows how best he may escape.*
> (Nun ist die Luft von solchem Spuk so voll,
> Das niemand weiss, wie er ihn meiden soll.)
> —Epigraph to Freud's *The Psychopathology of Everyday Life* (1901), from Goethe's *Faust*

In Freud's early writings, motivated forgetting is repeatedly characterized as a kind of burial, a forceful exclusion of material from consciousness. In *The Psychopathology of Everyday Life* (1901), for example, Freud suggests that forgotten material is submerged in the unconscious, and focuses on the way in which

---

[2]The forgetting-work has been the focus of the rich post-Freudian literature of the French Lacanian school and of British and American psychoanalysts. See, for example, Sullivan (1972).

the buried material returns to haunt discourse, in the celebrated "slip" or in other forms of parapraxis (hence the choice of the "ghostly" epigraph from *Faust*). In the essay "Delusions and Dreams in Jensen's *Gradiva*" (1907), we find the first explicit application of the network of excavation-burial-ghost imagery to a discussion of the nature of the writer's creative process. Freud likens the novelist's task to the work of the hero of *Gradiva*, an archaeologist who unearths precious artifacts of the past at the same time as he recalls "ghosts" of his own childhood. Specifically, Freud draws two parallels of interest for aesthetic theory: First, he compares psychotic delusion with normal acts of fantasy, like dreaming or writing; and second, he takes note of the similarity between psychoanalysis and writing, both of which are able to exhume past repressed experience. The *Gradiva* essay is particularly germane to a discussion of the role of forgetting in Proust's work because it deals with the phenomenon of repression as it relates to artistic fantasy, and because the network of imagistic associations both in *Gradiva* itself and in Freud's commentary–to dreaming, writing, discovery of buried treasure, and memory of ghosts of the past–recalls a web of related images in Proust's work.

All of these metaphorical associations are generated by the thematic content of the ghost story that Freud chooses as a starting point for his speculations about the similarity between delusion and creative fantasy. *Gradiva*'s archaeologist protagonist, while excavating the ruins of Pompeii in search of artistic finds, unintentionally "digs up" the memory of a forgotten childhood love. His delusion consists in mistaking his childhood sweetheart, whom he reencounters in Pompeii, for the ghost of the maiden Gradiva, an inhabitant of that ancient city buried centuries ago in the eruption of Vesuvius. He commits this error because the young woman bears a striking resemblance to a bas-relief figure of Gradiva, an art treasure disinterred in an earlier archaeological dig.

In actuality, Gradiva is not a phantom of Pompeii, but a living ghost of the archaeologist's own erotic past. Freud (1907) analyzes his delusion as an effect of forgetfulness:

> The childhood friendship dissolved ... and the memories of it passed into profound forgetfulness. ... The development of psychic

disturbance begins at the moment when a chance impression arouses the childhood experiences which have been forgotten and which have traces, at least, of an erotic content [p. 34].

The similarities between the action of *Gradiva* and the phenomenon of artistic remembrance in Proust (the celebrated *moment bienheureux* in which Marcel experiences a visitation of unsolicited memory, evoked by the taste of the madeleine or the view of the bell towers) are striking indeed; for in Proust's novel it is always a "chance impression" (to use Freud's term), such as the taste of the madeleine, which awakens forgotten memories associated with Marcel's infantile loves.

The parallel is reinforced by Freud's own analogy between the archaeologist's delusion and the artist's imagination. Suggesting that all fantasy is rooted deep in infantile experience, in latent unconscious memory, Freud maintains that aesthetic analyses are fair game for the psychoanalyst. In other words, Freud believes that a writer's fantasies are symptoms of repression. Like the ashes of Pompeii, which have retained imprints of the ancient city and its inhabitants, the unconscious stores traces of the individual's past. Indeed, Freud (1908) asserts that "there is no better analogy for repression, which at the same time makes inaccessible and conserves something psychic, than the burial which was the fate of Pompeii and from which the city was able to rise again through work with the spade" (p. 40). The artist's task, then, like the analyst's, is to excavate these stores, to recall the ghosts of the past. Freud seems to suggest that writing, as an instance of the return of the repressed, functions as a kind of seance, evoking and revivifying "shades" of forgotten experience.

Proust's work, of course, is fashioned from such shades of the past, evoked by the encounter with "artifacts" such as the madeleine. But in Proust's account of the creative process, memories often seem to be contained in these artifacts themselves, rather than in the writer's unconscious. Insofar as Marcel's ghosts seem to dwell in these objects, outside of the narrator, they actually seem alienated from him, disowned: "Is it not true," Proust asks his reader, "that the best part of memory is outside of us?" ("N'est-ce pas que la meilleure partie de la mémoire est hors de nous?" I, 643). At moments in the text, however, Proust explicitly identifies these alien impressions as internal sensations projected onto external objects (as in the case, most obviously, in the description of the magic latern shown in the child Marcel's room). These objects, then, which seem to be vessels in which the past is stored externally, are really screens for the projection of a past that is preserved within the artist-writer himself. As Freud points out in his discussion of *Gradiva*, the artist may often misrecognize his own memories, believing them to have come from beyond (like the apparent "ghost" of Gradiva herself), when in reality they have been resurrected only from repressed memory.[3]

Traditional Proust criticism has tended to ascribe Marcel's impression of alienated memory, encased in external objects, to a Symbolist tendency in the work, a kind of transcription of Baudelaire's concept of *correspondances* into the novelist's prose. This classic interpretation may, however, be supplemented with (or counterposed to) Freud's (1919) insight on the nature of artistic perception as a kind of "uncanny" visitation which, even when it seems to come from beyond, is actually drawn from the writer's own psychic *beyond,* his unconscious. In other words, the impression of alienated memory in Proust's narrative could be considered to derive from its alien source: namely, the writer's "other," his repressed store of experience. Proust himself describes the writer as a sort of corporeal repository of forgotten experience, buried and storied through time. Paradoxically, he characterizes this bodily store as being at once the very deepest stratum of memory, preserved intact from the corrosion of time, and the most profound product of the work of forgetting which has deposited the material there: "Bygone days cover up, little by little, those which have preceded them and are themselves buried under those which follow. But each day has remained deposited in

---

[3]This kind of "misrecognition" brings to mind Lacan's theory of *méconnaissance* in the therapeutic situation, as well as Freud's notion of resistance, according to which consciousness resists the reentry of repressed material and denies the validity of such material when it does resurface.

us, as in an immense library" ("Les jours anciens recouvrent peu à peu ceux qui les ont précédés et sont eux-mêmes ensevelis sous ceux qui suivent. Mais chaque jour ancien est resté déposé en nous comme dans une bibliothèque immense" III, 544).

This passage might almost serve as an illustration of Freud's theory of motivated forgetting, which attempts to account for the process by which forgotten material is retained in the unconscious. Indeed, the alien quality of this latent material when it resurfaces in Marcel's discourse – the "strange accent" ("accentuation étrange" I, 94) which haunts the literary work – might be attributed in part to its status as repressed material, and could likewise account for Marcel's tendency to disown or misrecognize the source of this material. It is as though Marcel's consciousness continues to have difficulty owning up to this problematic material, which has strong associations with pain as well as pleasure, even when it reasserts itself in the surface of his narrative thought. The work of forgetting/repression is not easily undone, and it thus exerts a profound influence on Marcel's narrative.

In "Mourning and Melancholia" (1917), Freud expounds a view of mourning as an instance of the forgetting-work, a type of repression which involves a decathexis, or unbinding, of libido from the absent loved one. This work is both prolonged and repeated, since it involves learning to do without the beloved in each situation once lived in his or her presence. Proust likewise refers to mourning as a type of work ("oeuvre"), citing "the work of forgetting" in reference to Albertine ("l'ouevre de l'oubli en ce qui concerne Albertine" III, 596). For Proust, then, mourning is a "work" in the dual sense of an applied effort and of a creative act. The obliteration of the painful memory of Albertine, for example, is described as a prolonged labor that requires the successive mourning of each of the beloved's multiple selves: "When I had managed to bear the grief of losing the first Albertine, I had to start again with another, with a hundred others" ("Quand j'étais arrivée à supporter le chagrin d'avoir perdu celle-ci, c'était à recommencer avec une autre, avec cent autres" III, 478). In this instance, the forgetting-work is an anaesthetic task that must be accomplished before Marcel's transformed memory of Albertine can become the generative core of his own "work."

The eventual result of this work of decathexis, for Proust as for Freud, is the lover's return to the world, freed from the detaining fascination with the deceased beloved. For Marcel, the indolent artist-dreamer, this liberating mourning work is yet another instance of work to be put off as long as possible; he dreads the moment when forgetfulness will divest him of his "protective covering of caresses, kisses, friendly slumbers" ("tout ce tégument de caresses, de baisers, de sommeils amis" III, 482). Indeed, Marcel's love, "having recognized the only enemy by which it could be vanquished," cowers before that forgetfulness which threatens to devour it like a famished serpent ("Et mon amour, qui venait de reconnaître le seul ennemi par lequel il pût être vaincu, l'oubli, se mit à frémir, comme un lion qui dans la cage où l'on l'a enfermé, a aperçu tout d'un coup le serpent qui le dévorera" III, 447). But in spite of Marcel's struggle against this beast of prey, this forgetfulness, the dreaded *oubli*, does succeed in swallowing his most cherished of ghosts: "It seemed to me that a cherished shadow had just been lost among the other shadows ... like Orpheus abandoned I repeated the name of the dead beloved" ("Il me semblait que c'était une ombre chérie que je venais de laisser se perdre parmi les ombres ... comme Orphée resté seul je répétais le nom de la morte" II, 136). Like Eurydice, Albertine vanishes ("Albertine disparue") from her lover's mnemonic sight.

Yet this voracious *oubli* paradoxically offers a mode of retention of the very love it menaces with extinction: Indeed, Proust characterizes the body itself as the vessel of memory, a corporeal deep-freeze "stuffed with memories" ("les bras, les jambes sont pleins de *souvenirs engourdis*" III, 699). Forgotten yet retained, Marcel's past loves are like a mold that "will determine the form of the love which follows" ("car un amour a beau s'oublier, il déterminera la forme de l'amour qui le suivra" III, 677). Thus even while it deprives Marcel of his active bond with Albertine, forgetfulness creates a new and lasting bond with the absent beloved. Shades of the past color the writer's present experience and haunt his future text. Just as the earth's topography is determined by the geological configurations beneath its surface, Marcel's current affective patterns are influenced by the buried past, the "deposits" of forgotten experience.

DISMEMBERED MEMORY: NOVEL AS MINE

> *I knew well that my brain was a rich mining basin, where there was an immense and richly diverse region of precious deposits.*
>
> (*Je savais très bien que mon cerveau était un riche bassin minier, où il y avait une étendue immense et fort diverse de gisements précieux.*)
> —Proust, A la Recherche du temps perdu, III, 1037

In the final volume of his work, Proust compares the writer's task to the mining of buried deposits: The artist draws upon stored material, which, like the immured treasure of the *Arabian Nights* so often mentioned in *Combray*, yields itself only in response to the proper magic formula. In terms of this mining/excavation imagery, forgetfulness comes into play in three ways in the production of the literary work. First, it buries or represses the memory of lived experience, preserving such memory as a "deposit" in the unconscious. Second, it causes the stored material to be worked or transformed by virtue of this consignment to the unconscious, in a crystallization of sorts, analogous to the formation of precious gems from ordinary mineral substances. Finally, forgetfulness—as artistic absent-mindedness—bores holes in the surface of conscious censorship, providing "shafts" to the underlying "deposits"; Proust insists that repressed memories are most likely to surface at moments of distraction, when consciousness is momentarily off-guard, confounding presence of mind. These three functions of forgetfulness in the creation of the text relate, respectively, to the retention, the transformation, and the retrieval of material in the artist's own unconscious; and these functions are most often suggested, in Proust's novel and in Freud's aesthetic writings as well, by the use of geological metaphors and mining imagery, to describe the exploitation and excavation of the artist's own latent memory.

In one particularly striking example of geological imagery, Proust refers to predetermined patterns of affective experience as "great uniform paths" that have been "melted long ago in the volcanic fire of ardent emotion" ("grandes voies uniformes par où passe chaque jour notre amour, et qui furent fondues jadis dans le feu volcanique d'une émotion ardente" III, 677). Thus current loves fellow paths that have already been gouged by the white heat of intense emotion. This view, according to which love is bound to repeat itself, conforming to patterns predetermined by the deforming wounds of early love, is of course consistent with Freudian theory, which asserts that one's primal love experience—particularly the oedipal drama, which "wounds" its protagonist with the threat of dismemberment—is formative of all future affective experience.

Now for the artist—whom both Freud and Proust consider to be particularly susceptible to the influence of the past on present experience—this means that creative vision, the artist's perception of the world, has been forged in the crucible of lost love. When Proust writes that the artist sees the world "through the eyes of an other" ("les yeux d'un autre, de cent autres" III, 278), he may be suggesting that the alien or "other" eyes through which the writer views the world are always, in a way, the "forgotten" eyes of an earlier self who once gazed upon the beloved. Moreover, since the artist strives to open the store of corporeal memory, to delve into the *"souvenirs engourdis"* preserved in the body, writing is always, in a sense, the reopening of a primal wound, which it retraces in the writer's own flesh. The self is the bodily vessel of memory, a vessel which must be ruptured in order to extract the precious deposits with which the text is forged.

Like the poet Orpheus to whom Marcel repeatedly compares himself, the writer pays the price for resurrecting his "cherished shades" ("ombre chéries"); he is consumed by the act of giving life to his beloved ghosts. Like Orpheus, Marcel discovers that the remembering of fragmented impressions into a whole corpus entails his own dis-membering. His drawing of his own Eurydice from the underworld of the unconscious involves a bodily exhaustion, poignantly portrayed in the final passages of the novel. This excavation saps the life of the poet, who "undermines" himself as he exploits his memory, working against time. The fragmenting of explosive nature of the creative moment, in which the self spews forth its content, is underscored by its occurrence at those moments when Marcel is most vulnerable, disturbed by unfamiliar surroundings or weakened by illness. When Marcel is thus violently "moved," his submerged layers surface in a poetic rupture, characterized as a "blossoming" of the narrative train of thought: "Our self," Proust writes, "is made up of the superimposition of our successive states. But this superimposition is not unmoveable like the stratification of a mountain. Perpetual upheavals cause a blossoming of ancient layers at the surface" ("Notre moi est fait de la superposition de nos états successifs. Mais cette superposition n'est pas immuable comme la stratification d'une montagne. Perpetuellement des soulèvements font affleurer à la surface des couches anciennes" III, 544).

But this creative upheaval, while disorienting and difficult, is also a felicitous experience, precisely because the work of art permits the artist to prolong or renew his relation with his forgotten beloved. Albertine, although *disparue*, will remain present not only as the mode of all of Marcel's future loves, but as the generating subject of his work (as will his mother, his grandmother, Gilberte – all the lost loves). In Marcel's work, Albertine becomes poetically accessible only when she is no longer the obsessive center of his emotional life but has been displaced; like a Freudian slip she emerges as the object of a *lapsed* attention. Moreover, all of Proust's lost past determines and overdetermines his artistic vision, which, through the passage of time, and the process of burial and stratification effected by the forgetting-work, has become a fecund tangle of layer upon layer of emotional memory: "Beyond a certain age our memories are so entwined, one with the other, that the subject of one's thoughts, or the book which one is reading, are no longer important ...everything is fecund, everything is dangerous" ("A partir d'un certain âge nos souvenirs sont tellement entrecroisés les uns sur les autres que la chose à laquelle on pense, le livre qu'on lit n'a presque plus d'importance ... tout est fécond, tout est dangereux" III, 543). Thus Proust ultimately suggests that the writer not only deposits experience within, in a forgetful store, but also permits repressed experience to spill out in the eruption of a seminal vision which alters the world: "one has put something of oneself everywhere, everything is fecund, everything is dangerous, and one can make as precious a discovery in an advertisement for soap as in the *Pensées* of Pascal" ("On a mis de soi-même partout, tout est fécond, tout est dangereux, et on peut faire d'aussi précieuses découvertes que dans les *Pensées* de Pascal dans une réclame pour un savon" III, 543). In the creative process, the work of mourning/repressing/depositing the past is channeled into the play of the text: Forgetfulness not only creates a new relation with that which is forgotten or missing, but it also transforms the forgotten material, and permits the dissemination of the transformed material—the stuff of the artist's "alien" vision—in the world. Perhaps the most striking example of the forgetful relation which the text provides with an absent character is the reader's own curious rapport with the missing person of Proust himself. The novelist is at once absent—as the "real" Proust never mentioned in the text—and present—as the narrating persona Marcel—in this autobiographical fiction. The reader is called upon to "forget" the facts of Proust's real life, in order to become engrossed in the experiences of Proust's fictional counterpart.

DISGUISING THE SOURCE: NOVEL AS MASKED BALL

> *This name—almost mythological for me—of Swann....*
> (Ce nom, devenu pour moi presque mythologique, de Swann....)
> —Proust, *A la Recherche du temps perdu*, I, 144
>
> It seems clearly probably that myths are distorted vestiges of the wish-fulfillments of whole nations.
> —Freud (1908), "Creative Writers and Daydreaming"
> [*S.E.* 9, p. 152]

At the same time that forgetfulness provides a mode of retention of absent people and forgotten experience—elements that continue to exert an influence on current experience not in spite of being forgotten, but because they have been forgotten—it also performs a transformative function, as the agent of repression. For forgetting acts as a kind of pressure which commits surface or lived experience to a period of gestation in the underworld of the unconcious, an active latency which works and transforms the forgotten material. During this latency, repressed material is subjected to a deforming and poeticizing contact with the unconscious; or as Freud (1907) puts it in the essay on *Gradiva*, repressed material is subject to transformations by primary processes such as condensation and displacement, operations characteristic of the unconscious. This transformation may be seen as a key element of the creative process, for it is the very deformation of repressed material that eventually allows it to reemerge into consciousness, eluding censorship thanks to its disguise. Indeed, Freud (1907) writes in "Delusions and Dreams" that artistic fantasies, as well as ordinary daydreams, are "offshoots of repressed memories ... which manage to become conscious by heeding the censorship of resistance and undergoing transformations and distortions" (p. 58).

The transforming work of forgetfulness is perhaps most clearly elaborated in Freud's discussion of the genesis of myth, a collective fiction that Freud compares to writing. In "Moses and Monotheism," Freud (1939) likens the whole of culture to a phylogenetic storehouse of forgotten events, and suggests that the mythmaking process makes use of these stores in the same way that the writer draws upon personal forgotten infantile experience. He describes the creation of the legend of Moses as the reworking of historical fact through collective repression: The "fact" (the death of the Egyptian prince Moses at the hands of the Jewish people whom he has championed), once repressed and reworked, reemerges as the hidden kernel of the legend of Moses, "disguised" henceforth as the patriarch of the Jewish people. Thus, for Freud, the forgetting of a traumatic or problematic event is an essential step in the creation of myth, or of fiction, which, like the screen memory of childhood events, is symptomatic of the true event it conceals (see also Freud, 1917). In myth, as in the phenomenon of screen memory, the fact is both obscured and preserved, absented and presented, thanks to a deformation which allows the historical event to elude the censorship of consciousness, returning—like Marcel's old friends at the ball in the final part of Proust's novel—in an unrecognizable avatar of its former self. As Freud (1907) puts it in "Delusion and Dreams," "after the compromise with censorship is complete, the former memories have become fantasies which may be easily *misunderstood* by the conscious person" (p. 61).

Proust's own forgetful artistic process seems analogous to mythmaking on at least two levels. First, Proust performs a transforming work on the givens of his own life, disguising and displacing such facts as his Jewish origin or his own homosexuality. Second, Marcel's writing, the creation of the text within the text, is facilitated by the return of the repressed elements in the writer's life, by Marcel's retrieval of his lost past transformed in the person of Mlle de Saint-Loup.

Gilberte's daughter is Swann's granddaughter, and as the new mythic object of Marcel's attention, she reinvests the name of Swann, maligned by time and effaced by her mother's marriage, with the mythic force it held in Marcel's childhood. Like a myth, Mlle de Saint-Loup, granddaughter of the forgotten man whose memory her mother has repressed, is herself a cryptic message, a visual code that Marcel deciphers. Her physiognomy both reveals and obscures her multivalent origins: "Her eyes were deep-set and piercing, and also her charming nose, slightly curved and beak-like, not perhaps exactly like that of Swann, but more like that of Saint-Loup" ("Elle avait les yeux profondément forés et perçants, et aussi son nez charmant légèrement avancé en forme de bec et courbe, non point peut-être comme celui de Swann, mais comme celui de Saint-Loup" III, 1031). She is the reassertion of the forgotten in Marcel's life, the nodal point of his forgotten love for Gilberte, his esteem for the forgotten Swann, and his long-forgotten friendship with Saint-Loup. Marcel refers to the overdetermined web represented by the young girl as "one of those starlike crossroads where the most diverse points of our lives converge" ("carrefours où viennent converger des routes venues pour notre vie aussi, des points les plus différents" III, 109). Thanks to her situation at this crossroads, Mlle de Saint-Loup is herself starlike, radiant: Marcel writes that these "roads were many for me, those which lead to Mlle de Saint-Loup and which radiated around her" ("les routes ... étaient nombreuses pour moi, celles qui aboutissent à Mlle de Saint-Loup et qui rayonnaient autour d'elle" III, 1029). She is thus imagistically associated with Proust's concept of art: the astral voyage ("d'étoile en étoile") to which Bergotte's work is compared in *La Prisonnière* (III, 258).

Indeed, the appearance of Swann's granddaughter serves as a catalyst for Marcel's creative effort. As the incarnation of Marcel's "lost years" ("formée même des années que j'avais perdues"

III, 1032), she is the carnal evidence of the passage of "lost time" ("temps perdu"). The transformed and disguised past inserts itself into the present, in a form resembling but not identical to the forgotten material from which Mlle de Saint-Loup has been fashioned ("She looked like my Youth" ["elle ressemblait à ma Jeunesse" III, 1032]). As the return of Marcel's now fictionalized youth, worked by forgetfulness, Mlle de Saint-loup prefigures and represents the fictional work itself, the excavated treasure of rediscovered years. Like Freud's Gradiva, she is the ghost of past love refound.

Thus the final vision, the apotheosis that Mlle de Saint-Loup seems to represent, is beholden to dismembered memory in at least two ways. First, the name of Swann is able to regain its mythological quotient by association with the radiant girl, at the same time that it revitalizes Marcel's memory of youth, only because it has been repressed for a time: Gilberte's marriage with Saint-Loup, of which this girl is the offspring, had been considered socially permissible only because Mlle Swann had "forgotten" the name of her Jewish father, adopting her stepfather's name to improve her social position. Second, Marcel's experience of Mlle de Saint-Loup as his own regained youth is possible only because he himself has been a forgotten man of sorts, out of the social arena for some time, so that he is suddenly and unexpectedly confronted with the fully grown image of his past. His own absent-mindedness and sequestration precede and facilitate his discovery of the treasure of youth.

Finally, it is only thanks to an absent-minded poetic consciousness—a non-linear and non-rational mode of thought that is capable of suppressing years of elapsed time and thus of defying chronological and rational order—that Marcel experiences the totalized insights of the final passages, insights that create the sort of "dimensionalized" account that Proust favors:

> In a book which would attempt to relate a life, it would be necessary to use, in opposition to that flat psychology which is usually used, a sort of psychology in space ... since memory, by introducing the past into the present, suppresses precisely that great dimension of time in which life unfolds.
>
> (Dans un livre qui voudrait raconter, il faudrait user, par opposition á la psychologie plane dont on use d'ordinaire, d'une sorte de

psychologie dans l'espace ... puisque la mémoire, en introduisant le passé dans le présent ... supprime précisément cette grande dimension du Temps suivant laquelle la vie se réalise [III, 1031]).

In other words, it is forgetfulness that has permitted the evolution of the Proustian character ("thanks to our forgetfulness they evolve" ["au gré de notre oubli ils évoluent" III, 981]) as well as the spatial quality of the novel's fictionalized time. The "total," "refound" panorama at the end of the novel is actually a forgetful vision, riddled with holes.

Moreover, the final treasure—the precious memories from which the work is formed—is retrieved only through a *loss*, a tapping of the writer's resources that entails a painful and exhausting derepression. In the final scenes, this depression requires that Marcel recognize his own decrepitude and impending death, and that he "undermine" his remaining strength by undertaking the monumental task of rewriting his past. The artist, as bearer of the submerged treasure, is pierced so that the past may emerge. Again, Proust writes that it is forgetfulness that is symptomatic of this artistic porousness: "An emptiness in the head, a forgetfulness about all those things which I could only now stumble across by chance ... made me like a treasury whose broken coffers would allow its riches to flow out, little by little" ("une vide dans la tête, un oubli de toutes choses que je ne trouvais plus que par hasard ... faisaient de moi comme un thésaurier dont le coffre-fort crevé eût laissé fuire au fur et à mesure ses richesses" III, 1037). Thanks to forgetfulness, the writer stages his own masked ball of forgotten guests. In the final weeks of Marcel's life, a fecund *oubli* cracks the coffers from which pour forth the treasure of the novel.

FORGETTING AS GENERATIVE OBSTACLE

> *Albertine had seemed like an obstacle, posed between me and all else.*
>
> (*Albertine m'avait semblé un obstacle, posé entre moi et toutes choses.*)
> —Proust, *A la Recherche du temps perdu*, III, 483
>
> *The artist is originally a man who turns from reality because he cannot come to terms with the demand for*

> *renunciation of instinctual satisfaction as it is first made, and who then in phantasy life allows full play of his erotic and ambitious wishes.*
> —Freud (1911), "Formulation on the Two Principles of Mental Functioning" [*S.E.* 12, p. 224]

Even though writing, for Proust, almost seems to be a sacrificial gesture which drains the life of the writer, it is nonetheless characterized as a supremely satisfying act. Indeed, Marcel's writing could qualify as a classic example of Freudian wish-fulfillment, since it is a fantasy which, in Freud's words, "allows full play of his erotic and ambitious wishes," in what seems to be a compensation for an incomplete life. Marcel writes: "It seemed to me life could be illuminated ... even *realized* in a book" (emphasis added) ("la vie me semblait pouvoir être éclaircie ... en somme *réaliseé* dans un livre" III, 1032). For Marcel, the literary act becomes a fictional supplement to a deficient reality.

Freud would of course concur that art affords a fantasy gratification of desire thwarted in life, maintaining that "in art alone it still happens that a man who is consumed by his desires performs something resembling the accomplishment of those desires ... just as though it were something real" (*S.E.*, *14*, p. 187). But Freud insists that the artistic fantasy, which replays reality in a more satisfying version, is nonetheless always a *substitute* gratification, which countervails an initial renunciation. In other words, art is the result of a compromise between the artist's desire and the restraints that reality imposes upon it. A desire that is at first deflected or repressed (by the reality principle) subsequently becomes the impetus for artistic production.

In Freud's view, then, art, like all forms of fantasy or delusion, is symptomatic of the originally repressed desire which motivates it. In *Introductory Lectures on Psycho-analysis* (1916–17), Freud even suggests that art is akin to neurosis ("The writer is in rudiments an introvert not far removed from neurosis" [p. 376]), but he stipulates that the artist, unlike the neurotic, rechannels energy back into the external world through production of a work of art designed to produce enjoyment in others. In our terms, this means that motivated forgetting, or repression, is actually the precondition of any literary text; or, to use Schiller's words as cited by Freud in "Moses and Monotheism": "All that is to live in endless song / Must first be submerged in life." A certain forgetful deflection of desire precedes and engenders the aesthetic symptom which is art.

In the celebrated essay *Beyond the Pleasure Principle* (1920), Freud also posits deflected desire as the source of human play: The child's game is a creative response to an unpleasant reality (the mother's absence) over which he has no active control. In the aesthetic and anaesthetic activity of play, the child compensates for deficient reality by evoking his mother's presence symbolically, manipulating the toy over which he exerts complete control and himself determining the rules of the game, a "re-play" of reality.

Thus Freud's work seems to present two possible responses to painful deprivation or frustration of desire: grief—the mourning-work described in "Mourning and Melancholia"—and play or artistic activity, which creates a new and circuitous relation with the absent beloved. The play response would seem to be essentially aesthetic, since it is analogous to the process of literary creation, as Freud points out in "Creative Writers and Daydreaming" (1908). A motivated forgetting, in response to the encounter with obstacles posed by reality, leads to a transformed (hence faulty) remembering, the artist's absent-minded play.

Here again Proust's work substantiates Freud's view. For in Proust the obstacle to gratification is seen as absolutely crucial to the artistic process: "One waits for suffering in order to work, one is afraid of each new work in thinking of the pain that it will be necessary to bear in order to imagine it" ("on attend une souffrance pour travailler, on a peur de chaque nouvelle oeuvre en pensant aux douleurs qu'il faudra supporter d'abord pour l'imaginer" III, 909). Ultimately, obstructed desire—like the courtyard paving stones that trip up Marcel on the way to the final ball, touching off one of the last *moments bienheureux*—functions as an obstacle that at once disrupts the smooth surface progress of daily activity and jolts or activates forgotten memories, opening up the sources of the work of art. And forgetting plays a crucial role in this obstructive process: Marcel either loves, is deprived, forgets, and reloves (the result of the mourning-work), or he loves, is deprived, gains distance from the experience by buying its memory, and eventually writes about it—when the memory is unearthed, transformed by the forgetting-work. In neither case is forgetting tantamount to losing the beloved, since, in the first instance, forgotten love determines the form of the present love, and in the second, passion attenuated by forgetfulness determines the eventual form and content of the creative work, which is a replay of transformed reality.

This textual replay is, of course, a kind of memory, but it cannot be a recapturing of "lost time" *as it was*: The erotic past must be dismembered, undergoing the transformative operation of the forgetting-work before it may reemerge in the text. Thus Marcel's writing—and Proust's novel itself—is an opening of the forgotten store in a relibidinization of all experience ("everything is fecund, everything is dangerous...."), including work experience. Indeed, Proust's work demonstrates that the boundary between work and libidinal play is permeable (as does Freud's use of pun, anecdote, and metaphor in theoretical texts): Creative forgetting transforms the work of mourning into the play of the literary text. In Proust's case, the text-play is exhausting and exhaustive; the creative outpouring saps the writer's very life. But it seems that some of Proust's artistic fellows and heirs—and one might count Freud among them—have learned to survive artistic dismemberment, by "forgetting" to carry the text-play to completion, playing and replaying a game (the "interminable cure?") in which the outcome is always deferred and the end product nowhere to be found.

REFERENCES

Freud, S. (1901). *The Psychopathology of Everyday Life. The Standard Edition of the Complete Psychological Works of Sigmund Freud*, 6 (24 vol., Strachey, J., trans.) . New York and London: W. W. Norton, from 1953.

_____ (1907). Delusions and dreams in Jensen's *Gradiva*. *S.E.*, 9, 1959.

_____ (1908). Creative writers and daydreaming. *S.E.*, 9, 1959.

_____ (1911). Formulations on the two principles of mental functioning. *S.E.*, 12, 1958.

_____ (1915). The unconscious. *S.E.*, 14, 1957.
_____ (1916-1917). *Introductory Lectures on Psycho-Analysis*. *S.E.*, 15 & 16, 1963.
_____ (1917). A childhood recollection from *Dichtung und Wahrheit*. *S.E.*, 17, 1955.
_____ (1917). Mourning and Melancholia. *S.E.*, 14, 1957.
_____ (1920). *Beyond the Pleasure Principle*. *S.E.*, 18, 1955.
_____ (1930). Civilization and its discontents. *S.E.*, 21, 1961.
_____ (1939). Moses and Monotheism. *S.E.*, 24, 1964.
_____ (1953). The psychopathology of everyday life. In J. Strachey (Ed. and Trans.), *The standard edition of the complete works of Sigmund Freud (Vol. 6)*. London: Hogarth Press. (Original work published 1901)
_____ (1959). Creative writers and daydreaming. In J. Strachey (Ed. and Trans.), *The standard edition of the complete works of Sigmund Freud (Vol. 9)*. London: Hogarth Press. (Original work published 1908)
_____ (1959). Delusions and dreams in Jensen's *"Gradiva."*. In J. Strachey (Ed. and Trans.), *The standard edition of the complete works of Sigmund Freud (Vol. 9)*. London: Hogarth Press. (Original work published 1907)
_____ (1958). Formulations on the two principles of mental functioning. In J. Strachey (Ed. and Trans.), *The standard edition of the complete works of Sigmund Freud (Vol. 12)*. London: Hogarth Press. (Original work published 1911)
_____ (1957). Mourning and melancholia. In J. Strachey (Ed. and Trans.), *The standard edition of the complete psychological works of Sigmund Freud (Vol. 14)*. London: Hogarth Press. (Original work published 1917)
_____ (1957). The unconscious. In J. Strachey (Ed. and Trans.), *The standard edition of the complete works of Sigmund Freud (Vol. 14)*. London: Hogarth Press. (Original work published 1915)
_____ (1963). Introductory lectures on psycho-analysis. In J. Strachey (Ed. and Trans.), *The standard edition of the complete psychological works of Sigmund Freud (Vols. 15 & 16)*. London: Hogarth Press.(Original work published 1916-1917)
_____ (1955). A childhood recollection from *Dichtung und Wahrheit* In J. Strachey (Ed. and Trans.), *The standard edition of the complete psychological works of Sigmund Freud (Vol. 17)*. London: Hogarth Press. (Original work published 1917)
_____ (1955). The uncanny. In J. Strachey (Ed. and Trans.), *The standard edition of the complete psychological works of Sigmund Freud (Vol. 17)*. London: Hogarth Press. (Original work published 1919)
_____ (1955). Beyond the pleasure principle. In J. Strachey (Ed. and Trans.), *The standard edition of the complete psychological works of Sigmund Freud (Vol. 18)*. London: Hogarth Press. (Original work published 1920)
_____ (1961). Civilization and its discontents. In J. Strachey (Ed. and Trans.), *The standard edition of the complete psychological works of Sigmund Freud (Vol. 21)*. London: Hogarth Press. (Original work published 1930)

———— (1964). Moses and monotheism. In J. Strachey (Ed. and Trans.), *The standard edition of the complete psychological works of Sigmund Freud (Vol. 24)*. London: Hogarth Press. (Original work published 1939)

Proust, M. (1954). *A la recherche du temps perdue (Edition de la Pléiade), Vols. 1-3*, P. Clarac, & A. Ferré. Eds.). Paris: Gallimard (Original work published serially in seven volumes from 1913-1927).

Sullivan, H. S. (1972). *Personal Psychopathology: Early Formulations*. New York: Norton.

12 Modes of Lacanian Fragmentation in Three Texts

Leopold Charney

> *The Moving Finger writes; and, having writ,*
> *Moves On: nor all your Piety nor Wit*
> *Shall lure it back to cancel half a Line,*
> *Nor all your Tears wash out a Word of it.*
> — *The Rubáiyát* of Omar Khayyám (E. Fitzgerald, Trans.)

I

However clichéd it might seem, this verse of *The Rubáiyát* creates an image at once terrible and seminal. Fragmentation rules: The omnipotent Finger, shorn from a body, does what it pleases, and nothing we whole humans do can erase the fateful words it has written.

The image Khayyám's verse immediately evokes, of course, is the ominous writing hand in Chapter V of the Old Testament Book of Daniel, the hand which suddenly appears in the middle of the air and writes the incomprehensible "Mene Mene Tekel Upharsin" on the wall of King Belshazzar's palace, mystifying words that Belshazzar must call Daniel to interpret. That "Moving Finger" is in fact five fingers, but its message of doom and destruction for Belshazzar is as indelible as any Khayyám might have imagined.

The Daniel chapter powerfully demonstrates the process of discovering the truth through deciphering what is most incomprehensible, the same process used in interpreting dreams, and, essentially, the same process used by Dupin in Poe's (1845) tale "The Purloined Letter" to solve the purloining of the letter. The tale is in fact an active schematization, in its fashion, of the way in which what appears to be so simple that it becomes endlessly complicated may in fact be that simple, but in different, transposed ways.

Lacan stated at one point in his career that "ce qui compte, c'est ce qu'on ne comprend pas" ("what counts is what one doesn't understand"), and so it is no coincidence that the Daniel chapter, Poe's tale, and Freud's Dream of Irma from Chapter II of his *Interpretation of Dreams* (1900-1901) – the first and paradigmatic dream for interpretation – are all discussed in his *Séminaire II* (1978). But Lacan was a critic who rarely made his mental associations clear, and who rarely revealed his real and full intentions in bringing texts or issues into discussion. His use of the Book of Daniel, for example, constitutes half a sentence in the midst (appropriately enough) of discussion of the Irma Dream. The reader of Lacan is left to infer the links between Lacan's theories and the texts he brings into discussion, to extrapolate the ways in which these texts, as signifiers, are meaningful to him.

I would like to conduct exactly this kind of extrapolation with the three aforementioned texts, hoping, by discussing them in dialogue, that they will illuminate each other and the central Lacanian issues that bind them together. The texts have many similarities beyond their use of the incomprehensible, but the most profound, and the one that intersects most strikingly with Lacanian theory, is their common exploration of fragmentation as it relates to writing (as in the Moving Finger) and its personal and societal effects, to power structures and their disruption, and to fragmented numerological units of covert and overt narrative. Nothing is quite as it seems in any of these texts (already an initial fragmentation): Some seemingly whole, hermetic unit is apparently disrupted (fragmented) by some other unit. But what if that seemingly whole unit is already fragmented? And what if the unit that fragments it is itself a fragment? And how does all of this relate to Lacan? The aim of this short essay is not only to illuminate the individual texts and the Lacanian theories, but also to try to understand why these texts are important to Lacan and to his theory beyond the points he manifestly makes about them.

II

The overt mystery of "The Purloined Letter" is clear: A letter has been taken from the Queen's apartment, a letter which, if its contents are publicized, will cause scandal and downfall for the royal family. Who took the letter? This is known: As Inspector G, the Prefect of Police, explains to the narrator and his friend Dupin, Minister D, "who dares all things" (p. 209), openly took the letter from under the eyes of the Queen when the presence of a third person in the room made it impossible for the Queen to protest. Thus it is also known how the robbery was comitted. And, presumably, why: It is a power play, and Minister D, of course, "dares all things."

So what is the mystery? Simply: *Where* is the letter? "The fact is," Inspector G tells Dupin, "we have all been a good deal puzzled because the affair *is* so simple, and yet baffles us altogether" (p. 209). Dupin, like Lacan, does not feel that this categorizing is at all valid: "Perhaps it is the very simplicity of the thing which puts you at fault" (p. 209), he suggests, and the Prefect merely laughs. Just as Lacan believed that the incomprehensible was the ultimate key to comprehensibility, here comprehensibility, in the form of the most obvious of robbery cases, becomes incomprehensibility, as the very simplicity of the case inhibits its solution, and will ultimately return to comprehensibility only in the form of Dupin's re-solution.

Inspector G and his police have expended all their resources to find the letter: "For three months," relates the Prefect, "a night has not passed, during the greater part of which I have not been engaged, personally, in ransacking the D____ Hotel.... I fancy that I have investigated every nook and corner of the premises in which it is possible that the paper can be concealed" (p. 211). But despite their searching, the police have found nothing. It is Dupin who finds the letter and who then turns it over to the Prefect. He has discovered its location not through searching the inside of the

Minister's lodging, but rather through searching the inside of the Minister's mind (though he has still given us no clue as to what is inside the Minister's envelope). He has attempted to understand what he would do if he were the Minister and has discovered that his initial comment to the Prefect that "perhaps the mystery is a little *too* plain" (p. 209) has assumed a very literal truth: The letter, in a new envelope with a new seal and a new address, was contained in "a trumpery fillagree card-rack of pasteboard, that hung dangling by a dirty blue ribbon, from a little brass knob just beneath the middle of the mantel-piece" (p. 220) in Minister D's apartment. Dupin's attention was attracted to the letter by its very *excessiveness*:

> But, then, the *radicalness* of these differences, which was excessive; the dirt; the soiled and torn condition of the paper, so inconsistent with the *true* methodical habits of D____, and so suggestive of a design to delude the beholder into an idea of the worthlessness of the document; – these things, together with the hyperobtrusive situation of the document ... were strongly corroborative of suspicion, in one who came with the intention to suspect [pp. 220-221].

The letter was obvious to Dupin because it was trying too hard not to be obvious.

The methods of analysis presented in the tale are one respect in which the tale must be important to Lacan. The police are like bad analysts: They hunt through everything, examine "the rungs of every chair" (p. 212), pore over the clues "by the aid of a most powerful microscope" (p. 212). But they find nothing because they understand neither the individuality (the textuality, if you will), the unique mind of the man they are investigating, nor the structure of the problem at hand, a structure that is, as Dupin perceives, mental, geographical, chronological, and itself structural. Dupin, a model analyst, can identify with the "patient" and can understand the structures involved. (Lacan also might say that the police's actions in "The Purloined Letter" represent the very way in which Freud's theories have become distorted over time – society picking up the small details without attempting to understand the larger, more disturbing picture of the mind of the man who created the theories.)

12. LACANIAN FRAGMENTATION 241

But Dupin, of course, is not perfect, and this is perhaps the most important element in our Lacanian understanding of him as an ideal analyst. (And we see too that he will not give the Prefect the letter until he receives the reward, just as the Freudian analyst is told always to demand payment from the patient under all manner of dire circumstance.) We can perceive this issue in simple, commonsensical terms: Perfection, in a person, is its own negation, for literal perfection is seen as too inhuman or stiff to be what we consider perfection. It is an endless paradox in which what we see as "perfection" is not the true, literal, objective perfection, but rather a subjective perfection that is not perfection at all but rather, perhaps, an awareness of one's faults and an ability to admit them. As Lacan notes in his seminar on "The Purloined Letter," Dupin, once the letter is in his possession, becomes almost as devious and cagey with it as was Minister D himself. He is human and fallible, and for Lacan, this aspect is central to understanding the analyst's role not as a deity but as a fallible human. Freud himself, in analyzing his own Dream of Irma in *The Interpretation of Dreams*, states that, even though (quoting Delboeuf) "every psychologist is under an obligation to confess even his own weaknesses, if he thinks that it may throw light upon some obscure problem" (p. 105), "in scarcely any instance have I brought forward the *complete* interpretation of one of my own dreams, as it is known to me. I have probably been wise in not putting too much faith in my readers' discretion" (p. 105). In other words, Freud will extend professional interests only as far as they will not intrude excessively upon his private life. He is ultimately human and does not hesitate to admit it.

III

The most interesting question in "The Purloined Letter," though, is not where is the letter, but rather: Who *wrote* the letter and what does it say? If the message in the Book of Daniel is written by a disembodied hand, the letter in "The Purloined Letter" is written by no hand at all and its contents are not just incomprehensible but invisible. The letter and the hand in Daniel are both fragmented units, as is the formula of trimethylamin in Freud's

Dream of Irma. This dream is quite literally the starting point of psychoanalysis: To the extent that the interpretation of dreams and its corresponding book are the beginnings of psychoanalysis, "this is the first dream," to quote Freud himself, "which I submitted to a detailed interpretation" (p. 106).

Irma, the main figure of the dream, was a young hysterical patient of Freud's to whom he proposed a "solution"—solutions to hysterical cases in those days were always sexually related—which she would not accept. I reproduce the dream in its entirety:

> A large hall—numerous guests, whom we were receiving.—Among them was Irma. I at once took her on one side, as though to answer her letter and to reproach her for not having accepted my "solution" yet. I said to her: "If you still get pains, it's really only your fault." She replied: "If you only knew what pains I've got now in my throat and stomach and abdomen—it's choking me"—I was alarmed and looked at her. She looked pale and puffy. I thought to myself that after all I must be missing some organic trouble. I took her to the window and looked down her throat, and she showed signs of recalcitrance, like women with artificial dentures. I thought to myself that there was really no need for her to do that.—She then opened her mouth properly and on the right I found a big white patch; at another place I saw extensive whitish grey scabs upon some remarkable curly structures which were evidently modelled on the turbinal bones of the nose.—I at once called in Dr. M., and he repeated the examination and confirmed it.... Dr. M. looked quite different from usual; he was very pale, he walked with a limp and his chin was clean-shaven.... My friend Otto was not standing beside her as well, and my friend Leopold was percussing her through her bodice and saying: "She has a dull area low down on the left." He also indicated that a portion of the skin on the left shoulder was infiltrated. (I noticed this, just as he did, in spite of her dress.) ... M. said. "There's no doubt it's an infection, but no matter; dysentery will supervene and the toxin will be eliminated." ... We were directly aware, too, of the origin of the infection. Not long before, when she was feeling unwell, my friend Otto had given her an injection of a preparation of propyl, propyls ... propionic acid ... trimethylamin (and I saw before me the formula for this printed in heavy type).... Injections of that sort ought not to be made so thoughtlessly.... And probably the syringe had not been clean [p. 107].

There is an enormous amount that can be said about this dream, and it is a fascinating topic in its own right. But let us concentrate, for a moment, merely on that floating formula of trimethylamin. With the purloined letter and the hand in Daniel, it forms a triad of disembodied images in these tests, images which find connection only as symbols, only in their impact, in their transferential impact, in their transferential and transponential power.

These images of fragmentation immediately evoke two central Lacanian concepts. One is his view of the unconscious as a "sujet acéphale" ("headless subject"); and the other, related one is his theory of the "mirror stage." Lacan had noticed in his research that human infants became preoccupied with observing their own image in the mirror, while infants of other species found no such delight. He realized that, while primate infants are born with finished bodies, human babies are born physiologically premature. But when a human infant first sees himself in a mirror, he sees a whole, a totality, and with this not only a vision of some future potency and capability but also, perhaps, an illusory feeling of *present* capability. He sees, in essence, not himself, but his mother, the person who, for him at that point, epitomizes full adult perfection and capability. There is no distinction in his mind between himself and his mother, which is the same kind of confusion between self and other that forms, after all, the basis of the Narcissus myth. This kind of narcissistic structure, for Lacan, is a key element of the mirror stage as a metaphor for the idealization that occurs throughout human lives: We perceive ourselves as whole, potent, effective human beings, but this view of totality is a vain illusion. All humans are fragmented.

IV

With these two central Lacanian concepts, the headless subject and the mirror stage, we can advance toward a theme that dominates all three texts: the very theme of fragmentation versus totality expressed in Lacan's mirror stage. Let us look closely at the schematized structure of each of the texts. Each is centrally concerned with power in various forms. Yet those who possess and symbolize power are figures of ignorance, impotence, and often outright foolishness who are unaware, like the ego postulated by Lacan, of the confusion and covert anxieties seething beneath them. Dr. M., the figure who Freud has said was "the leading personality" in his "circle" and in whose hands therefore lay the potential rejection of Freud's years of work, is stripped of his beard in Freud's dream, an image, of course, of castration, but also of serious loss of professional stature, since all important men of that time had beards. The King in "The Purloined Letter" is a noncharacter, his narrative invisibility embodying his insignificance, oblivious and powerless with respect to the events that could unseat him (and the Queen, of course, is the one who created the whole chaos in the first place through carelessness of one kind or another). King Belshazzar in Daniel watches helplessly as Daniel's translation of "Mene Mene Tekel Upharsin" finds Belshazzar's kingdom "finished" and "divided," his life "found wanting." He is later slain. These three men are all "sujets acéphales," not so much in Lacan's sense but in the more literal sense of ignorance, lack of insight, "headlessness," referring to the head at the seat of thought and understanding.

The power structure represented in each of these texts is always seen as disrupted by some fragmented unit. Each of these fragmented elements is important only in a symbolic way, only in its effect upon what goes on around it. The letter in "The Purloined Letter" changes everything, transposes relationships, disrupts the standard power structure: The Queen is powerless, at the mercy both of one of her Ministers and of her own police, and rescued ultimately by the disinterested Dupin; the King is invisible, the ultimate castrated father, without power or identity; the Prefect, Inspector G, sees his standard methods prove useless. The writing in the Daniel chapter disrupts the power structure in an even more literal fashion, as it correctly prophesies the death of King Belshazzar and the accession of a new ruler.

In Freud's Dream of Irma, the relations between writing and power structure take several forms. We can isolate two different kinds of writings—Freud's writing in *The Interpretation of Drams*, which is the trigger of the dream's latent content, and the actual writing of the formula in the manifest dream. In his thorough and persuasive analysis of the dream, Erikson (1954) argues that its latent meaning is not so much related to professional failure on the daily, medical level, as Freud himself believed it to be, but rather to a more general professsional rejection of Freud's new ideas and ostracism of Freud himself. This is why Dr. M., symbolic of the psychology power structure in Vienna, appears shaven; this is why Otto is shown as a careless practitioner, using an unclean syringe. Freud is enacting some kind of future revenge on a power structure that he supposes will be disrupted by his writing just as the power structure in Daniel is disrupted by the writing of the disembodied hand. To move to a more narrow, more literal level, the writing that actually appears in the dream—the formula of trimethylamin—disrupts medical ethics ("Injections of that sort ought not to be made so thoughtlessly"), disrupts our expectations of Otto, as a good practitioner, and, of course, disrupts the dream by ending it.

V

"Two motives, each of a given value, have not necessarily a value when united equal to the sum of their values apart" (p. 218), says Dupin in "The Purloined Letter," and this notion of parts and whole is also an important aspect of the fragmentation versus totality theme in Poe's tale. "If the Minister had been no more than a mathematician," says Dupin in explaining his ability to solve the mystery of the letter,

> the Prefect would have been under no necessity of giving me this check. I knew him, however, as both mathematician and poet, and my measures were adapted to his capacity, with reference to the circumstances by which he was surrounded. I knew him as a courtier, too, and as a bold *intriguant*. Such a man, I considered, could not fail to be aware of the ordinary polical [sic] modes of action [p. 218].

I said earlier that the key to Dupin's understanding of the case is structural; we can now view this structural understanding in a more specific way. For it involves both a structure of personality, as Dupin perceives the contradictions involved in the person, and a structure of transference, as he transfers his theories on parts and whole to apply to human endeavor.

We can use this same kind of structural transference to investigate the fragmented personalities of the three texts. The metaphorical logic used by Dupin in interpreting the Minister's motivations is more or less the same as the logic of the mirror stage. He has perceived, as the police have not, that human totality is nonexistent, and has understood the Minister in terms of his component parts. Yet the same kind of fragmentation exists in Dupin himself, a man who appears to be a quiet intellectual yet can decipher a criminal case more skillfully than the police; a man who seems scholarly and reflective yet commits the same crime as the man he is hunting, never tells the police about his crime, and makes sure he has his reward before returning the letter to the police. Surely Dupin's personality is equally fragmented.

Freud, as seen by Erikson in the Irma Dream, is a classic case of non-totality expressing itself as impotence. As Erikson explains it, the Irma Dream represents the alternatives of Freud's life at the time when it was dreamt: He can continue to pursue his professional goals and run the risk of ignoring his family (impotence both literal and figurative) or concentrate on his family and face professional impotence. The worst possibility, of course, would be rejection of his ideas by the power structure, an event that would cause both professional and personal impotence. We should not forget, in this regard, the parallels drawn in Section IV between the writing in the Daniel chapter and the writing in the Freud dream. The writing in the Daniel chapter was achieved by a hand not connected to any body, a hand epitomizing human fragmentation and metaphorical castration (and the emblems of fragmentation in all these texts, after all, involve writing). The "castrated hand" has no responsibilities. It need not worry about what will happen to the rest of its body when it writes, for it has no rest of its body. But is the castration, instead, an *emblem* of the writing? Where is the author of the purloined letter? Where is the body connected to the hand in Daniel? Where is the origin of Freud's dream? Is castration what enables one to write, or is it the result of the writing? Or is it both?

While on this topic, it is worth nothing the prevalence of images of division in the Daniel chapter. On balance, this prevalence should not be surprising. It is, after all, a chapter filled with death, violence, and shock; division can be seen as merely a part and an emblem of these events. But it might also be an archetypal rendition of Lacan's metaphorical mirror stage. That is, Belshazzar, the King who believed himself omnipotent and untouchable, is being made aware that his illusion of totality is indeed an illusion. Fragmentation rules: The hand that writes the words is free-floating, unconnected to a body; the message is divided into three or four sections ("Mene" appears twice in the writing [=4] but has only one meaning [=3]; the message itself consists of images of division: "God hath *numbered* thy kingdom" (one act) "and finished it" (two acts); "Thou art weighed in the *balances* and found wanting" (the absence of some vital section of moral life); "Thy kingdom is *divided* and given" not to one person or even to one group but "to the Medes and the Persians" (italics added).

VI

Among all these numbers, the number 3, in whatever different form, appears with the greatest frequency. It is the number of the oedipal triad, of course, but this is hardly its only psychoanalytic manifestation—in Freud's essay "The Theme of the Three Caskets" (1913) he analyzes several myths, tales, and plays in which triads appear and discovers primarily that when a choice exists among three objects, as in *The Merchant of Venice* or *King Lear*, it is always the third that is chosen, and that third always seems to be an emblem or a representative of Death, as in the Three Fates, of whom the third, Atropos, is the inexorable one. The frequent presence of triads in these texts is unquestionable. We have already seen the triadic structure at the key moment in the Daniel chapter. Let us look now at Freud's Dream of Irma.

Lacan himself, in his analysis of the dream in Chapters XIII and XIV of the same *Séminaire II* that contains the chapter on "The Purloined Letter," divides the dream into two sections: the "trio mystique" of the three women followed by the "trio de clowns" of the three bumbling men. But it is with the formula of trimethylamin that the triadic structure reaches its height. The sequence "propyl ... propyls ... propionic acid" that precedes Freud's first mention of "trimethylamin" already constitutes a structural triad which, we think, composes trimethylamin. But what exactly, is the chemical formula of trimethylamin? It is:

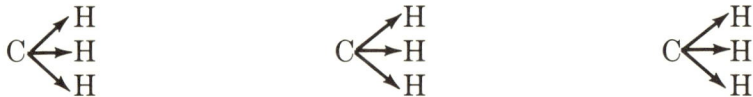

H is a letter composed of three strokes; C is also composed of three parts (top, middle, bottom) and is the third letter of the alphabet; the methyl group repeats the H three times; trimethylamin repeats the methyl group three times.

The presence of triads in "The Purloined Letter" is no less striking. The story opens "au troisième, No. 33, Rue Dunot, Faubourg St. Germain" (p. 208). We are already in the land of the triple three. (Could Poe have been thinking of 666, the Biblical number of the Antichrist?) Inspector G has been investigating the Minister's home "for three months" (p. 211). If the reward for the letter's recovery "were trebled" (p. 214), this same Inspector states, he would still be unable to find the letter. These incidents might seem trivial, even meaningless, were it not for a more consistent *structural* pattern of threes running throughout the text. The tale opens with two men sitting "au troisième, No. 33" when they are suddenly joined by a third man, Inspector G. He tells them a story about a letter, but Dupin does not understand why this letter is so important. The Inspector explains, "The disclosure of the document to a third person, who shall be nameless, would bring in question the honor of a personage of most exalted station; and this fact gives the holder of the document an ascendancy over the illustrious personage whose honor and peace are so jeopardized" (p. 209).

The Inspector proceeds to tell the story of the letter's theft: The Queen was alone with the letter when someone entered; she tried to hide it but failed; Minister D entered and stole the letter; the Queen, as Inspector G relates, "dared not call attention to the act, in the presence of the third personage who stood at her elbow" (p. 210). The Prefect describes his detailed search for the letter in not only the Minister's house but also "the two houses immediately adjoining" (p. 212). A month later the Prefect returns to see the two men and is told by Dupin that he has the letter, which is then handed over from Dupin to the Prefect to (presumably) the Queen. Dupin tells the narrator the story of his discovery of the letter, a tale that involves three digressions for various philosophical examples and three subsequent returns to the topic. Dupin's story of actually substituting the letter describes his coming upon Minister D and the letter alone in the room, and involves a man set up in the street to fire a shot that would distract the Minister while Dupin substituted the letter for the purloined letter.

What are we, then, to make of these threes? It is a difficult question, a task far harder than merely noting them, for one easily runs the risk of overanalysis. But in both Freud's dream and Poe's tale, the triadic patterns emphasize roles and modes of responsibility and the ways in which these change and shift. The methyl group formulas are like diagrammatic renderings of the covert issues of the dream. For example:

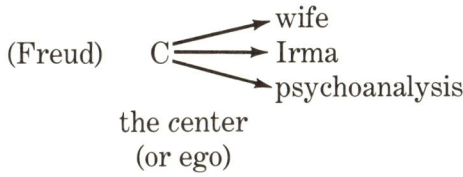

This diagram would reflect the fragmented structure of birth in the dream. The dream, as Freud relates in his analysis of it, is an anticipation of the celebration of his wife's *birth*day; his wife is also pregnant at the time. The dream is also the birth of the theory of psychoanalysis, a birth which, by this dream, will be performed by Freud not with his wife but with Irma (and also, of course, with Fliess, but that is a thorny issue). Thus there is a shifting triad of birth revolving through the dream.

This is but one example of a triadic structure in the dream. One could as easily present Irma, Freud's wife, and Fliess; or, for those who are familiar with Freud's lengthy analysis of the dream, Irma's friend, Freud's governess, and Freud's dead patient (in which triad, of course, the third figure is Death, as in "The Three Caskets"). Or one could make the triad the three men who appear in the dream, a triad which, if one includes Irma or even Fliess in the general picture, might assume some oedipal triad proportions. And if Dr. M. were the third figure, he might represent Death, at least in a professional sense. We must be careful, though, to maintain the integrity of Freud's text in the best Lacanian manner. In other words, Freud was writing in "The Three Caskets" about specific fictional situations in which a choice always seemed to fall on the third, and was attempting to speculate on the reasons for this seemingly inexorable choice. This does not mean that the third one must be Death in any situation in which three units are involved; not only is the connection fallacious, but, as often as not, one can, as I did in the Dr. M. example, manipulate the triad so that the desired element will come out third.

Whatever triads can be formed from the Irma Dream – and the repetition of the methyl groups in the trimethylamin formula, taken together with the formula's free-floating nature, encourage us to form as many as we can – all deal in some form with responsibility. The form is significant:

That is, Freud is dispensing responsibility; rather than fully accepting it (human fallibility) he disperses it to others, and they, whether his wife for the family, the patient he killed for his guilt, Irma for his theories, or Dr. M. for rejection of his theories, divide it in a shifting way among themselves. The dream is a paradigm of human fragmentation, an active schematization of Freud's own non-totality and his own, if subconscious, realization of it. Guilt, responsibility, and emotion circle around in their own significant triad, and Freud, only human, must diffuse some of these overwhelming emotions; non-totality leads to greater non-totality.

The structural triads in "The Purloined Letter" seem also to disperse responsibility among the characters, articulated and non-articulated, of the tale. Poe's tale is as centrally divided as the Irma Dream, divided not only into two distinct sections (the first scene and the scene one month later) but also into two distinct

12. LACANIAN FRAGMENTATION   251

modes of narration—the firsthand present (the two scenes among Dupin, the narrator, and Inspector G) and the secondhand past (Inspector G's narration of how the letter was stolen, Dupin's narration of how he stole the letter back, etc.). Within the present group, Inspector G is always the third: In both scenes, he bursts in on Dupin and the narrator as they sit in their scholarly contemplation. But it is in the secondhand, recollected scenes that the figure of the third seems crucial: "The disclosure of the document to a third person, who shall remain nameless" (p. 209) would destroy the Queen and her royal power structure; when Minister D steals the letter, the presence of a third, unnamed person in the room prevents the Queen from stopping him; the key to Dupin's retrieval plot is the third, unnamed person whom Dupin has asked to fire a shot in the street to distract the Minister. Note also that the third is not always human. Minister D's house becomes a third when Inspector G speaks of investigating "the two houses immediately adjoining" it; Dupin's house is the house of the triple threes; and the letter itself is a constant metaphorical "third," even when it is not, as in the scene with the Queen and the intruder, a literal third.

Why is the crucial third always unnamed? Why is it often even an inanimate object? Lacan addresses this question, elliptically as usual, in his view of the letter as an unarticulated character in the tale. This view is, in turn, a clear, if again elliptical, allusion to his tripartite theiory of analytic dialogue in which, essentially, $2 = 3$, or even 4. That is, for Lacan, the whole of an analytic dialogue is not at all equal to the sum of its parts. The unconscious creates a third force—a third, unarticulated personage, if you will—that makes the whole of the dialogue quite different from the sum of the analyst and the analysand.

Might this theory give some clue to the function of the thirds in "The Purloined Letter"? The unconscious, for Lacan, is the force that changes everything, transposes relationships, creates new modes. Certainly the same functions are filled by the nameless third person whose knowledge of the letter could destroy the Queen, by the nameless third person whose presence prevents the Queen from stopping Minister D, and by the nameless third person who fires the shot in the street. One could even say it about the Minister's house and about the letter itself. Like the triad of fragmented images discussed earlier, none of these elements has an independent effect; they achieve importance and potency only in the effect they have upon others. This, of course, is also the primary significance of the letter: The letter's effect, and therefore the Minister's power, are lost as soon as its contents are revealed.

VII

Triads in these texts are modes of change and of shifting responsibility from a central source onto different independent actors. If we look, then, at the total picture, a clear pattern emerges: In each of the texts, and through whatever sequences, repetitions, or forms, the elements that disrupt totality (ego, if you will) are all fragmented. We have seen the writing hand shorn from the body; the formula of trimethylamin free from medical, spatial, or manifestly contextual unit; the letter removed from any author or content; even the structural triads themselves, which disperse order, divide and scatter totality.

Lacan states in his chapter on the tale that the purloined letter "n'a pas le même sens partout" ("does not have the same meaning everywhere"). He did not even need to (although he does) state his allusion explicitly. The unconscious, of course, is *the* element which "n'a pas le même sens partout" for Lacan. This is why it is so important for the analytic paragon Dupin, as for the analyst, to understand the individual case, because the unconscious will exert a different impact upon everyone. Ultimately, as we see from these texts, the unconscious, the fragmented "sujet acephale," is what controls the ego with its illusions of totality. "The Moving Finger writes" and "all your Piety not Wit," all the devices of a clever ego, cannot "wash out a Word of it."

REFERENCES

Erikson, E. H. (1954). The dream specimen of psychoanalysis. *Journal of the American Psychological Association, II*, 5–56.

Freud, S. (1953). The interpretation of dreams. In J. Strachey (Ed. and Trans.), *The standard edition of the complete psychological works of Sigmund Freud,*

(Vols. IV & V). London: The Hogarth Press. (Original work published 1900-1901)

———— (1958). The theme of the three caskets. In J. Strachey (Ed. and Trans.), *The standard edition of the complete psychological works of Sigmund Freud* (Vol. 12). London: Hogarth Press. (Original work published 1913)

Lacan, J. (1978). *Le Séminaire Livre II: Le moi dans la théorie de Freud et dans la technique de la psychanalyse.* Paris: Seuil.

Poe, E. A. (1965). The purloined letter. In H. Allen (Ed.), *The complete tales and poems of Edgar Allan Poe.* New York: Modern Library. (Original work published 1845)

13 Phantasm and Narration in Marguerite Duras' *The Ravishing of Lol. V. Stein*

Susan Cohen, Ph.D.

Among the more than twenty novels and ten plays and films which have established Marguerite Duras as one of the most prominent literary and cinematic figures in contemporary France, *The Ravishing of Lol. V. Stein* is widely considered one of her masterpieces. Written in 1964, it forms a pivotal point in her work, and has elicited admiration and commentary both from literary critics and from psychoanalysts such as Lacan (1975) and Montrelay (1973).

On the night of a summer ball at the T. Beach Casino a nineteen year old girl named Lola Valérie Stein is abandoned by her fiancé, Michael Richardson, who goes off with another woman. Lol is precipitated into a profound existential crisis, from which she does not emerge. On the contrary, she progresses from shock to illness (neurosis) to madness (psychosis). These are the bare coordinates of the "story" *The Ravishing to Lol V. Stein* recounts. It would be a mistake, however, to consider the text a simple illustration of psychoanalytic concepts. While an understanding of the dynamics of Lol's malady is certainly necessary, it hardly suffices for a thorough appreciation of the novel. Lacan (1975), who devotes an expert article to unravelling and piecing together the "knot" of Lol's phantasm, neglects the specifically literary value of the text. Yet he warns against the pitfalls of abusive reductionism into which psychocriticism can fall. Referring to the "caddishness" of psychoanalytic "pedantry," he affirms with Freud that art takes precedence over psychology, the former opening new vistas to the latter, rather than the reverse.

Several factors internal to the text indicate that Duras herself hinders simplistic approaches. The prerequisites for a "case study"—patient and analyst—are lacking. Though Lol clearly becomes mentally ill, she never has the role of patient. Moreover, the text, as though to sabotage efforts to ascertain clinical etiology, provides no information on what might have composed Lol's childhood, and almost none on her adolescence. Equally significant, the little we are told comes not from Lol—for part of her dilemma consists in not having access to discourse—but from a narrator who, in sharp contrast with the predicated distance of a professionally dispassionate analyst, is someone quite passionately involved with her. Finally, we shall find that the reader's initial conception of the novel as the story of Lol's descent into madness becomes problematical in light of its narrative structure.

Yet because the novel shows Lol's personal style of Being-in-the-World and of Being-with-others, it is justifiable to put narrative voice into brackets for the moment in order to consider a first level of the text: Lol in the world. For the reader does have access to Lol's gestural presence in the world, if not to her voice, and access to her absence as well, to her manner of living in the world and of leaving it. Disclosing the specificity of her spatial and temporal constitution of the world, rather than seeking causality in a past not provided by the author and therefore unpresupposable, can help to elucidate the dynamics of this complex text. In this regard, a modified form of Binswangerian Daseinsanalysis proves a most useful approach. Binswanger (1968) based his method on the composite concept of Being-in-the-World as elaborated by Heidegger in *Being and Time* (1927/1962). Starting from the premise that human existence is inseparable from the world in which it finds itself, always already implicated in it and in a being-with-others, Heidegger avoids the word "subject" because of its Cartesian overtones of abstraction from the world. He employs instead the term Dasein (literally "being there"). Neither the world nor Dasein are things in themselves. Rather, Dasein projects out of itself, simultaneously constituting temporality, spatiality, world, and Selfhood in a movement of ex-tasis that defines existence (or ek-sistence, written in hyphenated form in order to mark its pro-jectional character).

Concerned with the *how* of an individual's Being-in-the-World, Daseinsanalysis describes the manifest level of experience rather than translating it into symbols and symptoms of the repressed, latent level, and thereby discounting it. It is the lived level of Lol's ek-sistence that is open to us and that has significance in this novel. The first section of my essay, then, will be devoted to its study. Subsequently I shall turn to the intricately related questions of her phantasm and the narrator's relation to it. The final section will treat the narrative element as such.

I. LOL IN THE WORLD

A. The Trauma

Lol's illness revolves around a precise moment, the end of the ball at the T. Beach Casino, and is articulated initially along the axis of verticality, which phenomenology considers primordial. The departure of Michael Richardson and Anne-Marie Stretter ejects Lol from a world until then entirely structured by the Being-with of love. With her fiancé, an essential component of Being-in-the-world is violently wrenched from her (a terminology of violence marks every textual reference to the scene) and, existentially speaking, Lol sustains a mortal wound. When, at the dance's end, the new couple leaves, Lol, no longer having the existential strength to maintain her vertical stance, falls down, "disappearing" in a "dead" faint: "When she could see them no longer, she fell to the ground in a faint" (p. 22; all translations are mine). In French the word "s'évanouir" means both to faint and to vanish, and it is imperative to an understanding of Duras' style that the reader forbear from eliminating any of the possible meanings of what I call her word-images. In Duras' work the single word often functions like compound poetic images, in the Bachelardian (1943, 1948) sense—that is, literally, materially, and dynamically, its various significations reverberating simultaneously. Lol, having fallen, having fainted, has indeed vanished: She ek-sists no more, with all that implies of absence and a certain death. Her bodily fall is the perfect concretization of the ontological collapse occasioned by the sudden sundering of her world. Binswanger (1968) has pointed out the aptness of the expression "to fall from the clouds." When used to express severe existential shock or disappointment, and, as in this instance, when the image is accompanied by its physical realization (Lol really does fall down), it has special pertinence: "The nature of poetic similes lies in the deepest roots of our existence where the vital forms and contents of our minds are still bound together. When, in a bitter disappointment, we 'fall from the clouds,' then we fall – we actually fall. Our existence actually suffers, is torn from its position in the world.... We say, later, after we have regained our equilibrium that it is as though we had fallen from the clouds" (Binswanger, 1968, p. 222-223).

Lol's personal disaster consists in the fact that she remains in the having-fallen: At no point does she "regain equilibrium" or recover her Self. Absent for good, she cannot re-place her Self or her world. She has been replaced, literally. That substitution here means elimination in the strongest sense of existential death is repeatedly attested by the text. The ball is a "massacre" (p. 54); Lol's friend Tatiana, who witnessed the event, is the evening's "sole survivor" (p. 123); the ball "destroyed" Lol's "nature" (p. 131) and, at the end, "buries her" (p. 210), etc. (I take issue with Montrelay's [1973] contention that Lol was like a "jealous woman who sees herself transported into the other" (p. 13). If she is transported it is not into another woman but, as the text makes clear, out of the world and ek-sistence altogether, replaced.)

B. Exile

Although she has died existentially, Lol nevertheless continues to live. Phenomenology has taught the crucial distinction between the two. When one constitutes Self, choosing freely from among one's possibilities in authentic temporality oriented toward the future, then Dasein as such ek-sists. But for Lol temporalization has been arrested at a point in the past that she cannot situate as past. She remains caught for ten years in a motionless, timeless hovering, exiled from the surrounding world (*Umwelt*), from the world of others (*Mitwelt*), and from her personal world (*Eigenwelt*). She lives mechanically ("On aurait dit qu'elle allait de soi. . . ." [p. 24]), a survivor of her own ek-sistence, stuck in an immobile limbo of repression and symptom. Maldiney (1973) has defined living in the past as "posthumous living": "What do symptom and repression signify? That the patient inhabits the World . . . in the past. Not that he lives as one says 'with his memories' but his entire history . . . is contradictorily preoccupied as though posthumously by the anxiety of a non-integrated past [passé non dépassé] (p. 52). Yet it cannot even be said of Lol that she inhabits the past, because she projects into none of the temporal ek-stasies at all. While she certainly is "posthumously preoccupied," she has repressed both the past and the anxiety attendant upon it.

How, then, does Lol live in this worldless world? Inhabiting, which is the most fundamental characteristic of how Dasein *is* in the world (Heidegger, 1958, p. 192), is now defined by its own negation. Unable to temporalize or spatialize, Lol sinks into a state of passive unfreedom devoid of choice. Marriage "happens" to her ("Lol found herself married without having desired it . . . without . . . choice" [p. 33], and she lives for ten years in U. Bridge in a total existential void. If inhabiting implies projecting into a room or a house or a place that becomes inseparable from Self and bears the imprint of Dasein, then to be sure Lol does not inhabit. Nowhere does this become more apparent than in her houses, in her relationship to things. Rather than expressing presence, her house, the mirror image of department store showrooms (p. 137), reflects the absence of a constituting individuality. Lol doggedly conforms to the impersonal norm of Everyman, imitating the inauthentic Heideggerian "they," in an attempt to simulate normal life: "Lol was imitating, but whom? Others, all the others, the greatest possible number of other people" (p. 37).

At the cost of great effort Lol seeks limited refuge against the madness and consequential institutional confinement she fears, in a semblance of ordinariness and in a semblance of order. Rigorous order, both in the positioning of objects in her house and in an unalterable hourly schedule, serves to mask her existential disarray. Concomitant with the need for order, Lol harbors a dread of disorder, the only thing that causes her to suffer (pp. 197-199), and her horror of it functions phobically as protection against the collapse of her fragile, hollow edifice: "Phobia is always an attempt at safeguarding a restricted, impoverished world" (Binswanger, 1958, p. 205). When, ten years later, back in S. Tahla, Lol refurbishes the house she had lived in as a child, she invests it with the same lifeless atmosphere, "strict care" and "frozen order" (p. 139), in which everything functions according to mechanical rather than personal time.

Of capital importance to understanding the intricacies of this text is the fact that the material manifestations of Lol's existential anonymity are informed with empty silence. For along with having lost world, Lol has lost authentic, Self-expressive discourse. Language, intrinsically related to inhabiting, as Heidegger (1958) pointed out in his famous dictum, "language is the home of being" (p. 115), mirrors and simultaneously constitutes our manner of Being-in-the-world. When Lol falls at the ball she falls silent as well, and remains locked in what might be termed existential aphasia. She "ceased speaking" (p. 24); she is "silent in life" (p. 54), an "uncomplaining wife" (p. 36), who "doesn't talk" (p. 69), etc. If she speaks at all, it is only when pressed, and at such moments, just as she retreats into the material organization of the "they," so she adopts the verbal order of its inauthentic thought. Called upon to describe her years in U. Bridge, she resorts to an overly detailed, overly ordered "recitation" (p. 95) of the objects in her rooms, her speech corresponding to the too meticulous regime of her household. Seeking the same reassurance in imitation of ready-made discourse as she does in showroom furniture, she speaks of her life "like a book" (p. 99). But this exaggeratedly rigorous reproduction merely emphasizes her anonymity, disturbing rather than reassuring those around her, who sense it to be the expression of alienation it is. It becomes clear that far from describing inhabiting, Lol is actually "telling the story" of how her arrival "depopulates" her dwellings (p. 95).

Thus in S. Tahla, Lol's edifices, both material and linguistic, begin to develop fissures that give her away. Asked by a dinner guest whether she misses her house in U. Bridge, Lol forgets to play the part of the "they," and answers that "she has never known inhabiting" (p. 168), a slip she then attempts to pass off as a joke. On the corresponding concrete side, the slip (or "crack in the ice" [p. 37]) takes the form of an error she makes in the outlay of her garden, when she "forgets" to provide for connecting paths between the main walks, which, consequently, do not "communicate" with one another and cannot be used until the "mistake" is corrected (p. 39). Lol's oversight is a necessary and revelatory corollary of her incapacity to communicate on any level. This parallel between the concrete and linguistic aspects remains surprising only if we take the word "language" in the restricted sense of speech, rather than understanding with Duras that gesture and silence are as constitutive of expression as are words, and that, especially in societies where it is incumbent on women to arrange the home as well as to be consigned to it, the "house is a language." (Duras 1982)

C. Return

Despite their ostensible reparability, these incidents have far-reaching consequences, for, quite aware that the world to which she had conformed for ten years has shattered, Lol "gives up" trying to maintain herself in it: "The only thing I know anything about is the immobility of life. Therefore, when that breaks, I know it" (p. 51). In diametrical contrast to her previous behavior, she begins to go out, taking long walks. That this daily leave-taking constitutes definitive departure is underscored by the accompanying birth imagery. Lol "stirs in God's stomach" (p. 50), etc. Yet both the nature of her promenades and of that toward which she directs her steps soon reveal the limitations of this rebirth. Lol's walks do not reinsert her in the world, for they lack the quality of movement projected out from the present into the future. Rather than enabling her to perceive her native city, they serve quite the opposite imperative, that of covering it with a sort of blank palimpsest, of making it invisible. Beneath her tread the city becomes "frozen," not reactivated (p. 71). Progressively she succeeds in making of it a "pure palace of the forgotten," an "oblivion" (p. 48). Moreover, in perfect existential reciprocity, the city's disappearance has her own absence as complement. She makes herself invisible, and no one recognizes her. For recognition presupposes the reciprocity of perception, as described by Maldiney (1973): "Perceiving is moving towards things on the foundation of a being-in-the-world where we are present, in space and time, through the expressive motility of our bodies" (p. 75). But Lol turns not toward but away from. More precisely, she turns back.

That toward which her peregrinations are directed, that space and time which lead her out of the artificiality of the anonymous "they" and the only setting in which she can reconstitute personality is, of course, the ball. She sets out to revivify it so that it can receive her: "The ball recovers a bit of life ... she warms it, protects it, nourishes it, it grows ... one day it is ready" (p. 51). Thereafter she enters it daily.

Quickly it becomes apparent that Lol's is not a rebirth into future-oriented ek-sistence but into a blocked past not experienced as such from a situation of presence. As Straus (1966) notes: "Only in contrast with the present, then, does remembering gain its meaning" (p. 65). Lol turns her back on both present and future, and returns literally to the past, preserving no distance from it: "She no longer has at her disposal the invariable distance of memory" (pp. 47-48). The past, in which she now sets up house, becomes her home: "She begins the past again, puts it in order, arranges it, her true dwelling" (p. 51). Thus when Lol emerges from the "they" world, she is reborn only to regress. She moves, but only backward. It can be argued that her preference for the past over the "they" world stems from the fact that the former affords her a spatio-temporal arena that is personal, while the "they" offers only an anonymous "afterlife." The (still "posthumous") return to the past is meaningful to the extent that it is, at least, hers. To be sure, Lol's new life provides only deficient ek-sistence, for, as Binswanger has shown, phantasms or delusions provide limited means of finding or understanding oneself, but they eliminate future-oriented potential and condemn one to unfreedom. Nevertheless, since Lol could not ek-sist in the "they" at all, and functioned in it only mechanically, her phantasm, insofar as it provides a minimum of insertion into meaning, however solipsistic, is preferable.

II. THE PHANTASM(S)

A. Hers

Lol's entire undertaking is motivated not by Eros but by Thanatos, and scrutiny of her new "home" further confirms that it partakes phantasmically of the dynamics of dying: The time she devotes the remains of her being to reconstructing is not the happy period of shared love but the impossible moment of her own death, which she had experienced at the ball, but the finalization of which the departure of the couple had prevented her from witnessing. The physical concretization of her own replacement – the moment when Michael Richardson will undress another woman in her place – this unseen gesture represents for Lol the consummation at once of her own end and, paradoxically, of her life. The end of the ball and what follows – invisible, unthinkable moments, since we cannot see or think our own death – constitute the contradictory "scene" into which Lol now projects.

Yet by herself, she cannot overcome the contradiction and never succeeds in visualizing it (p. 56). Imagination proving insufficient, she seeks more concrete support in "real life" for her phantasm. By way of another couple, Jacques Hold and Tatiana Karl, Lol reconstitutes the situation she will now "see," not materially but experientially. When she follows them to the hotel the knowledge of her exclusion from their lovemaking puts her in the presence of her absence, since, as Heidegger (1962) stated, "knowing is having seen in the wider sense of seeing" (p. 36). Grasping this prereflexively, Lol positions herself too far from the hotel actually to see inside the window, which is "a mirror reflecting nothing" (p. 43) except the "non-existent, invisible spectacle" (p. 73) of not being there. What renders this non-visual scene paradoxical is that it unites opposites which, though they are mutually implied, are mutually exclusive – presence and absence, existence and death; the duality of the imagery attests to the bivalency involved. When Lol lies in the rye field outside the hotel window, she is simultaneously alive and dead. Her very exclusion guarantees her existence, making her "real" as Lacan (1975) notes, but only on the negative axis of death, which, because it is at last her own, feels sweet to her. Indeed, it affords the only sensuality she is capable of. Thanatos couples with Eros but the former dominates: "Living, dying, she breathes deeply, tonight the air is honey, of an exhausting sweetness. She does not wonder where the marvellous weakness that made her sink down in the field comes from. She lets it act, lets it fell her until it suffocates her, roughly, pitilessly rocking her into the sleep of Lol. V. Stein" (p. 72). The scene finally enables her to live what she sought, the "velvet annihilation of her own person" (p. 56).

In order to ensure Lol's new ek-sistence two essential factors must be present—repetition and triangulation, and together they lead to what I consider a key to the novel. Clearly, experiencing her "dying" one more time cannot suffice. Instead, it must be renewed cyclically so that, phoenix-like, Lol may rise up to die again and again. Once her phantasm is externalized, however, it is not merely a question of any couple making love without her. The "scene" cannot form the required triangular "knot" (the word is Lacan's, who also saw this necessity of being three) unless Lol is personally connected to the participants, so that her exclusion presuppose her inclusion. The initial link must, as was originally so, be one of love. To that end, Lol selects the couple and sets out to make the man fall in love with her, an undertaking quickly crowned with success. But this man must love her and abandon her, and do both repeatedly. Therefore, having obtained Jacques Hold's love, she arranges the second part: She begs him not to leave Tatiana (p. 136), insists that he continue to see her (p. 137), tells him that Tatiana must be essential to his life (pp. 153–157), and that therefore he and Lol cannot form a couple (p. 161). Because the phantasm is her last refuge, perpetuation of the threesome forms the sine qua non of her identity. Indeed, when she consents to spend the night "alone" with Jacques Hold, an existentially fatal error is committed, which breaks the fragile equilibrium and ignites the crisis that plunges her definitively into madness. Suddenly Lol and not "the other woman" is being undressed. Utterly unable to identify with the part, Lol can no longer sustain identity. Beset by the intense "anxiety at the onset of psychosis, when the patient is literally experiencing the threat of dissolution of the self" (May, 1958, p. 50), she asks frantically who she is: "Who is there in the bed, who?" (p. 217). Dread, in the doubly intolerable circumstances of being two instead of three and of being the wrong one in the twosome, becomes so unbearable that Lol is compelled to rectify matters and bring in Tatiana. She accomplishes this onomastically, by naming herself Tatiana, splitting her own identity in order to effect her own eviction and substitution. Becoming Tatiana enables her also to be Lol, simultaneously loved, abandoned, and replaced. Calling herself alternately Lol and Tatiana, she reestablishes the triangle, but at the price of the irremediable ruin of her psychic unity. As

Tatiana she participates in the coupling; as Lol she begs to be left alone, left out, and attempts to flee the room, after which, switching again to Tatiana, she rushes back (p. 219). That Lol calls out her own name(s) instead of her partner's emphasizes the fact that she is not making love but descending into the solitude of madness.

B. His

The success Lol has in assembling the structural components of her phantasm raises a nexus of questions whose consideration displaces our initial focus. Because it revolves around a scene in which her prescribed role is that of someone being acted upon in the sense of being abandoned, the entire venture depends on the cooperation of the male actor. Moreover, in order to meet the requirements, he must become an accomplice highly aware of his function, which he does rather too willingly. Complying unquestioningly with each of Lol's bizarre requests, Jacques Hold consents to refrain from leaving Tatiana (p. 137), pretends that he cannot do without her (p. 152), lies to her, suddenly pretending to love her, brings her to the window of the hotel room, thus exhibiting her without her knowledge to Lol as proof that the triangle is being maintained, and even assures Lol that when in bed with Tatiana he does not mentally substitute Lol for her, which would psychically destroy the threesome (p. 158). It is precisely Jacques Hold's eagerness to play his designated part that is problematical. Added to the point, which I explore in the next section, that his is the voice of the narrative, this willingness elicits the multifaceted question of "who": Who lives the phantasm? Who is implicated? Who speaks? Who sees? Whose story is being told? The answer to these questions is, on the one hand, double, for Hold becomes part of the phantasmal world, and, on the other hand, single, for Lol is neither the one who sees nor who speaks. Indeed, the "story" focused on in the text is not Lol's. It is that of Jacques Hold's entry into phantasm.

If he cooperates so eagerly it is because he has become fascinated to an extreme degree by an unlived moment in a past that is not his. What he desires most ardently is to penetrate that past: "She is the night of T. Beach—soon, when I kiss her, the door will open, I will enter" (p. 121). Not content to echo Michael Richardson's conduct, he wants inordinately to blend with him and experience directly those past events, both real and imaginary. He means to accompany Lol figuratively and literally on her voyage back to T. Beach, actually to follow her into her imagined memory: "Here is the moment of my entry into Lol. V. Stein's memory" (p. 202). However, in his overwhelming rush to partake of her phantasm, he does violence both to himself and to her. Love and fascination cross the boundary into obsession and disregard. For Hold overlooks the fact that one does not come and go at will in the world of insanity, that the entrance fee for full membership is the integrity of Self as such. Utterly mesmerized, he embraces and even longs for the loss of authentic Being-in-the-world: "I desire to be part of the thing Lol lies about. Let her carry me off ... let her pulverize me with the rest..." (p. 124). His depersonalization is enacted onomastically in a sort of ritual de-naming ceremony with Lol. At the very moment he realizes that her name designates a non-ek-sistent Dasein, he experiences a personal fissure – his own name names him no longer: "Who had noticed the inconsistency of the belief in that person so named if not she.... For the first time my name pronounced does not name" (p. 131).

While this extraordinary scene marks Hold's passage into phantasm, it does not herald real participation in a world shared with Lol. By its very nature, which severs one from the world of others and of things, from the present and the future, phantasm isolates the former Dasein, shutting one into a state akin to dreaming: "The individual's images, his feelings ... belong to him alone, he lives completely in his own world, and being alone means, psychologically, dreaming – whether or not there is at this time a physiological state of sleep" (Binswanger, 1968, p. 243). Since "the dreamer is alone in his dream world," since "no one else can enter it, nor can the dreamer leave it" (Straus, 1966, p. 116), Lol's world remains perforce sealed to Hold, and his impressions that he can share what he himself refers to as her dream ("Lol dreams ... this dream contaminates me"[p. 217]) become obsessive illusions. All the more so given that Lol lives attuned to the eminently private moment of her own extinction, an exclusion the role assigned to Hold only reinforces, and which therefore precludes togetherness in the very phantasmal configuration. We conclude, then, that Lol and Hold do not share quite the same phantasm.

Although space does not permit thorough study of the characteristics of Hold's particular phantasm, we can rapidly sketch its dynamics. In his case, the phantasm is marked by a complex nexus of cruelty and (Self) destruction, even perversion. ("The perversion, if there is any, is on Jacques Hold's side" [Montrelay, 1973, p. 21].) It is articulated around a desire for knowledge, within the dynamics of possession according to which to know is to possess. Above all, Lol represents a mystery ("What was this tranquil ghost hiding...?" [p. 92]) which he would like to penetrate and elucidate for the knowledge it will bring him about *himself*: "But what is it about myself that I am ignorant of to such a degree and that she summons me to know?" (p. 123). His is an essentially epistemological undertaking, as Montrelay (1973) remarks: "Jacques Hold ... knows that a woman's 'madness' attracts him most vitally [le sollicite au plus vif] because it turns his anxiety into that burning curiosity which is the epistemological drive" (p. 21). And the text is punctuated with moments of frustration at the impossibility of knowing Lol, coupled with the excitement afforded him by a woman who eludes full "possession."

Thus he feels despair on the one hand, and delight on the other, for the dialectics of masculine possession turn women into objects of knowledge to be had, and, once "had," discarded with ennui. Clearly Jacques Hold tires of Tatiana and despises her because he thinks he knows her, and her body, "better than she knows it herself" (p. 155). The discovery that he will never succeed in knowing Lol ("... I know ... that for me she is unknowable" [p. 192]) acts to secure his interest, which lies in the perpetual repetition of his own phantasmal, and contradictory, quest for knowledge, renewable precisely because it goes unsatisfied. And here is where cruelty and perversion come into play. Since he is moved by a desire for endless possession rather than by authentic love, Hold has no thought of helping to bring Lol out of neurosis into free Being-with. Instead, her "fascinating" state must be perpetuated, for it is her very madness that causes her continually to escape his "trap": "My hands become the trap in which to immobilize her..." (p. 125). Thus, just when Lol voices her fear of imminent insanity, and, in a sort of appeal, confides her loss of identity, he exhorts her not to change: "I don't understand who is in my place. – Don't change" (p. 160). Elsewhere, he purposely refrains from helping her in a moment of great suffering: "I say nothing, do not come to her aid" (p. 153). And, beyond encouraging her to remain neurotic, he provokes the final crisis. It is he who persuades her to spend the night alone with him, and who, once the crisis begins, aggravates it, lying to her to keep her in the room, touching her despite her protestations of pain, and provoking her final personality split by suggesting the name of Tatiana Karl: "She said: who is it? ...–Tatiana Karl, for example" (p. 218).

Disregard for Lol is matched by perverse cruelty to Tatiana, both in his manipulation of her and in his fantasies relating to her. Aware that Tatiana realizes he does not love her, and that she desperately wishes he did (p. 175), he nevertheless takes pleasure in indulging in a grotesque parody of love. Without bothering to appear convincing, he begins to claim he loves her, enjoying the certainty that she does not believe him: "Doubtless she did not believe that they [his words] were addressed to her" (p. 142). He persists far beyond the exigencies of Lol's phantasm, reveling in the insult contained in his false declarations, and fantasizing more and more violent effects. Now he sees his lying protestatims of love as a kind of annihilating punishment that will cover Tatiana's "shame" (pp. 182-183); now as a cup of poison he administers slowly, the better to relish her suffering: "I say: I love you. Once the words were pronounced, my mouth remained open so they would pour out to the last drop" (p. 185); now as a violent blow that fells her: "... but the blow is dealt, and Tatiana is felled" (p. 185). Finally he reaches a paroxysm of imagined violence when, during the sexual act, he simulates her murder. Covering her head with the bed sheet, he proceeds to "possess" her "decapitated body," symbol of severed Selfhood, of the reduction of women to a brainless mass of flesh: "He hides Tatiana's face under the sheets and thus has her decapitated body in his hands, at his entire disposal. He turns it, raises it, disposes of it as he wishes..." (p. 156). His fantasy progresses in brutality until he sees himself gagging her, pumping her blood: "Her hot, gagged body, I pump Tatiana's blood ... beneath me she slowly becomes bloodless" (p. 194). Thus

Jacques Hold's particular phantasm moves along the lines of sadomasochism, and occupies, of necessity, a space different from Lol's.

III. THE NARRATOR

The preceding discussions have shown that the "who" of the phantasm is not simply Lol, that there are actually two phantasms, however much they overlap. We have yet to examine the question, who is "speaking," who "tells" the "story?" The narrative voice belongs to Jacques Hold. Yet although narrator and character are the same human being, we shall see that they do not coincide. Moreover, as in the "new novel" in general, there exists no story prior to the writing; speaking/writing and episodes fuse, forming a reality of which voice constitutes an integral part. Because the structural configuration of *The Ravishing of Lol. V. Stein* focuses on the interrelationship of voice and "content," a narrative analysis is necessary.

The book is written in the first person. However, the identity of this "I" remains concealed for more than one-third of the 221-page text: Only on page 85 does the narrator disclose his name. An explanation can be advanced: concerned with creating suspense and with respecting the chronology of a story he relates through the eyes of the ostensible heroine, the narrator reserves introduction of his name for the moment when Lol actually learns it. But this hypothesis collapses when we recall that the text contains two "main" characters, Hold and Lol, when we note that the former is given more weight by virtue of his narrative stance, that the narrator maintains no distance from his text, which turns out to be non-linear, and that, contrary to first impressions, the eyes through which everything is seen and the voice expressing that vision are always only his.

On the one hand, the name "Jacques Hold" resolves more than one mystery. Several pronouns converge—the speaking "I," "me," but also "he," and "the man," Tatiana's lover, whom Lol followed through the streets of S. Tahla. On the other hand, if purposeful narrative deceit ends on page 85, unity of person is not effected.

Even after naming himself, the narrator does not merge "I" with "he." Elucidation of this problem will become feasible after a description of the narrative situation.

Before page 85 the reader does learn that the narrator enjoys an intense personal relationship to Lol. Still, enough ambiguity is maintained so that the moment of onomastic identification comes as a shock. The pause created by the blank space on page 85, followed by page 86 which is entirely blank, breaks the textual flow and draws the reader backward rather than forward. It becomes necessary to reread the text up to that point in order to realize the extent to which narrative deception has been practiced and to appreciate the complexity of the narrator's relationship to his text. Suddenly we learn that "Jacques Hold," "he," is also the "I" who is writing, who, having explicitly asserted himself as author, has been manipulating information he already possessed. Yet the narrator makes no attempt to present his text as objective; he proclaims the opposite repeatedly. Although, especially at first, he often documents his information ("Tatiana says," "they say," etc.), quite soon (p. 12) he repudiates the principal source informing the reader that he no longer believes what Tatiana says. Having thus dissipated the factual stance, he announces that the story of the ball will be a mixture of her report and his own invention. Then, throughout the book, he furnishes a sort of antidocumentation, punctuating the narrative indiscriminately with a melange of "outside" sources and subjective statements such as "I think," "I'm making this up," etc., so that fact and imagination merge. What emerges is a single vision and existential truth—reality, in other words, as projected by the narrator, who states as early as page 12 "I am going to tell *my* story of Lol. V. Stein" (emphasis added).

Departing from objective fact permits him to write from his point of view instead of Lol's. In this declaration of intent he informs us that he has filtered what he has learned about Lol's past, choosing to tell only a minimum. He also explains why: Lol's life as such does not interest this writer. Only that in her existence which relates to him contains value. What he wishes to communicate is not Lol. V. Stein as a person, but her importance in *his* life. If he devotes so much space to the ball it is because it determines his "entry" into Lol's life, that is, into phantasm. "I don't want to know the nineteen years preceding that night any more than I say ... because the presence of her adolescence in this story might attenuate in the reader's eyes this woman's crushing presence in my life" (pp. 12-13). Using, again, a vocabulary of possession, he then explains how he will manipulate Lol textually: He will "take her," "at the moment she seems to *me* to begin moving toward meeting *me*" (p. 13; ephasis added).

Lol's "crushing presence" in Jacques Hold's diegetic life as character and in the text communicated by him as narrator is, we know, passionately, phantastasmically projected. And the key to the narrative resides in the word "presence." From the very first sentences, the textual discourse is situated in a "here" and "now" ("Lol. V. Stein was born [est née] here, in S. Tahla" [p. 9]). The verbal tense that predominates is the present, in which I include the "passé composé," for, as Benveniste (1966) has shown, the latter establishes a "living link" to the speech act in the process of being made (in the present) and, therefore, to the speaker. This makes it an "autobiographical form par excellence" (p. 244). Moreover, the frequency with which passages that begin with the "passé composé" slide into the present and are peppered with deictics (signs which reveal the narrator's presence in his text) proves that they are "meant as present" and, as Straus (1963) states, "cannot be detached from myself as the one who is narrating, experiencing, thinking" (p. 391). This "story," then, is written in the present, not by someone simply reporting past events, nor by a narrator experiencing them for the first time as he writes, but by someone living and reliving them in a perpetual present, a perpetually repeated present. Here its function is iterative, and recalls the form used in scripts for the theater or cinema.

On the level of concrete expression reiteration characterizes the narrative, from content to syntagmatic configuration. Repetition of scenes, or paragraphs, sentences, and words is thus not to be situated on the diegetic level but on the level of the narration itself. Pontalis and Laplanche (1967) define phantasm as an "imaginary scenario in which the subject is present and which portrays [qui figure] in a fashion more or less distorted by defensive processes, the satisfaction of a desire.... [it is] repetitive behavior" (p. 152). On the level of the narrative, the subject of the phantasm is none other than the "I" announced in the first paragraph of the text, and who speaks in the perpetually repeated present of the waking dream that constitutes the novel. From the very beginning everything is articulated in relationship to this "I": "I have never seen him, I never heard," etc. (p. 1). Information furnished by others acquires importance only when incorporated in "I"'s single perspective.

The continual repetitions in this text come not from Lol but from the narrator, who, as speaker, is already caught in the phantasmal world he constructed as character. For example, on page 93 the narrator repeats data concerning Lol's adolescence that were already provided in the first pages of the text. The same information reappears yet again on page 119, so that the phenomenon cannot be explained as a desire to inform the reader. Given the narrator's stated intention to speak but little of Lol's past, this triple reiteration becomes additionally symptomatic, especially when one observes that each time something is repeated it is repeated practically verbatim. Thus it would appear that the narrative is not being manipulated with a great degree of control. Indeed, narrator as well as character are too passionately and obsessively involved to be able to divorce what is being said from how it is being said. Far from being the simple narration of a phantasm, *The Ravishing of Lol. V. Stein* is a phantasmal narrative, in which the narrator himself is caught.

The phantasmal nature of the narrator's discourse also makes itself felt in repetitions of the ball scene, which is continually redescribed and re-evoked, in addition to being simulated repeatedly at the hotel. Initially he relates it in the "passé simple" (pp. 13-21), the tense of the historical, "objective" past. The ball is thus set as a temporal zero, a point from which the narrator's "chronicle time" will be measured. Benveniste (1966) explains that "chronicle time," which founds communal life, fixes an axis, which must remain stationary, and counts time in regular intervals before and after it. Yet even as he first recounts it, the narrator has ceased to project the ball as past. It has already invaded his present. It is already "famous" and present, as the deictic indicates: "this famous ball" (p. 10). The constant recapitulations of the scene (thereafter in the present tense) show that it has already passed from historical event to a phantasmically repeated present which "haunts" both narrator and narrative from the start. The ordered discourse of chronicle time gives way to phantasmal discourse, as Benveniste has shown it must when the axis of temporal references is displaced by an individual.

Almost nothing in the text occurs just once. Episodes of pursuit and of "voyeurism" recur frequently, often in inverted form: Lol follows Jacques Hold, who in turn follows her, only to be followed again by her, etc. Lol takes up the position of false voyeurism outside the hotel, and Hold literally spies on her and Tatiana on two occasions (pp. 105, 171); he also acts as voyeur of his own life when he observes himself making love to Tatiana. And the last event of the text, when Lol again lies outside the hotel window of the room where Hold awaits Tatiana, is less a final episode than the same scene ceaselessly repeated, opening on yet another immobile series situated inside the walls of the ballroom where time does not advance.

On the syntagmatic level repetition occurs so frequently that it constitutes a stylistic device of the narrative. To cite but a few random examples: "and it begins again, begins again" (pp. 62–63); "this ball, this ball" (p. 84); "the sea subsides, subsides" (p. 211); the phrase about Tatiana "naked under her black hair, naked, naked, black hair" is repeated so often that the words escape the narrator and all meaning is lost to him: "... the sentence explodes, it bursts meaning ... I no longer even understand that it doesn't mean anything..." (pp. 134–135).

We are now better equipped to propose an explanation of the phenomenon of non-coincidence between the narrating "I" and Jacques Hold. In his now famous linguistic analyses Benveniste (1966) demonstrated that first-person narratives contain a double "I." One must distinguish between the speaking "I" and the "I" the utterance refers to, the character acting in what is being related. Although this distinction applies here, because temporality is not limited to the comparatively simple opposition of narrative present to the past of plot, this text has a more complex structure, marked by the multiplicity of references to be reconciled. Before the name "Jacques Hold" appears, the speaking "I" contrasts with an unidentified character "I," but also with a "he" and "the man."

The naming of Jacques Hold, instead of simplifying matters, only complicates them further. Moreover, later, other allusive pronouns such as "we" and "one" ("on") must be accounted for.

A possible explanation lies in the truth, noted above for Lol, that linguistic disarray reflects existential malaise. The splintering of narrational self-reference conveys fissures in the narrator's Dasein. It is impossible for the various "persons" to merge because the pronouns do not allude to a unified Self. Existentially speaking, Jacques Hold is not the same person as the narrator, because the latter has, in a sense reminiscent of Lol's own "posthumous living," "survived" the scattering of his personality that was ritually enacted in the "de-naming scene." Once he divests himself of his name there remains no appellation for him besides "I." This "I" has a role to play which, because it consists in replicating the actions of another, Michael Richardson, in the phantasmal hope of blending with him, blurs identity into anonymity as communicated by that most ambiguous of French pronouns "on," translated as "one," "we," or "they": "The eternal Richardson is going to be useful ... [on] will mix with him ... all that will merge into one ... [on] will no longer recognize who is who ... [on] will lose oneself from sight, lose one's names..." (pp. 131-132). Thus "I" assumes anonymity, as is made even more evident when the narrator says who "I" is in a way that precludes identity: "Her choice is free of preference. *I* am the man in S. Tahla she decided to follow" (p. 131; italics added). Precisely because "I" is no longer Jacques Hold the two cannot merge at the time of narration. Indeed, in its very structure, the sentence on page 85 in which the name "Jacques Hold" first appears both alludes to a unity that no longer holds and emphasizes present disunity. Rather than expressing coincidence via a simple "I am Jacques Hold," it proffers a series of splintered elements, leaving "I" unmentioned and implicitly separate: "Tatiana introduces her husband, Pierre Beugner, to Lol, and Jacques Hold, one of their friends, – the distance is covered – me" (p. 85). One must not consider "me" the equivalent of "I," for the autonomous pronoun "moi" in French has a role of emphasis that distinguishes it from "I": "... the value of emphasis or contrast peculiar to 'moi' with respect to 'je'" (Benveniste, 1966, p. 197). Here "me" functions appositively and onomastically; its antecedent is not "I" but "Jacques Hold," and it establishes equivalency not with the first person but with the third. This has great existential significance. On the "I" side of the "I-Jacques Hold" opposition we have found a certain anonymity. On the other side gradual depersonalization will also be the case. No longer naming "I," Jacques Hold (he, "on") will name no one, as we shall see.

Closer scrutiny shows that the designation "Jacques Hold," which continues to appear regularly, is reserved for the man who sleeps with Tatiana. When presenting scenes of them together, the narrator persistently refers to himself in the third person: "... behind Tatiana, Jacques Hold, me ... Tatiana turns toward Jacques Hold—are you coming? Jacques Hold says no" (p. 128). This division and the gradual emptying of the name "Jacques Hold" are most evident in the hotel scenes. In the second scene, for example, as long as the narrator projects toward Lol the first person predominates, as when "I" takes Tatiana to the window in order to show Lol they are there: "I asked her to come with me to the window ... thus I showed Tatiana to her" (p. 141). But "I" vanishes when he turns from Lol and "possesses" Tatiana: "Jacques Hold possessed Tatiana Karl mercilessly..." (p. 142). The contrast deepens as the pace of alternation quickens: "*I* went back to the window ... [to look at Lol]. *He* went back to the bed and lay down next to Tatiana Karl," etc. (p. 145; emphasis added).

But the dichotomy is difficult to maintain, and in the third hotel scene existential disintegration coincides with its linguistic manifestation: In discourse the third person indicates absence of personhood (Benveniste, 1966). The narrating "I" separates himself so thoroughly from Jacques Hold, whom he no longer wants to be, that he can no longer be him. Jacques Hold has become nobody: "She [Lol] loves, loves the one who must love Tatiana. No one" (p. 154). In this scene the name "Jacques Hold" has disappeared and with it the person who sleeps with Tatiana. Therefore he finds himself impotent. Only Jacques Hold can "take" Tatiana; "I" cannot even try: "*I* don't even try to take her, *I* know *I* wouldn't be able to" (p. 188; emphasis added).

Were he to adhere to his original plan to tell a story in which events unfold chronologically, the fourth scene would be the last. Jacques Hold, having disappeared, "I" would logically remain impotent; Tatiana, already suspicious, would know why; they would separate, and the phantasm would come apart. But phantasmal need for repetition prevails over linear, chronological discourse. The brevity with which the fourth scene is evoked allows the narrator to avoid describing any structural alteration of the triangle that a break with Tatiana would entail. Reproducing only the outlines of the original scene, he suggests that it will be enacted as yet another in an implicitly ongoing series. The participants reassemble and we are led to suppose they will behave in the prescribed manner, regardless of what has happened in "objective," external time. The sketchy quality of this episode, with which the novel ends, thus serves less to conclude than to refuel the perpetual repetition intrinsic to the phantasm(s) involved.

Thus the primary subject of this novel is the story of the narrator's plunge into phantasm. But the narrator is subject in another sense; he and only he says "I." Being the only one in possession of discourse, he alone constitutes subjectivity, however phantasmally (Benveniste [1966] has shown the essential link between subjectivity and the capacity to posit it by saying "I"), whereas Lol remains the voiceless object of his acts, of his text. It is the narrating "I" that notes Lol's silence, and that asserts itself in contrast to it. Indeed, "I" discovers his "love" just when he ascertains her muteness, delighting in it, for it permits him to articulate everything as a function of his subjectivity, to which both Lol and Tatiana are sacrificed: "I went back to the window, she was still there ... in a way she could express to no one. I discovered that about her at the same time I discovered my love for her" (p. 145). Thus the narrator, not Lol, tells Lol's story and, in the process, appropriates it. Finally – and the gender of the author becomes pertinent here – the narrative structure of the novel exposes the violence done to women when they are deprived of discourse. Recalling Freud's (1913, S.E. 12) declaration that muteness in dreams is a common representation of death, and that this novel is a sort of phantasmal dream, we see that Lol's silence, upon which the narrative "I" is predicted, is correlated to her "death" as necessary for the narrator.

In conclusion, let me point out the extraordinarily well chosen title of this text. In French "ravissement" has meanings of delight (as in "ravishing beauty"), of rapture, theft, and violation. Further, the title's syntax prevents one from deciding whether it is in the active or passive voice, or who the subject is: Who ravishes whom and in what sense(s)? As so often with Duras, elimination of alternative meanings is unnecessary; words function pluralistically. Because space does not allow for lengthy stylistic analyses here (which I have conducted elsewhere), for the moment it will suffice to draw attention to the aptness of this title, which corresponds in complexity to the text it names.

REFERENCES

Bachelard, G. (1943). *L'air et les songes*. Paris: Corti.
_____ (1948). *La terre et les rêveries de la volonté*. Paris: Corti.
Benveniste, E. (1966). *Problèmes de linguistique générale* (Vols. 1 & 2). Paris: Gallimard.
Binswanger, L. (1958). The existential analysis school of thought. In R. May, E. Angel, & H. Ellenberger (Eds.), *Existence: A new dimension in psychiatry and psychology*. New York: Basic Books.
_____ (1968). *Being in the World: Selected Papers of Ludwig Binswanger*, Ed. J. Needleman. New York: Harper & Row.
Duras, M. (1964). *Le ravissement de Lol. V. Stein*. Paris: Gallimard.
_____ taped interviews between Marguerite Duras and Susan Cohen. (unpublished)
Freud, S. (1933). *Essais de psychanalyse appliquée*. Paris: Gallimard.
_____ (1958). The theme of the three caskets. In J. Strachey (Ed. and Trans.), *The standard edition of the complete psychological works of Sigmund Freud* (Vol. 12). London: Hogarth Press. (Original work published 1913)
Heidegger, M. (1958). *Essais et conférences*. Paris: Gallimard.
_____ (1962). *Being and Time*. New York: Harper & Row. (Original work published 1927)
_____ (1962). *Chemins qui ne mènent nulle part*. Paris: Gallimard.
Lacan, J. (1975). Hommage fait à Marguerite Duras du *Ravissement de Lol. V. Stein*. In *Marguerite Duras*. Paris: Albatross.
Maldiney, H. (1973). *Regard, parole, espace*. Lausanne: Age d'homme.
May, R. (1958). The origins and significance of the existential movement in psychology. In R. May, E. Agle, & H. Ellenberger (Eds.), *Existence: A new dimension in psychiatry and psychology*. New York: Basic Books.
Montrelay, M. (1973). *L'ombre et le nom*. Paris: Minuit.
Pontalis, J. B., & Laplanche, J. (1967). *Vocabulaire de la psychanalyse*. Paris: P.U.F.
Straus, E. (1963). *The Primary World of Senses*. London: Collier-Macmillan.
_____ (1966). *Phenomenological Psychology*. New York: Basic Books.

Notes on Contributors

ZELDA BOYD is Professor of English at California State University, Hayward. She has written on language and language in literature.

LEOPOLD CHARNEY is at Yale currently working on the application of psychoanalytic theory to various cinematic genres.

SUSAN COHEN, formerly associated with Rutgers University and with New York University in Paris, is now on the faculty of the French Department at Barnard College. This article is part of a book in progress on Marguerite Duras. She has lectured on Marguerite Duras's fiction, interviewed the author several times, and published "Marguerite Duras: La Présence de Rien" in *Les Cahiers Renaud-Barrault.*

ARTHUR COLLINS is Professor of Philosophy at the City College of New York.

TOM CONLEY is Chair of the Department of French and Italian at the University of Minnesota. His work on issues of word and image in the arts and literature studies the psychoanalytical dimensions of language. Some of his recent work has appeared in *Hors Cadre, Yale French Studies,* and *MLN.*

NOTES ON CONTRIBUTORS

JERRY ALINE FLIEGER completed her doctoral work in French literature at the University of California, Berkeley, and is currently at Rutgers University where her teaching duties include seminars on Lacanian theory and psychoanalytic approaches to literature. She has published articles in *Diacritics, Sub-Stance, Critical Exchange, French Forum, Contemporary Literature,* and *Structuralist Review* on the role of the unconscious in literary production, as well as on recent developments in psychoanalytic criticism in France. She is the author of a forthcoming study on the comic mode and deconstructive theory as applied to contemporary French literature.

MARGARET GANZ, a Professor of English Literature, has focused in essays and reviews on the interplay of literature and psychology, particularly in comedy, with a special emphasis on Freud and Rank. She is working on a book exploring the psychological interrelations of humor and irony.

ELISSA GREENWALD, Assistant Professor of English at Rutgers University, is completing a study of the political and psychological backgrounds of American romance. She has also written on Hawthorne's influence on Henry James and on Virginia Woolf. Her Ph.D. is from Yale, where she was influenced by Harold Bloom's readings of Freud.

ROGER B. HENKLE is the author of *Comedy and Culture: England 1820–1900* (1980). He has published on comedy theory in *The Sewanee Review, The Virginia Quarterly Review, Critical Quarterly, Mosaic,* and *Thalia: A Journal of Humor.* He is Professor and Chairman of the Department of English at Brown University and serves as Managing Editor of the critical journal *Novel: A Forum on Fiction.* He is presently working on a book which defines middle class ideology in 19th century English literature, stemming in part from his work in Brown's interdisciplinary Program in Modern Literature and Society which he co-founded.

DONALD M. KARTIGANER is Professor of English at the University of Washington. In addition to a number of essays on modern literature, he is the author of *The Fragile Thread: The Meaning of Form in Faulkner's Novels* (1979), a monograph, "Process and Product: A Study of Modern Literary Form" (*The Massachusetts Review*, XII, 2 & 4), and is co-editor of *Theories of American Literature* (1972).

PETER L. RUDNYTSKY is Assistant Professor of English and Comparative Literature at Columbia University and Executive Secretary of the Association for Applied Psychoanalysis. He has published numerous essays on literary and psychoanalytic topics in such journals as *Raritan, American Imago,* and *Renaissance Drama,* and is completing a book on *Freud and the Myth of Oedipus.*

IRVING SCHNEIDER is a psychiatrist/psychoanalyst practicing in the Washington, D.C. area. For the past five years he has been the Chairperson of the Subcommittee on Films of the American Psychiatric Association. He is Associate Clinical Professor of Psychiatry at Georgetown University Medical School, faculty member of the Washington School of Psychiatry and member of the Washington Psychoanalytic Society and the American Academy of Psychoanalysis.

MADELON SPRENGNETHER is an Associate Professor of English at the University of Minnesota. She has published numerous articles on Renaissance literature as well as a book of poetry, *The Normal Heart,* and a book of essays, *Rivers, Stories, Houses, Dreams* under the name Madelon S. Gohlke.

Author Index

A

Abraham, N., 194, *213*
Apollodorus, 144, *147*

B

Bachelard, G., 257, *277*
Bales, K., 149, *165*
Barthes, R., 204, *213*
Bayley, J., 97, *106*
Baym, N., 149, *165*
Beckett, S., 207, *213*
Beers, C., 54, *66*
Bell, M., 149, *165*
Benjamin, W., 91, *106*
Benveniste, E., 107, 112, 114, *123*, 271-276, *277*
Bersani, L., 102, *106*
Binswanger, L., 256, 258, 260, 266, *277*
Boose, L. E., 171, 176, 184, *189*
Breuer, J., 9, 10, 15, 16, *35*
Brooks, P., 20, 33, *35*
Brunswick, R., 21, *35*
Bullough, G., 184, *189*
Butler, S., 127, 131, 132, 133, 135, 137, 138, 140, 143, *147*, *148*

C

Carroll, D., 33, *35*
Cassirer, E., 94, *106*
Cavell, S., 171, 182, *189*
Chabot, B., 16, 19, *35*
Conrad, J., 5, *35*
Crews, F., 159, *165*
Culler, J., 33, *35*

D

de Certeau, M., 194, *213*
de Man, P., 46, *48*, 171, *189*
Dennison, G., 39, *48*
Derrida, J., 45, 46, *48*, 170, 186, 187, *189*
Duncan, J. L., 149, *165*
Duras, M., 201, *213*, 255, 261, *277*

E

Eakin, P. J., 149, *165*
Erikson, E., 39, *48*
Erikson, E. H., 244, *252*

F

Finas, L., 198, *213*
Finley, J. H., 135, *148*
Fitzgerald, F. S., 6, *35*
Fitzgerald, R., 135, *148*
Franzosa, J., 149, *165*
Freud, S., 3, 9, 10, 11, 13, 15, 16, 18, 19, 20, 30, 34, *35*, 72, 77, 86, *87*, 92, *106*, 108, 110, 113, *123*, 130, 131, 133, 143, *148*, 150, 151,

152, 153, 154, 155, 158, 160, 161, *165*, *166*, 185, *189*, 215, 216, 218, 219, 220, 222, 227, 228, 232, 233, *234*, *235*, 238, 247, *252*, *253*, 276, *277*

G

Gabbard, G., 57, *66*
Gabbard, K., 57, *66*
Gadamer, H.-G., 14, 18, *35*, 169, *189*
Gardiner, M., 32, *35*
Graves, R., 131, 144, 145, *148*
Green, A., 171, 180, 185, 187, 188, 189, *189*
Greenacre, P., 131, *148*
Greenblatt, S., 171, 179, 180, 182, 188, *189*
Grene, D., 130, 132, 135, *148*

H

Hartman, G. H., 172, 175, *189*
Hawthorne, N., 151, *166*
Heidegger, M., 256, 259, 260, 263, *277*
Heilman, R. B., 172, 174, 179, 182, *189*
Hemingway, E., 122, *124*
Herndon, J., 39, *49*
Hodgson, J. A., 176, *189*
Holt, J., 39, *49*

J

James, H., 153, *166*
Jameson, F., 211, *213*
Johnson, B., 46, *49*, 169, 170, 187, 188, *189*
Jones, H. F., 135, 146, 147, *148*
Jordan, G. G., 149, *166*

K

Kafka, F., 90, 98, *106*
Kartiganer, D., 8, *36*
Kawin, B., 3, *36*
Kellogg, R., 3, *36*
Kierkegaard, S., 16, *36*
Kirk, G. S., 135, *148*
Kirsch, A., 171, 177, *189*
Klein, R., 205, *213*
Koestler, A., 95, *106*
Kohl, H., 39, *49*
Kozol, J., 39, *49*
Kris, E., 93, *106*
Kubie, L., 62, *66*

L

Lacan, J., 46, *49*, 111, *124*, 156, *166*, 170, 174, 175, 187, *189*, 211, *213*, 238, *253*, 255, 263, *277*
Lacoste, P., 193, *213*
Laplanche, J., 271, *277*
Lattimore, R., 135, *148*
Leab, D., 63, *66*
Leavy, S., 17, *36*
Lebensztejn, J.-C., 198, *213*
Levin, H., 175, *189*
Loewald, H., 18, *36*

M

Maldiney, H., 259, 261, *277*
Masson, J. M., 11, *36*
May, R., 264, *277*
Miess, M., 201, *213*
Milner, G. B., 95, *106*
Milner, M., 47, *49*
Money, J., 186, *189*
Montrelay, M., 255, 258, 267, *277*
Murdoch, I., 89, 97, *106*

N

Nowottny, W. M. T., 186, *189*

P

Piaget, J., 39, *49*
Poe, E. A., 238, *253*
Pontalis, J. B., 271, *277*
Proust, M., 224, 227, 231, *236*

R

Rabkin, L. Y., 54, *67*
Ragussis, M., 149, *166*
Rank, O., 133, *148*
Ricoeur, P., 109, 112, *124*
Rogers, R., 182, *190*
Ropars, M.-C., 196, *213*
Ross, L. J., 184, *190*
Rymer, T., 170, *190*

S

Schafer, R., 108, 114, *124*
Schimek, J. G., 13, *36*

Schneider, I., 53, *67*
Scholes, R., 3, *36*
Schur, M., 11, *36*
Shakespeare, W., 172, *190*
Snow, E. A., 171, 180, 188, *190*
Stanford, W. B., 135, *148*
Steiner, G., 135, *148*
Stockholder, K. S., 180, *190*
Stouck, D., 149, *166*
Straus, E., 262, 266, 271, *277*
Sullivan, H. S., 218, *236*
Sward, K., 62, *67*

T

Truffaut, F., 58, *67*

W

Wangh, M., 184, *190*
White, L., 201, *213*
Winnicott, D. W., 42, 44, 47, 48, *49*

Z

Zandvoort, R. W., 117, *124*

Subject Index

A

Abel, Karl, 111
Abraham, Karl, 59
Action language, 108, 115-116
Actor, 4-8, 16, 21, 29
Adler, Alfred, 27-30
Affect, 184-185
Amazing Dr. Clitterhouse, The, 60
Ambassadors, The, 201
Amnesia, 53
An Unmarried Woman, 66
Anscombe, Elizabeth, 115
Autobiography, 37, 48

B

Baudelaire, Charles, 221
Bernfeld, S., 60
Bernheim, 82-83
Biograph, 54
Blind Alley, 61
Bob & Carol & Ted & Alice, 66
Bonnie and Clyde, 210
Book of Daniel, 237-238, 241, 244, 246
Boomerang, The, 60
Brentano, Franz, 77
Bringing Up Baby, 60

C

Cabinet of Dr. Caligari, The, 58
Carefree, 60
Cartesianism, 71-87
Castration, 24-26, 31, 94, 185-186, 188
Christianity, 43, 200-201
Christmas Dream, The, 53
Cinthio, Geraldi, 177-178
Comic, 89-106
Consciousness, 74-75, 82, 91, 99, 155, 222
Conversion, 155, 160-161
Countertransference, 17
Criminal Hypnotist, The, 54-55, 65

D

Dali, Salvador, 58
Dark Delusion, 64
Dark Mirror, The, 64
Dark Past, 61, 64
Dark Waters, 64
Daseinsanalysis, 256-258, 266
Daydreaming, 150
de Saint-Gelais, Melin, 198
Death instinct, 152
Decathexis, 222-223
Delusion, 152, 219
Depression, 231
Descartes, R., 47, 72-73
Don Quixote, 98
Dora, case of, 31
Dr. Dippy's Sanitarium, 54, 63, 65-66
Dr. Kildare's Strange Case, 61
Dream analysis, 59
Dream screens, 53

287

SUBJECT INDEX

Dreams, 22–25, 27, 53, 58, 219, 238, 242, 244, 246
Drunkard's Reformation, A, 54
Dualism, 73

E

Edison, 54
Ego, 38, 92
Electra complex, 142
Escaped Lunatic, The, 54
Euphues, 41

F

Face to Face, 66
Faerie Queene, 40
Fantasy, 11, 13, 22, 24–27, 30, 33, 47, 127–147, 187, 219–220
Fetishism, 185–186
Fichte, J. G., 74
Fiction, 37, 48
Film noir, 60, 64
Fine Madness, A, 66
Fixation, 155
Flame Within, The, 60
Flashbacks, 53
Flaubert, G., 196
Fliess, W., 249–250
Foreman, Carol, 63
Forgetting, 215–234
Frame analysis, 53
Free association, 16, 19
Frye, N., 211

G

German philosophy, 74
Griffith, D. W., 54

H

Hallucination, 53, 160
Harvey, 62, 65
Hecht, Ben, 58
Hegel, G. W. F., 74
Hermeneutics, 18, 211
Historical truth, 151
Hitchcock, Alfred, 58
Holbein, H., 201

Home of the Brave, 63–65
Homosexuality, 24–26, 229
Hugo, V., 196
Huston, John, 64
Hypnosis, 9–10, 14–15, 55, 82–83

I

I Was A Teen-Age Werewolf, 56
Incestuous fixation, 178, 180, 183
Intentionality, 77
Internationaler Vorlag, 60
Irma Dream, 238, 241–242, 244, 247, 250
Irving, John, 211

J

James, Henry, 45, 201
Jesus Christ Superstar, 43
Jung, C. G., 27–30, 128

K

Kant, E., 74
Kaufmann, Nicholas, 59
Keats, J., 118
Kenny, Anthony, 115
King Lear, 109, 247
Kleptomaniac, The, 54
Kramer, Stanley, 63

L

Lady in the Dark, 61
Lang, Fritz, 58
Leibniz, G. W., 74
Levi-Strauss, C., 211
Literary criticism, as narrative, 37–48
Locke, J., 74
Love at First Bite, 66
Lukács, G., 211
Lumière, L. J., 53

M

M, 60
Man With Wheels in His Head, The, 53
Maniac Chase, 54
Maniac Cook, The, 54
Marot, C., 198

Marxism, 211, 213
Mazursky, Paul, 66
Méliès, George, 53-54
Memory, 83-84
Mental Mechanisms, 63
Merchant of Venice, The, 108-109, 247
Mind that Found Itself, A, 54
Miser's Dream of Gold, The, 53
Molinet, Jean, 198, 201
Montaigne, M. E., 38, 44, 206-207
Mourning, 222-223, 234
Mr. Deeds Goes to Town, 56, 60
Müller, Max, 111

N

Narcissus, 243
Narration, in Duras, 255-277
Narrative, 4-5
Nashe, T., 40
Neutrality, 17
New Arcadia, 40-41
New Criticism, 38
Nietzsche, F. W., 74
Nightmare Alley, 64-65
Now Voyager, 61

O

Obsessional neurosis, 160
Oedipus complex, 11, 19, 31, 142, 171, 178, 180, 187
Oedipus Rex, 13
One Flew over the Cuckoo's Nest, 66
Ordinary People, 63, 66
Other, 5

P

Pabst, G. W., 59
Pascal, B., 226
Pears, David, 115
Peter and the Wolf, 47
Phantasm, in Duras, 255-277
Philology, 111
Picaresque, 40
Porter, Edwin S., 54
Post-hypnotic suggestion, 87
Primal scene, 13, 24-26, 33, 181, 185
Private Worlds, 60
Psychosomatic, 173

R

Rajah's Dream, The, 53
Rat Man, case of, 31
Reformation, The, 54, 65
Religious myth, 43
Repetition compulsion, 46, 178
Repression, 27, 75, 220-221, 227-228
  in Hawthorne, 149-165
Rubáiyát, The, 237
Ryle, G., 82, 115

S

Sachs, Hans, 59
Schelling, F. W. J., 74
Schiller, F., 232
Schnabel, Julian, 211
Schopenhauer, A., 74
Screen memory, 22, 25, 178
Secrets of a Soul, 59, 65
Seduction theory, 11, 22
Self, 258, 268
Seventh Veil, The, 61
Sexuality, 153-156, 159, 178, 180, 185
Sidney, P., 40-41
Signifier, 171, 174-175, 187-188
Slips, 77-80
Snake Pit, The, 62, 64-65
Spellbound, 58-59, 61, 65
Spenser, E., 40
Superego, 153
Sweet, Henry, 117
Symbol
  analysis of, 107
  as symptom, 149-165

T

Tennyson, A., 118-119, 121-122
Testament of Dr. Mabuse, The, 58
Tin Drum, The, 210
Transference, 18, 20, 151, 153, 164, 246

U

Unconscious, Graphic, 193-213
Unconscious memory, 220-221, 224
Under a Hypnotist's Influence, 54
Unfortunate Traveller, The, 40

V

von Hartmann, Eduard, 74
Voyeurism, 177-178

W

Wanger, Walter, 60
Ward, Mary Jane, 62
Warhol, A., 211
Warning Shadows, 60
What Drink Did, 54
When Clouds Roll By, 58
Wittgenstein, L. J. J., 115
Wolf-Man, case of, 3, 8, 12-13, 26-35
Woman Under the Influence, A, 66
Word play, analysis of, 107
Wordsworth, W., 118